MW00805429

Behind
the Curtain
of Power

*How Karl Rove, David Axelrod, Roger Ailes, James
Carville, Dick Morris, and Lee Atwater Won the Toughest
Race in the World and Changed America*

by Rune Olsø

DORRANCE
PUBLISHING CO
EST. 1920
PITTSBURGH, PENNSYLVANIA 15238

Dorrance Publishing Co
585 Alpha Drive
Pittsburgh, PA 15238
Visit our website at *www.dorrancebookstore.com*

ISBN: 978-1-6366-1257-7
eISBN: 978-1-6366-1843-2

Behind
the Curtain
of Power

How Karl Rove, David Axelrod, Roger Ailes, James Carville, Dick Morris, and Lee Atwater Won the Toughest Race in the World and Changed America

For Aela & Maje

Contents

PROLOGUE

You Can Bet It Was Planned that Way!

Most of us can recite the names of the last US presidents. We remember them for their achievements, their faults and their scandals. But how did they come to capture the most powerful office in the land – who were the masterminds that catapulted them into the highest echelon of power? This book is about the operators that orchestrated those remarkable political victories: Lee Atwater, Dick Morris, Roger Ailes, James Carville, Karl Rove, and David Axelrod.

Six superb political craftsmen who all moved the electorate to shape history. This book is a behind the scenes look at the paths they chose – the way they manipulated, cajoled and maneuvered their way through the political battlefield. But it's also the story about where they came from, and the most important goals and fears that drove them as individuals. We will get a glimpse of how their childhoods and past experiences shaped them and made them go to such great lengths to succeed.

Every one of them left a trail of enemies and admirers, victims and winners. While some worked for candidates and issues close to your heart, others undoubtedly worked for candidates and issues you strongly disagree with. Most of them played dirty at times. But in all these fascinating stories, we can find important lessons about innovation, strategy, and tactics that will also be used in future presidential elections.

This book is not written for professional historians, who will find little in it that they don't already know. It is intended for those who want to have a look behind the curtain to see who's pulling the strings, and why. President Roosevelt once said, "In politics, nothing happens by accident. If it happens, you can bet it was planned that way."

On stage, we only see the actors play out their roles. But we know there are scriptwriters and directors shaping that story, working diligently in the shadows. We can't fully understand history without understanding them. These are the stories of six men whose achievements behind the curtain of power changed America and the course of world history.

Rune Olsø
Norway, 2021

CHAPTER 1

BAD BOY

Lee Atwater

*"Politics wasn't Lee Atwater's career,
it was his calling."*

- Former Vice President Dan Quale

Joe's Little Voice Lifted in Pain

Today, decades after his death, Lee Atwater is often remembered with fondness and gratitude by many Republicans and with pure hatred by many Democrats. He was very different from other political consultants of his time. He talked with a southern drawl, played the guitar like a rock star, and drenched his food in Tabasco sauce. He had an enormous amount of energy and self-discipline, yet would constantly overstep normal boundaries. He was young – only 37 when he ran the successful presidential campaign of George H. W. Bush in 1988 – and died at the early age of 40. It was a short life, but he still managed to achieve more than most of his peers could dream of in a lifetime.

Atwater is remembered as one of the architects behind innovative negative politics, often playing on the electorate's darker emotions of fear or disgust. But for scores of young Republicans, he was also a celebrity; a role model even.

"In Republican circles Lee Atwater was a rock star," Republican strategist Mary Matalin wrote. "He also had a following. Political groupies."[1]

In the words of biographer John Brady, Atwater "made it cool to be a republican. ...He was called mischievous, fiercely competitive, driven, focused, combustible, spontaneous, instinctive, smart, simple, complicated, both generous and ruthless to a fault. He ran 50 miles a week, no matter what the weather, no matter what the distractions He was a partner in a Washington barbeque restaurant.. ...He recorded a blues album with BB King that received a Grammy nomination, featuring a signature song called – what else? – Bad Boy."[2]

He had an almost psychic connection with middle-American political culture. Some saw him as a race baiter, while others made a record about him called "Black Like Lee." To some a villain, to others a hero – that was the life story of Lee Atwater.

He grew up in what he described as "the middle of the middle class" in the Forest Acres section of Columbia. In the 1950s and 1960s, it was a place for the middle-class dream of the good life. Good schools, safe streets, and plenty of space for a boy to make mischief.

Born in 1951, little Lee was a nervous bundle of energy, restless even as an infant. Atwater's parents – his mother a teacher and his father a retired insurance adjuster – owned a trim, one-story home.[3] He started talking early and had a sharp memory. At two-and-a-half, he could recite the Pledge of Allegiance. By the time he went to school, he knew all the presidents and loved history.

Still, he could never summon a real interest for the slow pace of academics. Lee simply didn't have time to spare. He was too busy playing antics, being center point of attention, and chasing girls. His classmate and lifelong friend David Yon said Lee was bright but unable to stay focused – he was always switching channels. His eleventh-grade English teacher, Robert C. Ellenburg, remembers the day when Lee was due to give a book report. After getting a two-hour extension on his deadline, the young man proceeded to walk to the front of the class and speak for 10 minutes on the literary merit of the Columbia Telephone Directory.

"He said it jumped around too much from character to character without sustaining any of them," Ellenburg fondly remembered. "He predicted it would have to be revised next year."[4]

It was classic Atwater.

The early years, Lee spent mostly with his little brother Joe, whom he absolutely worshipped. Little Joe was to have a deep impact on Lee's life. One afternoon, his mother promised the two boys fresh donuts. She put on the deep fryer, filed it with oil, plugged in the cord, and waited for it to reach 340 degrees. Curious, three-year-old Joe climbed up on the trash can to get a closer look.

"Joe, get down, the grease is hot," commanded their mother.

As Joe started to get down, the trash can tipped over. Starting to fall, he instinctively reached out and grabbed the cord. The fryer overturned. The boiling oil came down over Joe on the floor. In one horrifying instant, their mother knew that her son was going to die. Then the screaming began. Lee ran into the kitchen and saw his little brother lying there, his skin starting to peel, one of his eyes lost to the scalding liquid. Lee, stunned, could only watch in helpless desperation.

They wrapped little Joe in sheets and rushed him to the hospital. His burns covered 90 percent of his body, and he couldn't be saved. The terrible accident and the loss of his little brother shaped Lee in a profound way. It haunted him. Every day for the rest of his life, he could hear Joe's little voice lifted in pain.

Thirty-six years later, engulfed in pain of his own, as he lay in his hospital bed dying, Lee would scream out, not for his wife or children, but the name of his little brother.[5]

It's hard to say how much the episode and the ensuing never-ending-nightmares formed Lee's political psyche, but it's certainly one of the explanations of why he often would detach himself from empathy to become the most ruthless political warrior in American politics. To Atwater, politics became a holy war. He would bury himself in these battles, as if to escape everything else.

Growing up, money was tight in the Atwater household. As soon as Lee and his sister Anne, who was born after Joe's death, were old enough, their mother went back to teaching. Lee had to pitch in, too. In fifth grade, he started selling eggs door to door for 60 cents a dozen. Small jobs and chores became an ordinary part of life, and he would often work while his friends played.

One afternoon when he was out driving with his father, Lee was fiddling with the radio dial as James Brown's "Please, Please, Please" started pouring from the speakers. The music seemed to transfix young Lee. That night, he found the same station on the radio in his room. A lifelong love relationship with rhythm and blues had started, and after some back and forth with his parents, he finally got a guitar. Even though his relentless practice meant the wire strings made Lee's fingers bleed, he was completely consumed by the instrument. On weekends, he rose early and practiced until 7:00 in the evening.[6] When he played, there was nothing else in the world that mattered. Music made Lee happy. He would go on to become an accomplished guitar player, jamming with blues legend B.B. King. Once he even privately visited soul-music legend James Brown in a South Carolina state prison.[7]

But there was one love in Lee's life that music could never compete with: Politics. He experienced political action for the first time in eighth grade during a class trip to Washington, D.C. His teachers feared the young prankster would be trouble, but they couldn't have been more wrong. Lee seemed to blossom when he entered the political realm, thriving on the excitement, bombarding their hosts with intelligent questions. When the class posed for a photograph in front of the Capitol after a visit to Senator Strom Thurmond, Lee placed himself right in front of the senator. He came home inspired by Washington, by politics – and by the Senator.

Strom Thurmond had started his political career as a full-blood segregationist Democratic governor in South Carolina. He ran for president in 1948 as the States Rights Democratic Party candidate, as a supporter of racial segregation. He represented South Carolina in the United States Senate from 1954 until 2003, first as a Democrat, then from 1964 as a Republican. Atwater undeniably picked up some lessons from Thurmond on how to win over white racist voters in the South, without using an obvious racist message.

But it wasn't Thurmond's racial rhetoric that appealed so much to Atwater. On the contrary, he grew up in a household that taught equality and fellowship between people of all backgrounds and color. Throughout his career, his coworkers and friends never perceived him as a racist. He had several black friends, and in his years as chairman of the party, he tried to expand the GOP's black base. So, even though he would go on to use racial codes in a reprehensible way, he wasn't a racist as such. No, there was another reason Atwater felt so attracted to Senator Thurmond.

In his home state of South Carolina, the senator was a political force of nature, a true master of the political game. And *that* appealed immensely to Atwater. For him, it was like learning how to play chess for the first time – and cracking the code – from a master of the game. Lee soon understood that the way the pieces move is not the important part. The important part is understanding your opponent's moves and developing a strategy to counter and overrun your opponent. The masters can foresee their opponent's thinking and plan many, many moves ahead – sacrificing pieces along the way to finally reach their one and only goal: Winning. It was like a revelation to Lee. He had found his life calling.

The Game, the Competition, the Show

But Atwater's growing passion for politics didn't result in a more disciplined approach to his curriculum. Getting mostly Ds and Fs, and with no hope for improvement in sight, his parents sent him to Fork Union Military Academy on Virginia. After a year of hard drilling and strict discipline – both inside and outside of the classroom – he returned a little stronger and a little wiser. His grades had gone up, but deep down, he still had the same happy-go-lucky attitude.

Back in school with his friends, Atwater ran his first political campaign as a prank. He convinced his classmate David Yon to run for student body president under the alias of Dewey P. Yon. Then he wrote his candidate's platform. Even back then, Atwater understood what the voters wanted, and the platform promised students free beer in the cafeteria and no grades lower than B.[8] So "Dewey" won, and the principal had to annul the vote and call another election.

Atwater's bad grades were a reflection of the time he had spent chasing girls, making up pranks, and playing his guitar. In 1969, he ended up at nearby Newberry College. There, he became social chairman of his fraternity and began a short career in adult cinema; renting and showing black-and-white pornographic movies and charging admission.

"You can bet nobody asked for their damn money back on those flicks," he later said in an interview, while sitting with his wife and parents in the family living room. "We weren't like the guys who took your money and then showed a bunch of people horsing around in leotards."[9]

By the end of his freshman year at Newberry, Atwater's interest in politics was growing rapidly. Inspired by his friend Yon who got a summer job with Senator Hollings in 1971, Atwater decided to seek an intern spot in the Washington office of his idol, Senator Thurmond. Even if it was just for a month, he loved DC. The senator took a liking to the young man, teaching him – in Atwater's own words – "the game, the competition and the show" of politics. Back in college, he began reading works of political thinkers like Plato, Locke, and Jefferson. Struck by the senator's physical vigor at the age of 69, he started jogging. It was the start of a new, more disciplined life. It became part of his daily routine to run 50 miles a week.

The University of South Carolina had traditionally controlled the state's College Republicans, but that was before Lee Atwater entered the scene. Working diligently, quickly learning the ropes, he drew all the small constituencies together and staged a coup of sorts, getting elected state chairman. Under his leadership, the College Republicans started an historic recruitment drive, pure Atwater-style.

First Lee persuaded his best-looking fraternity brothers to drive to women's colleges to recruit new members. Then he would enlist the best-looking among the females to recruit new members at all-male schools. Sure, it was manipulative, but it worked like a charm. Atwater created an army of volunteers that he could call on whenever he might need them, and he used his office to establish college outposts for Thurmond's reelection campaign in '72. He did the same for Nixon's reelection in five southern states.

However, his fresh political career didn't mean he felt he had joined the establishment. In a state so heavily dominated by the Democrats, being a Republican to Atwater meant being anti-establishment. This was to be part of his success – never accepting the establishment's answers. Instead, he always searched for other approaches that were built on the deep understanding of the working-class people he had grown up with. Atwater dabbled in different political projects, helping elect a mayor of a small town, and going back to interning for Senator Thurmond again in Washington D.C.

By now, politics had become his absolute obsession, his way of defining himself. And the Senator sensed he was dealing with a prime student.

"Lee always was a good watcher," Thurmond later said. "He didn't miss a thing."

There was certainly a lot to pick up. As a delegate to the Republican National Convention in Miami the summer of '72, Atwater inadvertently drove the senator into a demonstration of peaceniks. Somebody yelled, "Hey, it's Strom Thurmond, the power pig of the South!" The car was trapped in the crowd, and they couldn't move. Atwater got shaky, but Thurmond kept his cool and got out of the car, entering the hostile crowd.

There were television cameras all over the place. An 18- or 19-year-old girl confronted Thurmond, calling him names like "fascist pig" and "cocksucker," but he just kept smiling, asking if her parents knew she was out there. With the girl still shouting obscenities, the senator got back in the car with a smile, and they drove away. The shaken Atwater asked why the senator had gotten out of the car in front of such a hostile crowd, just to be verbally attacked in front of the cameras. Thurmond smiled, "Young man, that'll be 25,000 votes when we get home." Atwater remembered the lesson for the rest of his life.

"Boy, did I learn from that man," he later recalled.[10]

By 1973, Atwater was heavily involved with the College Republicans. That summer, he became campaign manager for another power-hungry young man trying to build a political career; Karl Rove. At the time, Rove was running for chairman of the College Republican National Committee. The contest for the chairmanship was a serious matter; Rove left his job in order to spend five months, without pay, campaigning full time. Rove, who 30 years later would pick up the mantle as the Republican Party's chief strategist, was actually so consumed with the College Republicans that he didn't spend much time actually going to college; he didn't graduate until many years later.[11]

Atwater was a great asset to Rove's campaign. But as always with Atwater, there was something in it for him, too. The deal between Rove and Atwater went like this: First they would get Rove elected as chairman. Then Rove would appoint Atwater as executive director.

Karl Rove found it impossible not to like Lee. He was fun loving and amiable, and he was forever scheming. The two crisscrossed the South in the spring of 1973, lining up support in advance of the summer convention where the new chairman of the College Republicans was to be chosen. Atwater knew all the fronts and fissures of campus politics in the region: who was important and who was not. By the time they rolled into Missouri in June for the convention, they had a battle plan.[12]

There were two main candidates for chair: Karl Rove and Robert Edgeworth. Rove and Atwater knew they probably didn't have a clear majority going into the convention, so they made sure they controlled the credentials committee. Suddenly there was a flurry of challenges submitted to the committee.

"The credentials committee savagely went through and threw out, often on the flimsiest of reasons, most of my supporters," Edgeworth later complained.

As more and more delegates lost their case in the committee, tempers flared, and there were near fistfights. The next day, with everybody gathered in a large hall, the candidates were nominated and voting started. In the confusion over who actually had delegate rights, each side declared victory.

"I gave a nice acceptance speech, thanking everybody for electing me. Then I sat down," remembered Edgeworth. "Karl got up, gave a nice acceptance speech for everybody who had elected him. Then we both went to Washington D.C."[13]

Following the chaos at the convention, the issue of who was the rightful chair was to be decided by RNC Chairman George H. W. Bush. But before Bush could issue his verdict, Edgeworth's people planted information in *The Washington Post*, which claimed that Rove had been teaching dirty tricks to the young Republicans at political workshops. The *Post* published the story under the headline, "GOP Probes Official as Teacher of Tricks." [14]

This was 1973, and with the Watergate investigation looming, the story was a headache to Bush, a man who hated disloyalty. It was probably the dumbest move Edgeworth could have made. His disloyalty to the party had made him a non-starter as far as Bush was concerned. The RNC Chairman quickly finished the investigation, clearing Rove. Then he promptly appointed him the elected chairman of the College Republican National Committee. Real loyalty, after all, has always been the most important commodity in politics, rare as it might be.

After obtaining the chairmanship, Karl appointed Lee the new executive director, just like he had promised. It didn't take long before Atwater met George H. W. Bush in the RNC building. He strolled right up and introduced himself. To his surprise, the chairman invited him into his office where they had a long chat. The brash Atwater told Bush that his ambition was to one day sit in that very chair – as leader of their party. The forthrightness and folksiness of the young Republican made the chairman like him from the start, and they began meeting for chats on a regular basis.

He got on well with the Chairman. He even got Bush to help him impress a girl he had met. The girl was an intern working for Senator Thurmond, and Atwater got Bush to loan him his boat for one of their dates. Her name was Sally Dunbar. At first, she wasn't that impressed, but Lee grew on her. They fell in love. Eventually they were married. Atwater had found his companion, and he was to stay with her for the rest of his life.

That said, Atwater never became much of a family man. Politics was the core of his life, and he spent most of his time working. Allegedly, he also had frequent sexual encounters with a score of different women. At least, that's what the rumors claimed. In his absence from home, Sally became the anchor of their family, taking control, even managing their finances. When Lee was out running campaigns, she was at home running their family.

Guerrilla Tactics

Ever the restless soul, Atwater soon returned to South Carolina. In 1974 he set up his own firm. He named it "Baker & Associates." In fact, there was no Baker. Baker didn't exist. The only employees were Atwater and his friend Stuart Barnwell. But Lee felt it was a serious name that had the right sound for a political consulting agency. He quickly earned a reputation for a supreme strategic mind and hardball tactics. In just four years, he helped achieve 28 Republican victories across the South. He also lost two races; William Westmoreland, who didn't get the nomination for governor, and Carroll Campbell, who lost his run for lieutenant governor. Lee proved to be a terrible loser. After each drubbing, the young campaign manager literally had the dry heaves for two or three days.

"I got over it," Atwater said, "but I never want to get to where I can stomach losing."[15]

One of the successful races he ran was Joyce Hearn's campaign for the state house in 1975. Atwater impressed her.

"He really made politics fun," she recalled. "He dragged in all sorts of volunteers from the campuses around Columbia – the College Republicans were like a standing army to him – and they worked ungodly hours. When things got down to the wire, I remember going into the office and seeing Lee in midnight meetings with his staff. For them it was the excitement, the win factor. He had a real insight into motivating others."[16]

Atwater's remarkable skills were noticed by virtually everyone he worked with. Even though he had run Campbell's failed lieutenant governor campaign, when Campbell announced that he was running for a state senate seat in 1976, it was with Lee as his campaign manager. It was a remarkable show of faith and spoke volumes of Atwater's ability to impress. The Campbell state senate campaign provides a good example of how he worked.

Lee swore he would win the race. He mapped out a fivefold strategy. First, they would act as if Campbell was the front-runner throughout the campaign. He was well known from earlier races, and they did not want to help their opponent, Democrat Daniel Yarborough, get more attention. Therefore, Atwater decided, there would be no debates. Second, they would target the independents by building Campbell's image like that of an independent, rather than a Republican. Following the Watergate scandal, the national mood was not pro-Republican, so all the commercials, speeches, and campaign literature would avoid the R-word. Third, the campaign would focus hard on the suburban voters, not the rural democratic parts of the district. Fourth, they would start by raising money. This was more important than anything else. And fifth, they would use all available media outlets. That meant not relying too heavily on costly television ads.[17]

Most of the advertising budget went for radio spots that were run during news programs. Atwater bought a lot of radio ads for the morning and afternoon, when people would be in their cars, listening to the radio, driving to or back from work. He also bought 14 large billboards, the only campaign to use this form of voter communication, arguing, "Anytime one can totally dominate one form of advertising, impact upon the voter in enhanced tremendously."

Atwater considered large newspapers the least effective mass medium, as only one of five voters read them, and even fewer read the political ads printed in them. But small, weekly local papers were another matter altogether. They had much more local interest and were read by a broader public, so Atwater would use them for all they were worth.

Of course, timing also mattered when using paid media to market Campbell. Billboards would install name recognition, so they would go up one month before the election. Then radio spots would start three weeks before the election. With a few weeks left, television ads converting the candidates name into a human being were run. And the last week before Election Day, they published newspaper ads, serving as reminders. Atwater never had any faith in giveaways, like key chains, pens, and other "junk." They were good for the party congregation, not for reaching voters.

Lee ran the campaign like a master chef in a cooking contest – every little detail needed to be just right. And as always in an Atwater-managed-campaign, volunteers played a key role.

"A good political organization is worth 3 to 5 points in the election, and if that won't make a difference, you aren't going to win anyway," he said.

He led the Campbell campaign with gusto, inspiring volunteers, dispatching orders about advertising and operations, making sure his strategy was followed in everyday decisions. In a year when the Democrats were sweeping South Carolina, Atwater's candidate became the only Republican to win a new seat in the state house senate.[18] It was impressive, and it got noticed.

In 1978, the reelection campaign for Senator Strom Thurmond was shaping up to be one of the most challenging of his long political career. Thurmond's opponent was the young and energetic Democrat Charles "Pug" Ravenel. Pug was only 40, and the age difference to the now 76-year-old Thurmond was not lost on anyone. Thurmond understood he needed a real war-consiglieri if he was to crush his opponent, so he hired the now 27-year-old Lee to run the show. But – to make sure Atwater would not overstep or do anything rash – the Senator attached the Republican consultant Allison Dalton to oversee him. Dalton got the title "campaign coordinator." Chief consultant to the campaign was the renowned and feared strategist and pollster Arthur Finkelstein.

Atwater and Finkelstein did extensive polling and lay the strategy for the campaign. It was Atwater's first really big race – his shot at real national recognition.

"Lee came to the campaign with a negative, nearly evangelical pitch," wrote biographer John Brady. "He wanted to paint Ravenel as a young, liberal Johnny-come-lately who had never held elective office, had never done anything for the good folks of South Carolina."

But this approach was shot down by Dalton and the rest of the Senator's entourage. Thurmond scored high positives, so his closest confidants didn't want to shake the tree too much. After a lot of discussion, it was decided they would go with a positive theme.

For a while, Ravenel did well in the polls, and it seemed a close race. Too close for Atwater's taste. So, Lee contacted one of his old friends from the Young Republicans, Roger Stone, who was based in New York. Stone came over an article in a small New York publication "by accident." It was about a local fundraiser hosted by a New York couple for their Harvard classmate, Pug Ravenel. Addressing a crowd of 25 in their apartment, the article stated, Ravenel said that if elected to the US Senate, he would like to be "the third Senator from New York." To this day, it is still impossible to determine whether the story is real or if it was planted by Stone to help Atwater's candidate.[19]

Real or not, the story was pure gold. Lee put the wheels in motion, pushing the story around South Carolina and planting the right quotes to keep it growing. After a few rounds in the press, even a group of Democratic state legislators berated Ravenel for his comments. A negative ad was aired. Ravenel vehemently denied having ever made the comment, but no one listened. His negatives jumped from 12 all the way up to 43 percent. And just like that, Ravenel started sinking in the polls.

Far from getting irritated by Atwater's flagrant disobedience, Dalton was impressed by the young man's diligence and drive. He especially took notice of the amount of opposition research Atwater engineered and his ambition to constantly control the agenda.

"We knew as much about them as we knew about our own campaign," Dalton recalled. "Any news conference for us, he took no chance – he built a crowd of our own friendly people. For Ravenel's press conferences, Lee had our people there to raise though questions."[20]

The electorate was heavily democratic. That meant that even a popular Republican senator like Thurmond couldn't take its support for granted.

"We had to use guerrilla tactics," Atwater explained. "Republicans in the South could not win elections by talking about issues. You had to make the case that the other guy, the other candidate, was a bad guy."[21]

To Lee, going negative was simply about staying alive and winning the race. And Thurmond won with 56 percent of the vote. By now, Atwater was building a national reputation as a prime Republican strategist and campaign manager – someone who was hungry, aggressive, and successful.

Win It for the Gipper

Savoring his big win in South Carolina, Atwater entered an exciting contest. 1979 was the year for Republican presidential wannabes to gather on the arena before the primaries. And there were a lot of wannabes, because the 1980 presidential election seemed almost unlosable to the Republicans. The country was in recession, and America's strength in the world looked declining. The sitting Democratic president, Jimmy Carter, was weak. And Atwater had a favorite to replace him; Ronald Reagan.

Reagan hit a nerve in Atwater. He admired Reagan for his independence and his conservatism. But more importantly, he thought the Gipper could win. Atwater was sure that Reagan's main opponents, John Connally and George Bush, couldn't attract as many voters in November. He called up his old friend Carroll Campbell and suggested he become chairman of Reagan's South Carolina campaign, while Atwater would run it. Campbell said yes.

Before 1980, South Carolina selected its GOP nominee through a party convention, which was controlled by Senator Thurmond and his machine. And Thurmond supported Connally. Atwater knew he had to work around the old system if Reagan was to have any chance of bagging South Carolina. But he had a plan that would sidetrack his old mentor and secure the state in Reagan's column.

Atwater worked to push for a full-scale primary that would come after Iowa and New Hampshire, but before Super Tuesday. This would take power away from the Thurmond controlled convention, and it would place the South Carolina primary both late enough and early enough to completely reset the trajectory of the primary race. He used all his contacts and every conceivable angle to get it done. In August 1979, the South Carolina Republican Party agreed to Atwater's plan. The party switched to a primary system scheduled to take place on March 8, 1980, just days before Super Tuesday – so that the winner would get a huge boost at a key moment.[22] Now the result would be fully in the hands of the voters, and that much more important to the winner.

The timing of the South Carolina primary proved to be of tremendous importance to the Reagan campaign. George Bush had won in Iowa and Reagan had won in New Hampshire, so Connally desperately needed a win in South Carolina. Connally had the backing of Senator Thurmond and Governor Edwards, an obvious advantage in the Palmetto State. An article in *The New York Times* in December 1979 summed up the importance of the state's primary:

> *A new and early spot on the campaign schedule...has set up the South Carolina Republican Presidential primary as potentially the most important early showdown between Ronald Reagan and John B. Connally in the 1980 Republican Presidential nomination race. "We know Connally has got to make a stop Reagan effort here," comments Representative Carroll A. Campbell Jr. of Greenville, the state campaign chairman for Mr. Reagan. "He's got to throw in everything he's got. If he makes his stand here and we beat him, he's not going to stop us anywhere." [23]*

The article also made it clear that the other campaigns feared Atwater: "Each side has put heavy emphasis on organization. The field director of the Reagan effort is Lee Atwater, ...who is described by one Connally organization source as 'the best nuts-and-bolts man' in the state."[24]

Atwater was indeed the best nuts-and-bolts man in the state, as well as the superior strategist. Making the most of his resources, he set up a formidable organization. By March, they had called more than a quarter million voters to register them in their files.

Atwater started airing Reagan television spots in January and whisked the candidate through an array of appearances. Connelly's prospects started fading, just as Atwater had foreseen. But he feared that this could help Bush reemerge as the viable alternative and thereby give him the momentum. So, he directed his media consultant to run several ads that attacked Bush as too liberal for South Carolinians.

As always, Atwater had something up his sleeve. He had convinced his old pal Dick Greer to work with Bush's campaign manager in the state, for the purpose of subterfuge. So, there wasn't much mystery when an internal memo "suddenly" leaked from the Bush campaign just weeks before the primary. It stated that Connally had endorsed gay rights – a very controversial stand at the time in conservative South Carolina – and that Connally had engineered a plan to buy black votes. Connally called the Bush memo "a typical scurrilous, unfounded allegation" and shot back with some dirty allegations of his own.

To the outside world, the primary contest started looking like a mud-slinging contest between Connally and Bush, while Atwater's candidate was keeping his distance. Three days before voting day, *The Washington Post* summed up the mood of the campaign in the headline, "Reagan Keeps Clean While Bush, Connally Sling Mud in SC Race."[25] Through savvy tactics and dirty tricks, Atwater had pitted the Bush and Connally campaigns against each other, while his own candidate rose above it all – to a clear lead in the polls. Reagan won South Carolina handedly. Bush's momentum was halted. Connally withdrew a week later and endorsed Reagan. After a year of nonstop campaigning and spending $11 million, Connally had won only one delegate, Ada Mills, who became nationally known as "the $11 million delegate."[26]

Now, Reagan could focus on winning in November, and Atwater was named regional political director, overseeing South

Carolina, Alabama, West Virginia, and Georgia. His overall strategy for these four southern states divided the voters into three broad categories: First, the white-collar affluent, who usually vote Republican in presidential elections. Secondly, black voters, who were mostly Democratic. And thirdly, a huge in-between group of blue-collar or farmers, which included large numbers of "born-again" religious voters.[27] This last group was his main target.

Four years earlier, many of them had voted for Carter. After all, being a peanut farmer from Georgia, he had been one of their own. But now they were disillusioned with the Democratic president, and their votes were in play. Lee worked relentlessly to secure their support, using everything he had ever learned from his now 20 years of political experience. He secured Reagan a win in all his states, except Carter's home state of Georgia. On election day, Reagan beat incumbent President Carter in a landslide, winning 489 electoral votes, to Carter's 49.

While working for the Reagan presidential campaign in 1980, Atwater also signed on as a pollster for Congressman Floyd Spence's campaign against Democrat Tom Turnipseed in South Carolina's second district. Turnipseed had three years earlier been a contender in the Democratic gubernatorial primary, and before leaving that race, he had disclosed that he as a teenager had undergone shock treatment for his depression.

Atwater did a poll where (amazingly, though probably not accurately) Turnipseed got only 27 percent to Spence's 52. He published the results, saying that the race was as good as over before it had even really begun. This sent Turnipseed into a fury, claiming the poll was fraudulent. The battle between Atwater and the

Democratic candidate continued all through the campaign. At one press conference, Turnipseed accused Atwater directly of using objectionable push polls to smear him.

Atwater in turn responded by going around the state telling people that the Democratic candidate had once "been hooked up to jumper cables" and should not be taken seriously.[28] Turnipseed lost the election and the "jumper cable" remark went into political folklore as part of Lee Atwater's image. Years later, Atwater apologized to Turnipseed, writing in a letter before his death, "It is very important to me that I let you know that out of everything that has happened in my career, one of the low points remains the so called 'jumper cable' episode."[29] Yet at the time, it seemed a natural consequence of Atwater's relentless drive to win at any cost.

Inside the White House

With both Reagan and Spence winning their campaigns, 1980 was a good year for Atwater. He reveled in his image as the Republican Bad Boy, willing to do and say just about anything to win a race. As the President-elect set up his new administration, Reagan's chief of staff James Baker got a call from Senator Strom Thurmond, pushing him to find a position for Atwater as well. For Thurmond, it was a smart move – placing one of his friends on the inside of the new administration. For Baker, it was a chance to do the important Senator a favor. Lee was offered a job in President Ronald Reagan's Office for Political Affairs. He was still just 29 years old, and now he was definitely a player in the big leagues. Even so, he saw his new White House position as merely a steppingstone to greener pastures: "I really had two goals in life: to manage a presidential campaign and to be chairman of my party,"[30] he was later to say.

Ever since his days of organizing young college Republicans, Atwater always had a way of building strong teams and inspiring people around him. It was a valuable quality he embodied, a quality he now brought with him into the White House. He understood that for people to be willing to sacrifice, they had to feel they were a part of something bigger and more important than just their own aspirations. He would ask people if they knew what the three most important things in politics were, and give them the answer himself: "Loyalty, loyalty, loyalty."

Atwater lived by that creed: If someone was part of your team, you didn't desert them in the midst of a political battle, no matter what. A good leader always steps up to protect his soldiers. And Atwater almost always did. A very rare quality in politics, it is a trait that separates the truly inspiring leaders from the rest of the crop. Atwater would demand a lot from his staff and volunteers. But they got to be part of a real team, a political family, where they always mattered. And they knew Atwater recognized their skills and backed them up. That is why Lee Atwater always had such a huge following. His team became his second family.

Everywhere he ended up, he quickly organized his people and then worked around the clock to achieve his goals. His new role in the White House gave him proximity to the President and the opportunity to work on solving the political challenges of the day. But equally important, the Office for Political Affairs was in charge of distributing a treasure chest of over 4,000 administrative jobs in the new administration.

By the end of Reagan's first four years, a majority of these jobs had come through Atwater's office. Thousands of Republicans had gotten their job from him, which of course meant a tremendous amount of goodwill. And though most of them never met Atwater in person, he made sure every one of them knew whom they had to thank for their good fortunes. He made his secretary stop answering the phone with, "Office for Political Affairs," and start answering, "Lee Atwater's office." He sent congratulatory notes signed by him personally. If you got a job, you got it from Lee Atwater. They all owed him.

These were favors that could be collected whenever he needed them. Amassing influence, gathering IOUs, wasn't limited to those who got jobs. It could also be representatives, senators, governors – anyone who came across Atwater's path. Said Republican strategist Mary Matalin, who work closely with Lee, "Atwater always had a three-cushion shot. There was always something in it for the candidate, something in it for Atwater, and something in it for everybody else so they would be loyal to Atwater. It was quite a technique."[31]

When not dealing with policy or doling out jobs, Lee was busy fundraising. His first year in the Office of Political Affairs, he invited 150 of the top players from political action committees – from oil, manufacturing, paper, agriculture, and so on – and briefed them on the workings of his office. He didn't solicit money from them then of course, which would be a violation. He just got to know them, expanding his vast network of contacts.

But the next year was an election year, and his meetings with the PACs took a different turn. New meetings were set up outside the White House, and led by staffers from the Republican National Committee. Atwater would swoop into these meetings, give a speech, and leave. But not before ending his talk with a remark that, "I know you all want to discuss who you're going to support in these campaigns," and waving goodbye. The RNC staffers would then work the room, getting as many donations as they could.

This way, Atwater raised millions for GOP candidates. At the time, no one had ever raised money this way before. It was serious money, really large sums. Lee soon became part of an "assets and priorities group" that directed campaign money to chosen candidates. [32] A lot of senators and congressmen who desperately needed campaign money to stay afloat soon found out that Lee Atwater was a guy that could get things done.

It's Morning Again in America

The first years of the Reagan presidency were rocky waters. In the midterm elections in the Fall of '82, the Republicans lost 26 House seats. In January 1983, a Gallup poll had Walter Mondale – the would-be Democratic nominee – at 51 percent to Reagan's meager 33. From the White House's point of view, it was plain something had to be done.

Atwater was working on a concept he called "the permanent campaign" – setting strategy and building a core staff inside the administration that were ready and fired up for the reelection effort. He came across a memo sent by Clark Clifford to President Harry Truman in November 1947 on "The Politics of 1948," which accurately predicted both the nominees for the next year's election and that Truman would win. By looking at the Electoral College, Clifford had realized Truman could lose some of the big eastern states, normally assumed to be essential to victory, as long as he held the South and those Western states carried by the Democrats in 1944.

On the basis of Clifford's concept, Atwater wrote a memo of his own called, "The South in 1984." In it, he described how Reagan could get reelected in 1984 on much the same basis.

"The South's gut instincts are still Democratic," he observed. Southerners would "only vote Republican when they feel they must." But he noted that Reagan had managed to persuade southerners to vote against one of their own (Jimmy Carter) in 1980. He identified them as a key swing constituency which he described as "populists,"[33] and Atwater knew how to get them – by playing on traditional cultural issues.

In a second memo, Atwater again emphasized the South as the key to victory and urged driving "a wedge between the liberal Democrats and the [populist] traditional southern Democrats." What interested him most about the group of "populist voters" was that they didn't vote on ideology but rather a set of largely negative attitudes: "They are anti-Big Government, anti-Big Business, and anti-Big Labor. They are also hostile to the media, to the rich and to the poor."[34] Playing on these emotions, Atwater felt they could be persuaded to vote for Reagan rather than "the pro-Big Government, pro-Big Labor, liberal Democratic nominee." All they needed was some "wedge issues" that enhanced this divide, to convince them to vote for the Gipper.

With the '84 election one year out, Atwater quit his job at the White House and moved into the Reagan/Bush campaign headquarters. Though the Reagan inner circle was impressed by Lee, he was still only 32, and it was considered too much of a gamble to make him the campaign's Number One. Instead, he was named deputy campaign manager to serve under Ed Rollins. Atwater felt he could live with that. After all, he planned on running the campaign as it's de facto campaign manager, and he was going to make damn sure all the right people knew. He certainly wasn't going to let any of the credit go to Rollins, no matter what title was printed on his office door.

Rollins spent a lot of his time acting as the campaign's liaison with the crowd at the White House, while Atwater developed most of the campaigns strategy and ran the day-to-day operation. With his "Southern Strategy" in place (mostly along the lines of his previous memos), he developed plans for Republican victories in former Democratic strongholds, how to deal with key states, and addressed issues such as crime, unemployment, and the deficit. He also developed the campaign media strategy, which outlined Mondale's weaknesses and how to attack them.

Inside the campaign headquarters, the deputy soon overshadowed his boss. More and more, people saw Atwater as the man really pulling the strings in the campaign. Questions from the White House on strategy? Just ask Lee. How to deal with a serious media attack? Check with Lee. Operational problems? Lee would know what to do.

Atwater sent a score of prominent Republicans into attack-mode against the liberal Mondale, who was portrayed as "a tool for special interests and big government." All the while, as the attacks increased in strength, Atwater kept the President out of the scuffle – just like he had done back in the South Carolina contest.

Polling revealed that the GOP had a problem attracting women voters, so Atwater made sure the GOP Convention could boast of the fact that an unprecedented 46 percent of the delegates and alternates were women – at the time quite an achievement.

While their surrogates were out attacking Mondale and the Democrats as too liberal (capturing those populist voters in the South), the campaign focused most of its resources on building Reagan's positives in the overall electorate. They needed the voters to feel that Reagan had brought them better times, more jobs, and a resurging economy.

The campaign gathered some 40 top advertising executives together for a historic venture, creating "the Tuesday Team Inc." – an independent advertising agency named for Election Day. Working out of a temporary, shabby set of offices above Radio City Music Hall in New York, the team created a host of commercials. The most memorable was "Prouder, Stronger, Better," an ad more commonly referred to as "Morning in America."

It was nothing less than a feel-good-movie packed into a 60 second spot: The sun shines on San Francisco Bay, bustling people hurry to work, a bride and groom kiss softly at their wedding, a small town turns out for a flag-waving parade. The photography has a golden quality, as if it were all shot on a warm September day. A heartwarming soundtrack plays in the background, as the narrator in a deep comforting voice tell us:

> *It's morning again in America. Today more men and women will go to work than ever before in our country's history. With interest rates at about half the record highs of 1980, nearly two thousand families today will buy new homes, more than at any time in the past four years... It's morning again in*

America, and under the leadership of President Reagan, our country is prouder and stronger and better. Why would we ever want to return to where we were, less than four short years ago?

The ad communicated the exact message that Atwater wanted – safety, tradition, and optimism under Reagan, as opposed to dangerous new liberal Mondale experiments. Several other memorable ads ran as well, all designed to appeal to core emotional feelings. The campaign was to spend close to $25 million on the television ads, more than half of its budget.[35]

As aggressive as Atwater could be, he was first and foremost a smart and calculating strategist. He knew that attacks weren't always the smartest option. A crucial moment in the race came when Mondale's vice-presidential running mate Geraldine Ferraro said she would release her husband's tax returns, but then went back on the promise. The media smelled blood.

At an emergency meeting in the Reagan campaign, Atwater disagreed with suggestions that they attack Ferraro in public. His strategy was clear: "We don't have to do a thing, and this will destroy Geraldine Ferraro. The one thing that will save her, is if we get into it." He quoted Napoleon; "Never interfere with the enemy when he is in the process of destroying himself." The campaign did what Atwater ordered and kept quiet.

Mondale refused to order his VP-nominee to disclose the records, and the damaging media cycle lasted for weeks.[36] When Ferraro finally did hold a press conference to stop the bleeding, the Mondale/Ferraro ticket was already damaged goods. Atwater had succeeded in doing the most difficult thing in any heated campaign: He and his team had held their mouths shut.

The other crucial moment came toward the end of the campaign, when Reagan faltered in his first debate against Mondale. The President's speech was halting, he often paused and rambled. Luckily, after the campaign brought in the communication guru and strategist Roger Ailes to work with Reagan, things got a lot better. In the next debate, Reagan had gotten a lot of his old swagger back, looked better, and lay the whole age issue to rest in one of the most memorable moments of the campaign (more on this in chapter 3).

The debate spectacle was also the last bump in the road for the Reagan reelection campaign of 1984. Atwater's strategy had hit bullseye, the campaign had reached nearly all of its tactical goals along the way. Reagan ended up getting reelected in a historical landslide, winning 49 of the 50 states, capturing 59 percent of the popular vote.

The VP Aiming for the Oval

As the Reagan Presidency entered its last term, Vice President George H. W. Bush was already working to secure the 1988 nomination. Bush was a true loyalist in the Reagan White House. The VP logged more than 750,000 miles preaching the Reagan gospel.[37] But he was also something of a moderate – certainly far more moderate than Reagan and his court of economic libertarians. When he ran against Reagan for the nomination in 1980, there had even been a moment when he attacked Reagan's ideological belief in supply side economics (the belief that that economic growth could most effectively be created by lowering taxes on the wealthy and decreasing regulation) and decried it as "voodoo economics." But there was one dominant part of Bush's character that drowned out all the others – he was a survivor. And he understood that he had to appeal to the Reagan voters if he was to have any chance to win the presidential election in 1988.

Unlike most governors and senators, Bush had no electoral base ready to go. What he did have was an enormous network of friends in the Republican Party and the title of vice president. And last but not least, he had Lee Atwater angling to be his campaign manager.

Shortly after the 1984 victory, Atwater sent Bush a memo stating that, "The 1988 presidential nomination is the VP's to lose." The memo went on to describe how a '88 campaign had to be put together, including which main tasks needed to be completed and a timetable. But more importantly, he described the start of a strategy of duality – Bush needed to appeal to the Reagan followers yet at the same time "carve out a sharper and clearer identity as someone who is his own man, with his own ideas" for populist consumption.[38]

While Bush pondered on his choices, Atwater joined the Black Manafort Stone & Kelly consulting firm in New York. The firm worked for a bunch of other politicians, and as a result, the Bush clan had problems being at ease about where Atwater's loyalties lay. To reassure their anxiety, Atwater asked the VP's son, young George W. Bush, to become part of his team. While Atwater saw it as a great way to liaison with the Bush family, the younger Bush would be learning from the master campaigner. That sealed the deal. Atwater got the position he had always coveted: Manager of a presidential campaign.

In December of '85, the Vice President publicly announced that Lee Atwater would run his $4 million Fund for America's Future, the political action committee that would launch his presidential campaign. Atwater moved into the PAC's headquarter in an office building eight blocks from the White House, to lead his new staff of 20 paid staff members and numerous volunteers.[39]

President Reagan liked his VP. He appreciated Bush's loyalty and his willingness to contribute to the furthering of the Reagan agenda even when he was known to personally disagree. White House officials let it be known publicly that the President would anoint Bush without hesitation as the one most suited to carry his conservative revolution into the next decade, were it not for his role as party leader. This helped Bush make inroads into the party's conservative factions, who in the past had regarded him as too moderate. By the fall of 1986, several surveys showed that he was the first choice of GOP conservatives. Bush was also rated above any of the most frequently mentioned Democratic contenders.[40] In other words, a very good starting point for his presidential campaign.

But then, in November 1986, a story surfaced about secret arms-dealings between the US and the Islamic-ruled dictatorship of Iran. It soon became clear that the whole sordid affair also involved using the proceeds from the arms sales for illegal support of the Contras – a group waging guerrilla warfare against the democratically elected government of Nicaragua. Equally damaging were obvious attempts of a subsequent cover up.

Trying to contain the damage, President Reagan announced the creation of a Special Review Board to look into the matter – the so-called Tower Commission. Their report was published in

February 1987. It stated that Reagan did not have knowledge of the extent of the program, though it did criticize the President for not having enough oversight over his National Security Council staff.

The Democratically controlled Congress weren't satisfied with the report and started its own investigation into the Iran-Contra affair. The congressional majority report later concluded that:

> The United States simultaneously pursued two contradictory foreign policies - a public one and a secret one...The record of the Iran-Contra Affair also shows a seriously flawed policy-making process...There was confusion and disarray at the highest levels of Government...The Iran-Contra Affair was characterized by pervasive dishonesty and inordinate secrecy...The ultimate responsibility for the events in the Iran-Contra Affair must rest with the President.[41]

In a televised address to the American people, President Reagan tried to handle the issue as best he could, saying:

> A few months ago I told the American people I did not trade arms for hostages. My heart and my best intentions still tell me that's true, but the facts and the evidence tell me it is not. ...I take full responsibility for my own actions and for those of my administration. As angry as I may be about activities undertaken without my knowledge, I am still accountable for those activities. ...I'm still the one who must answer to the American people for this behavior.

The scandal tainted the White House. Atwater was most concerned about how it tainted the Vice President and how it would affect the 1988 election. Some reporters started digging into just how involved the VP had been. Bush denied any knowledge of the Iran-Contra affair, stating that he had been out of the loop. But the press wouldn't let go of the matter. It soon became clear that the issue would follow Bush throughout the campaign.

In January of '88, CBS News had scheduled a live interview with the VP. It was supposed to be a cozy profile interview. However, the campaign was tipped off that the interviewer, CBS News anchor Dan Rather, was about to ambush the VP on the Iran-Contra affair. Atwater had media guru Roger Ailes, who had helped Reagan four years earlier, train with Bush. They both urged the VP to come off strong, and Bush turned the tables on Rather, accusing him and CBS of misrepresenting themselves in obtaining the interview.

In the most memorable moment of the interview, Bush seemed to stun Rather by referring to the anchor's well-known walkout from the set of the Evening News the year before, which caused CBS to transmit a blank signal for nearly seven minutes.

"It's not fair to judge my whole career by a rehash on Iran," Bush seethed. "How would you like it if I judged your career by those seven minutes when you walked off the set in New York?" [42]

The strategy worked, and the interview ended the worst media attacks on Bush over the Iran-Contra affair, though it still left him with some damage. Having been a central part of Reagan's White House was no longer just an asset, as it now came with a hefty price tag.

Atwater was building his team of staff and volunteers, doing fundraising and developing the state-by-state apparatus. If he was the dark prince among political strategists, he met his match in Roger Ailes when it came to shaping the message. Ailes became part of the campaign, advising, drafting ads and co-creating strategy with Atwater.

"He has two speeds," Atwater said admiringly of Ailes. "Attack and destroy."[43]

Ailes and Atwater understood each other well. With an uphill battle ahead, Bush decided to strengthen the team further by also bringing in his old friend James Baker. Baker and Atwater worked closely together. But even with Baker and Ailes onboard, Atwater remained the grand master of strategy.

There were huge obstacles to overcome. As late as Memorial Day in '88, polls had Bush 16 points behind the Democratic nominee, Governor Michael Dukakis of Massachusetts. It was not the energetic start of the campaign that Atwater had envisaged. His biggest headache was that Bush had an image problem. To many, he seemed weak, bordering on a wimp. *Newsweek* magazine even put Bush on its cover under the headline, "Fighting the Wimp Factor." The showdown with Rather had shown Bush from a tougher side, but it wasn't enough to change the overall perception. In '88, Bush's negatives had reached 44 percent. In other words, there simply wasn't any way to build Bush's positives high enough to beat Dukakis in November.

Back in Democratic dominated South Carolina in the late '70s, Atwater had observed how Republicans struggled to win when they ran mostly positive campaigns. "You had to make the case that the other guy, the other candidate, was a bad guy," he had concluded. Now, with Dukakis far ahead in the polls and his own candidate embroiled in problems, Atwater turned to his old mantra. If he couldn't win by promoting his own candidate, he would win by taking down Dukakis.

So, when Atwater set up his "opposition research" team, he let everyone at campaign HQ understand that this was their highest priority. He had about 100 researchers – some professionals, some volunteers – working day and night in three shifts, with a budget of $1.2 million to spend on the sleuthing of Michael Dukakis.[44]

Often such research is done mainly to unearth any unfortunate surprises about your own candidate. After all, who remembers every statement they have ever made, every vote they have ever given, or every person they have been photographed with or fooled around with in their youth? So, you dig into your own candidate's records, and if you did solid research, you could build a defense and have answers ready for questions that could come from the press or attacks from your opponent.

While in the Dukakis campaign, the main point of the research was to know yourself; in Atwater's operation, it was all about knowing your enemy.

"The only group that I was interested in having report to me directly was opposition research," Lee later mused.

The team put together a 312-page textbook called *The Hazards of Duke*, which was openly distributed both to Bush's campaign county chairmen as well as reporters. The prison-furlough issue that later would become so huge, wasn't given much weight and came late in the book. Still, Atwater's plan of attack was, quite literally, an open book to both reporters and Dukakis' campaign.

That Atwater was about to declare full war and bombard his enemy with attacks shouldn't have come as a surprise to anyone. Pug Ravanel, who had some experience with Atwater's attacks, wrote a letter to the Dukakis campaign in May '88 stating:

> My very strong belief is that Lee Atwater is the premier neg-ative strategist in American politics .... I have a deep suspicion that Atwater will begin hitting at Dukakis very early, perhaps even before the convention ... If Mike [Dukakis] does not re-spond right away, he could risk having the negatives well set in the minds of Americans before he could begin to change them.[45]

But the warning didn't register in the Dukakis campaign. They still didn't understand that a master of dirty tricks, the Bad Boy from the South, was about to hit them right in the face.

Getting Away with Murder

Back in 1974, in Lawrence, Massachusetts, a young man named William Horton had been part of a brutal gas station robbery. Even though the 17-year-old gas station attendant had cooper-ated by handing over all of the money in the cash register to Hor-ton and his two accomplices, Horton still stabbed him 19 times before dumping him in a garbage can where he bled to death. Horton was convicted of murder, sentenced to life imprisonment and incarcerated in Massachusetts. Even though he had been im-prisoned without the possibility of parole, in 1986, he was allowed to take part in a weekend furlough program. Horton used this chance to escape. In 1987, he showed up in Maryland, where he attacked a young couple. He raped the woman twice after pistol-whipping, knifing, binding, and gagging her fiancé. Then he stole their car. Hunted down by the police, he was sentenced in Maryland to two consecutive life terms plus 85 years. The sentencing judge refused to return Horton to Massachusetts, saying, "I'm not prepared to take the chance that Mr. Horton might again be furloughed or otherwise released."[46]

The furlough program in Massachusetts had been enacted under a previous Republican governor, and Governor Dukakis had supported it steadfast. In 1976, while in his first term as governor, Dukakis had vetoed a bill that would have banned furloughs for first degree murderers like Horton. Massachusetts papers had been writing about the Horton case for a while, so it was a well-known case in the state. In a debate between the candidates during the Democratic Primary, Al Gore had even criticized the furlough program, though he did not mention Horton by name. Then the popular magazine *Readers Digest* made it a national case with an article about the murderer, the furloughs, and Dukakis, under the headline "Getting Away with Murder."

This was around the same time as Dukakis polled a 16-point lead on Bush, which would have been enough to depress any campaign manager. But Atwater wasn't gloomy. As he watched focus groups discuss the Horton case, hearing their reactions to questions about Dukakis' stands on capital punishment and on giving first degree murderer's weekend passes from prison, Atwater was in fact more elated than pessimistic. He had found a wedge issue more powerful than he had ever imagined.

Atwater went to see the candidate himself, laying out his proposed plans of full-scale attack, using Willie Horton as a political weapon of mass destruction. Bush hadn't entered the race to lose, and judging by the polls, they were in deep trouble. So, the VP signed on to Atwater's strategy – a plan of full annihilation.

"By the time we're finished, they're going to wonder whether Willie Horton is Dukakis' running mate," Atwater stated confidently.[47]

In a speech in the middle of June to the Illinois state Republican Convention, using unusually sharp language, Bush portrayed Dukakis as weak on crime. Bush asked rhetorically, "What did the Democratic Governor of Massachusetts think he was doing when he let convicted first-degree murderers out on weekend passes?". He continued:

> *Why, even after one of the criminals that he let out brutally raped a woman and stabbed her fiancé, why won't he admit his mistake? ...I think that Governor Dukakis owes the people of the United States of America an explanation as to why he supported this outrageous program.[48]*

In a speech to the National Sheriffs Association on June 23, Bush again invoked the terror of Willie Horton. "He was sentenced by a judge – sentenced to life in prison," the VP said of the murderer. "Before being eligibility for parole, Horton applied for a furlough. He was given the furlough. He was released. And he fled – only to terrorize a family and repeatedly rape a woman. So I'm opposed to these unsupervised weekend furloughs for a first-degree murderer."[49] In speech after speech, Bush continued to pummel Dukakis on the Horton case, portraying his opponent as too soft on crime.

But to get the Horton story out to the masses, journalistic accounts from the President's speeches weren't enough. The National Security Political Action Committee (NSPAC) was not directly linked to the Bush campaign, as it was legally barred from having any direct contact with Atwater, Ailes, and the rest of the Bush campaign. However, the NSPAC's media consultant Larry McCarthy had until recently worked for Ailes. Now he took his cue from Atwater's strategy and produced an ad called "Weekend Passes." It was brutally effective.

Since the ad was produced and the airtime paid for by the NSPAC, Atwater and the campaign could distance themselves from it. But many thought the coincidence of an independent ad that fit so well into the Bush campaign's strategy and narrative was more than a little peculiar. The author of the book *Boss Rove*, Craig Unger, claims Atwater was actively involved in the making of the spot. According to Unger's account, Atwater invited Republican operator Roger Stone over to see it. Stone is known for being one of the most merciless proponents of hardball politics, but even he advised against airing it because it was too racist. That didn't convince Atwater.

"Y'all a pussy,"[50] he allegedly replied. The ad would run.

Featuring pictures of Dukakis, a mugshot of Willie Horton, and on-screen text highlighting the message with words like "stabbing," "raping," and "weekend passes," the narrator told the viewers:

> Bush and Dukakis on crime: Bush supports the death penalty
> for first degree murderers. Dukakis not only opposes the death
> penalty, he allowed first degree murderers to have weekend
> passes from prison. One was Willie Horton who murdered a

boy in a robbery, stabbing him nineteen times. Despite a life sentence Horton received ten weekend passes from prison. Horton fled, kidnapped a young couple, stabbing the man and repeatedly raping his girlfriend. Weekend prison passes - Dukakis on crime.

The NSPAC's "Weekend Passes" spot ran for a while. Then, the day after it had been taken off the airwaves, Atwater and Ailes released an ad from the Bush campaign. It was called "Revolving Door," and featured prisoners walking through a revolving door of a prison, while the narrator intoned:

As governor Dukakis vetoed mandatory sentences for drug dealers; he vetoed the death penalty; his revolving door prison policy gave weekend furloughs to first degree murderers not eligible for parole. While out, many committed other crimes like kidnapping and rape. And many are still at large. Now Michael Dukakis says he wants to do for America what he's done for Massachusetts. America can't afford that risk!

On the screen, words like "268 escaped" and "many still at large" flashed as the narrator spoke, leaving the impression that hundreds of first-degree murderers were now at large, roaming the streets of Dukakis' home state. The advertisement didn't mention Horton or feature his photograph. It didn't need to. Everybody could make that connection for themselves.

The furlough issue was more than a highly effective wedge issue, harvesting voters and demobilizing democrats. It also became a lightning rod for the other difficult questions that arose throughout the last months of the campaign. One example was when Bush's running mate Dan Quale completely faltered in the VP-candidate debate. The Bush campaign simply went out the next day and stepped up the attack on Dukakis, describing him as the "Furlough King," criticized Dukakis as cold, saying that he had shown "an astounding lack of sensitivity" to crime victims.

"In the way that Bush earlier tried to question the patriotism of Dukakis, today he tried to depict him as a heartless man who prefers criminals to their victims," David Hoffman of *The Washington Post* wrote, adding, "Bush denied he was engaging in 'negative campaigning.'"[51]

But Bush obviously was engaged in negative campaigning, just as Atwater had prescribed.

Then, while under attack, Dukakis fumbled. In the second presidential debate between Bush and Dukakis, Bernard Shaw of CNN asked the Democratic candidate: "Governor, if Kitty Dukakis were raped and murdered, would you favor an irrevocable death penalty for the killer?"

It was a brutal question, and a hush went through the audience, people leaning forward to hear his answer.

The Dukakis campaign had, of course, known that such a question would come. With all the press coverage of the issue, as well as the attack ads, it was inevitable. Dukakis campaign manager Susan Estrich had rehearsed an answer with the candidate. Interviewed for the CNN series *The Race for the White House*, Estricht later recalled, "It was going to be a question coming of who's side are you on: The criminals or the victims. It was our last chance in front of a national audience of that size" to push back the attack.

In fact, Dukakis had good reason to show indignation. His own family had been victims of crimes, and he knew firsthand what this was about. So, his campaign wanted him to tell that story.

"This is what the answer has to be," Estrich said:

> *I know what it's like to be the victim of crime. I found my brother killed, by the side of the road, left to die by a hit and run driver. My father in his 70's was in his medical office. And they came in, they tied him up and robbed him - a 75-year old man. So believe me, I know what it's like to feel that pain.*

It was a great answer. But Dukakis didn't use it.

With the nation waiting on the edge of their seats, waiting to hear his reaction to the question about his wife being raped and murdered, Dukakis didn't tell the audience about his own family being victimized. Instead, he answered the question in a flat non-emotional tone: "No, I don't, Bernard, and I think you know that I've opposed the death penalty during all of my life. I don't see any evidence that it's a deterrent and I think there are better and more effective ways to deal with violent crime." As Dukakis showed no emotion at the brutal question, instead answering clinically and unemotionally, it was like all the air went out of the room. Even his own campaign manager thought: "He's dead."[52]

Maybe Dukakis's presidential hopes had died up on that debate stage, maybe not. Either way, Atwater wasn't going to ease up on the pressure. Throughout the whole campaign, up until the last voting station closed, he made sure the democrat felt his opponent breathing down his neck. Atwater made sure there was a volunteer in front of Dukakis's home each morning, carrying a Bush-campaign sign. The only billboard the campaign rented was the one behind the state capitol in Boston, so that Dukakis would have to see the "Bush 88" poster every time he went to work. College kids were hired to line up with Bush signs along the route to Logan Airport whenever Dukakis had a scheduled flight. Atwater set out to make Dukakis feel hunted.

His old unit, the College Republican National Committee, even distributed small yellow cards that depicted a man flying from an open cage like the drawing on a Monopoly game card, with the bold text "Get out of Jail, Free." Willie Horton was mentioned on the back of the cards, which were widely circulated in Dukakis's hometown of Boston.

Then, a false rumor was started that Dukakis had once secretly undergone psychiatric treatment for clinical depression. The rumor grew among journalists, and when President Reagan was asked about it during a press conference, he answered with a clever smile and a joke that seemed suspiciously well-rehearsed, "Look, I'm not going to pick on an invalid."[53]

All the networks ran with the story. The rumor didn't have to be true; the important thing was that it was out there, and now everybody had heard it. To some swing voters, it created real doubts about Dukakis' mental health. No one knew whether the rumor was masterminded by a dirty trickster or whether the President perhaps had been briefed before his "spontaneous" joke at the press conference. In the end, that didn't really matter. The rumor fulfilled its purpose either way, to Atwater's delight.

On the November 8, 1988, George Bush was elected the 41st President of the United States of America. Dukakis, who had been ahead by 16 points as late as Labor Day, won only 10 states, to Bush's 40. Atwater had promised to crush Dukakis, and he had. Now the Bad Boy of politics celebrated hard. He had won the race.

"Anyone who felt good about American politics after the 1988 election campaign probably also enjoys train wrecks, or maybe a day on the beach watching an oil slick wash ashore," *Newsweek* later wrote.[54]

Many saw the hyping of the Willie Horton issue as some sort of proof that Atwater was a racist, or at least an immoral person using race to divide the electorate. But Atwater biographer John Brady felt this was too harsh a judgment.

> *No one who knew Lee Atwater personally - either as a pol or as a good ol' boy - ever felt he was a racist. ... But of course, Lee wasn't prejudiced against people with emotional problems either, and he called Tom Turnipseed 'someone who was hooked up to jumper cables'... He prided himself on playing to voter's deep-rooted attitudes...[55]*

Atwater was a master strategist. He understood exactly how to move voters. And most importantly, he hated to lose, and absolutely had to win. How that victory was achieved seemed to be of secondary importance to him.

The Last Campaign

Atwater had stated he had only two goals in life – to manage a winning presidential campaign and to become head of his party. As a thank you from the newly elected president, he was named the new chairman of the Republican National Committee. Now he could check both boxes, and he hadn't even turned 40 yet.

As always, Atwater had big plans and was spurting with energy. The RNC had traditionally been more of a Party Bank, mainly organizing fundraising and distributing money to worthy Republican candidates. Atwater wanted to change that dramatically. He wanted to reshape the RNC into a party that resembled a permanent national campaign, a political force in itself.

He hired the highly talented operative Mary Matalin as his deputy. Wrote Matalin:

> Working with Atwater and running the RNC was a dream job for a political junkie... Lee was competitive in all things. He always said that losing made him physically ill... I learned more from Lee in that job than I did on the entire campaign.

And there was another reason why working for Atwater turned out a good opportunity for Matalin: "Atwater was interested in the bigger picture and had little inclination to run the day-to-day operation, he gave me carte blanche and free rein to set it up however I wanted."[56]

While Matalin ran the nuts and bolts of the organization at RNC headquarters, he could strategize, travel, give speeches, fire up the grassroots, and sell his grand vision of a GOP for the next century. He would use his drive and energy to build a political force that was unstoppable. He started building a machine designed to create new lasting voter coalitions.

Atwater was certainly feared by his foes, who were desperate to know what he was up to. The offices of the RNC had to be swept regularly for listening devices after they discovered that a telephone was bugged. Another time, Atwater had a strange feeling he was being tailed. The RNC hired a private investigator, who discovered that he was right. Lee lured the spies into a gas station, and while they were keeping an eye on him, had his aide stick a banana in their exhaust pipe.[57]

But his grand plan of a new and unbeatable Republican machine abruptly came to a halt on March 5, 1990. While giving one of his stump speeches, Lee suddenly collapsed on stage. He was rushed to a hospital, where the doctors discovered a large brain tumor. It came as a shock, totally out of the blue. Doctors sought to curb the tumor with radiation and chemotherapy.

Wrote Matalin, "He ran his illness like he ran a campaign. He made me, his wife Sally, and the rest of the people who cared about him research the best doctors and the treatments with the highest possible chance of success. He chose the most radical, the most risky."[58] As the cancer treatment wreaked havoc on Lee's body, making him bloated and unrecognizable, his existence became one of constant pain, a struggle to survive, minute by minute, day by day.

Something else changed as well. All his life, he had tried to drown out the image of his baby brother Joe, who had died in front of him that fateful day so long ago, and whose screams he had carried with him every day and night ever since. He had filled his entire adult life with work – from early morning to late at night, as well as most weekends, leaving little time for reflection. Maybe it was his need to escape those haunting memories from his childhood that had led him to also escape himself, immersing himself into the political battlefield.

If it was a form of escape, it had worked for a long time. But not any longer. Now he was fighting for his life. Sensing this was a battle he could lose, Lee started writing letters of apology to some of the people he had hurt during the vicious campaigns he had masterminded. In letter after letter, he acknowledged that he sometimes had crossed the line of decency in the constant quest for victory.

"Mostly I am sorry for the way I thought of other people," he told an interviewer. "Like a good general, I treated everyone who wasn't with me as against me."[59]

As the sickness overcame him, Lee finally had to accept his fate. In a piece in *Life* magazine in January he wrote, "My campaign-honed strategies of political warfare were simply no match for this dogged opponent. Cancer is no Democrat."[60]

He died on March 29, 1991, only 40 years old.

The Republican strategist Karl Rove, who had known Lee most of his adult life, wrote, "I am not certain how many really close friends he had, but loneliness may be the normal state of genius. And Lee was a genius at politics – at understanding people and what would move them."[61]

Atwater's old enemy Michael Dukakis, who was one of those who had received a letter of apology before Lee died, called the death a tragedy.

"We obviously were on opposite sides of a tough and negative campaign, but at least he had the courage to apologize," Dukakis said. "That says a lot for the man."[62]

Lee Atwater was immensely successful. He created a new and intense negative campaigning style. He was a strategic genius. He achieved more in his short lifetime than most dare dream about.

But had all that brought him happiness? Lee spent his last days at the hospital with his mother, talking about his little brother who had died that gruesome death more than 30 years earlier. When pain overcame him during those last weeks, he cried his brother's name.

Looking into his mother's eyes, Lee asked, "Mama, wasn't Joe lucky? Wasn't Joe lucky?"[63]

CHAPTER 2

GUNSLINGER FOR HIRE

Dick Morris

"In today's hype-addled world, the word 'brilliant' is tossed around too casually. But in this rare case, the adjective is right. Morris is brilliant – when he's not being stupid."

- Newsweek

The Monster, the Twister, and the Prostitute

In the summer of 1996, the tabloid *Star* magazine revealed that President Clinton's top strategist Dick Morris had regularly met with a prostitute at the Jefferson Hotel, just blocks from the White House. The article revealed that Morris, in conversations with the prostitute, had referred to the President and his wife in racy, disparaging terms.[64] The *Star* also published a photograph of Morris in an embrace with the girl on the balcony of his suite at the hotel. Morris' extramarital affair with a woman of the trade was one thing, bad enough in the middle of a campaign. But his indiscretions towards his employer – the leader of the free world – was far worse.

Just two days before the start of the Democratic convention, Morris had showed the girl copies of the speeches that both Hillary Clinton and Vice President Gore were to deliver a few days later. On another occasion, he had let the girl listen in on his confidential phone calls with President Clinton: "There was no doubt about it, it was The Man," the *Star* quoted her as writing in her diary. "I was finally impressed."

She claimed the President's chief strategist had even told her secret information concerning a NASA mission. Morris had called President Clinton "the Monster" on account of his quick temper, while the first lady got the label "the Twister," allegedly because of her tendency to stir things up.[65]

The story broke in the middle of the 1996 Democratic convention, and Morris immediately resigned his job as campaign strategist for President Clinton, issuing a statement that read:

> *While I served I sought to avoid the limelight because I did not want to become the message. Now, I resign so I will not become the issue. I will not subject my wife, family or friends to the sadistic vitriol of yellow journalism. I will not dignify such journalism with a reply or answer. I never will. I was deeply honored to help this President come back from being buried in a landslide and to make it possible for him to have a second chance at a second term. He is a great President and a great man. ...I want to thank the President and the Democratic Party for allowing me to return. I hope I have served them well.*

Served them well, he most certainly had. Clinton would most probably not have been a two-term president had it not been for Morris' mastery of political strategy. In fact, there may not have been a Clinton presidency at all. If Morris hadn't been around, Bill Clinton's political career might well have ended decades earlier. He was a major strategic force in the long and winding political life of Bill Clinton, going as far back as the late 1970s. He was there at many of those most crucial of moments, when the path to defeat seemed far more likely than the path to victory. But with Morris' help victory was achieved, nonetheless.

No one knew this better than the President himself. And despite Morris' grievous indiscretion, he was deeply thankful for their long political partnership. His statement showed his empathy in the midst of the raging scandal, "Dick Morris is my friend, and he is a superb political strategist. I am and always will be grateful for the great contributions he has made to my campaigns, and for the invaluable work he has done for me over the last 2 years."[66]

Years later, propelled into the far-right corners of American politics, Morris was to turn his back on the man who had treated him so graciously at that pivotal moment. The strategist's journey to the fringes of the political right was as much a product of his ousting by the Democratic Party, as anything else. But by then, Clinton's eight-year presidency was coming to an end, and Morris and Clinton had already created history together.

"Even if this episode destroys me," Morris told *Time's* Walter Isaacson at the time of the scandal, "I will have done one great thing in my life, which is to help [Clinton] get the chance to lead this country."[67]

Politics Has Been My Whole Life

Richard Morris was born in New York, the son of the writer Terry Morris and attorney Eugene Morris. Little Dick was born prematurely, weighting only two-and-a-half pounds. He walked late, learned to talk late, read late, wrote late. Still, he turned out to be a bright kid. His parents weren't especially interested in children, but they liked young adults, so Dick quickly adapted. He began reading *The New York Times* regularly when he was eight because, "commenting on international affairs was the only way for me to get my parents' attention."[68]

By fifth grade, Dick had written a short biography of each and every President. He later wrote:

Politics has been my whole life. I first worked for a presidential candidate in the fourth grade of elementary school, when I helped elect the president of the student council. His name was Mark Zarro. Capitalizing on the popular TV show of the time, my slogan was naturally "The Z that stands for Zorro."[69]

During the 1960 presidential race, Dick canvassed his Manhattan Upper West Side apartment building on behalf of John F. Kennedy. The 12-year-old dressed in a jacket and tie before visiting each of the 64 apartments, speaking to all the tenants. As a teenager, he set up amateur political organizations in the city's high schools and colleges. He made deals with kids he thought could be good candidates. He would write their speeches, help them organize their supporters, and advise them on campaign themes. He had only one condition; they had to recruit their followers to work with him. Many of these young candidates would go on to have successful political careers, like US Congressman Jerrold Nadler. Morris ran Nadler's first campaign – for class president.[70] Dick Morris may have been only a kid, but he had found his life calling.

Soon, Morris and some friends began expanding their political activity. The main goal of their adolescent organization was to take control of the West Side by challenging the Democratic Party district leaders in primary contests. By the age on 21, Morris ran seven successful challenges for the post of Democratic Party district leader. In one, he helped Richard Gottfried become district leader.[71] Gottfried would go on to represent the 75th District in the New York State Assembly for more than 40 years, making him the longest-serving member of that body.

Dick was much more liberal than the Democratic Party establishment of Manhattan. He even worked as a volunteer on the political staff of George McGovern in Chicago in 1968. When the machine politicians secured the nomination for Humphrey, he joined the demonstrators on the streets outside the convention to protest what he saw as arrogance and autocracy.

The young political operator had a temperament perfectly suited for negative politics. Being deeply enraged, he had no difficulty in empathizing with the anger and resentment simmering in the electorate. In his early career as a consultant, he became known in political circles for contributing to upset defeats of Senate and gubernatorial incumbents in New Mexico, Texas, California, Massachusetts, New Hampshire, and Florida.

At the same time, he worked for the New York City Budget Commission, a civic watchdog group dedicated to improving productivity and efficiency in city and state services.

"Here I saw massive inefficiency in government," Morris later wrote.

> I found [sewage] plants that had been under construction for twenty years, and had still not been completed. Sanitation trucks that had three men when they needed only two... It took longer to build a New York City school in the 1970s than it had taken to build the Empire State Building in the '20s. ...I discovered that government was not a good instrument for social progress.[72]

The work Morris did for the Budget Commission made a deep impression and left him reevaluating his liberal views on government's role and scope.

Working on Howard Samuels's unsuccessful race for governor in '74, Morris met a lovely young woman named Eileen McGann. They fell deeply in love and married three years later. As the turbulent years of LBJ, Nixon and the recession melted away into the new Reagan era, and as he found more personal peace through his marriage, Morris gradually changed from a negative tactician to a more complex, savvier strategist. He remained a hired gun but began seeking out new types of issues that could win the races he worked on. Most often these were positive issues that he could use as emotional triggers to rouse the voters.

In Texas, Morris worked for Democratic governor Mark White aiming to attract more independent voters with positive new initiatives. In New Hampshire, he worked with Warren Rudman as he became the first successful US Senate candidate to reject Political Action Committee (PAC) funds. He wrote an ad for Rudman asking voters, "Wouldn't it be nice to have a senator we could call our own?"

In New Mexico in 1982, Morris helped Jeff Bingham to an offset defeat of the incumbent Senator, Jack Schmidt. They made an ad simply saying:

Do you believe we should drill for oil in national parks? Jack Schmidt says yes because we need the oil. Jeff Bingham says no because we may need oil, but we need our heritage more. Two good men for Senate. On Election Day, vote for the one who agrees with you.

This was miles from the negative attack ads flooding the airwaves. And it worked. The issue-based campaign style, built on positive messages that at the same time contained a negative differentiator between his candidate and the opponent, became a Morris trademark.

One of his most prominent clients was the Republican congressman Trent Lott, who in 1988 was running for the US Senate from Mississippi. Lott's opponent, Democratic congressman Wayne Dowdy, ran an ad in which a Trent Lott lookalike was seated in the backseat of a chauffeur-driven limousine. As the limo drove through the countryside, it passed an old lady groping futilely in her mailbox for a check that had not come. The announcer attacked Congressman Lott for supposedly voting to cut Social Security benefits and upbraided him for having a chauffeur at public expense. The ad concluded, "Let's cut Trent Lott's chauffeur, not Social Security."

Morris always did his research. Now he found out that Lott's actual chauffeur wasn't a chauffeur at all, but a security officer named George Awkward. So, he created a brilliant counter-ad. It featured the real security officer in his shirtsleeves, with his shoulder holster and gun prominently visible, speaking directly into the camera:

> *I'm George Awkward. I've been a member of the Washington DC police force. Since an attempted terrorist bombing in the Capitol, Congress voted to provide security protection for its leaders. My job is to guard House Minority Whip Trent Lott. Now, in a negative ad in Mississippi, Wayne Dowdy is saying I'm Trent Lott's chauffeur. Mr. Dowdy, I'm nobody's chauffeur! Got it?!*

The ad changed the race. Morris had created a popular catchphrase. Kids all over Mississippi started saying, "Got it?!" whenever they could. Lott won handsomely.

A prominent national figure like Lott was an important client to Morris. But he wasn't *the* client. That was a charismatic Democrat from Arkansas, whom he had met years earlier. Morris had begun building his campaign business in the late '70s, soliciting clients from around the country, when he met the most important man of his career. His first real client became the unknown, newly elected Attorney General of the small state of Arkansas, William Jefferson Clinton.

The Youngest Governor

In the early fall of 1977, Bill Clinton was sitting in his office, drinking coffee with his chief of staff Steve Smith. The ambitious, energetic and hardworking attorney general, then only 31 years old, was pondering whether to run for governor of Arkansas or for the US Senate in 1978. Initially, Clinton was leaning towards the Senate, mostly because of the length of tenure. While the governor had to run again every two years, senators had six-year terms. This meant a lot more time to govern before you had to start gearing up for the next reelection campaign.

But the Senate race was shaping up to be a highly contested primary. Two Democratic congressmen, Jim Guy Tucker and Ray Thornton, had already declared their candidacies, and most expected the sitting governor, David Pryor, to run as well. Clinton thought he could help sway Pryor either way, depending on what position he wanted to run for himself. He just had to make up his mind. And to do that, he craved more data.

Clinton and Smith had heard about this young political consultant in New York, Dick Morris, who had some novel new ideas about how to use polls both to predict likely final outcomes of an election, as well as shape rhetorical arguments in campaigns. To get clients, Morris had called every Democrat in the United States that was running for senator or governor in 1978. He made 60 attempts and ultimately found three clients. Clinton was the first. So, when Smith called him, Morris was desperate to sign on. He made up some nonsense about having to be in the neighborhood anyway and flew to Little Rock to meet the ambitious attorney general in person.

At their first meeting, the two instantly clicked. Clinton jumped straight into a discussion on whether he should run for the senate or for the governorship and pressed Morris on how he could use a poll to help him decide.

"I said, what you do is you kind of run the whole campaign in front of the voters," Morris recalled. "You do the ads you're going to do, what your opponent will say, what you'll be attacked for, what you will attack your opponent for, your answers... you run the whole campaign for a group of voters and you poll them and you see how they vote."[73]

Though this was a new approach to political polling, it was done all the time in the entertainment industry, Morris remembered.

"It was an idea I had gotten from my partner at the time that polled for movies. When *Jaws II* came out, or the new James Bond, there would be a storyline and he would poll it," he explained. It was a total revelation to Clinton. "Here was someone who was focused on politics, and I was outlining a way that you could approach it rationally and systematically, and have some means of determining it... And we hit it off very well," Morris told the television host Charlie Rose years later.[74]

To say that they hit it off well was quite an understatement. In fact, Clinton had charmed Morris, who walked out of the office mesmerized. After their meeting, he flew home to tell his wife, "I've met a man who could become president of the United States." Clinton had a sense of seriousness, a charisma that was undeniable, Morris felt. He felt an almost "magical presence" about Clinton that he had to resist if he was to stay objective.[75]

Clinton was not the only one that had left a good first impression. Fascinated by Morris' scientific approach to the political game, the ambitious Arkansan hired him to do a poll on the two races. The results showed Clinton could win the governorship without any problems. Morris told him that there was a good chance he could win the Senate race too, though this was much more uncertain. Clinton's challenge, Morris told him, was not Governor Pryor, who most likely would "fade in a though primary against a young charismatic candidate"; it was the face-off with the other candidates. Morris's conclusion was in stark contrast to the conventional wisdom of the time that held the sitting governor as the strongest candidate in the Senate race.

Clinton also wanted to talk about how he should communicate with voters on issues. Morris told Clinton:

> ...you can't go out there and say, 'I love children.' Voters sense that's baloney. You can't even say, 'I'm for education.' Voters know you incur no risks with such a bland position. But if you say, 'I want to raise taxes to help schools,' then voters can believe you really care about kids because they see you're willing to take heat for them.[76]

Clinton was impressed, said he felt the same way, and that he would probably end up running for the governorship – if Governor Pryor decided to enter the Senate race.[77]

In a private meeting a few weeks later, Pryor told the young attorney general he had decided it was time to end his time in the Governor's Mansion and run for the Senate. He asked Clinton to stay out of the Senate battle, reassuring him that he would be elected governor. Pryor even tried to make the governorship sound more attractive to Clinton, telling him he could break the state record and serve longer than anybody else had ever done.[78] With Pryor's decision made, Clinton decided to follow Morris' advice and run for governor. But he would not go on to break the record for longest serving governor of Arkansas. Unbeknown to Pryor, Clinton had much higher ambitions.

With his potential contenders busy fighting over the Senate nomination, Clinton had no real opposition in the gubernatorial primary. He gained support both from the labor unions and the business community. The campaign also led in fundraising. Morris working closely with Clinton through the whole race, flying to Little Rock frequently to strategize and handle new developments. As the two got to know each other better, Morris learned to appreciate and take advantage of Clinton's openness to new and bold ideas, and he came to view the candidate as a shrewd political operative. Clinton's willingness to approach the political fray like a constant developing battle, where you have to stay on the alert and change course whenever necessary – sometimes swallowing your pride to get to fight another day – was hallmark traits of his political mind. It was also a quality that created an ideal space for the unconventional, brusque and often antagonizing Morris to operate within.

That the young attorney general had the ability to change positions when necessary, seemed a contradiction to his pronounced idealism. In the late '70s, he was a devoted liberal, who had worked both on the George McGovern race in 1972 and as a Jimmy Carter state campaign manager in 1976. Wayne King of *The New York Times* described him as, "Tall, handsome, a populist-liberal with a style and speaking manner as smooth as Arkansas corn silk." Clinton had a long range of progressive government programs he wanted to enact. But he always understood that to make a better world, first you have to seize power. That meant winning elections. And to do whatever was necessary to win. It was this quality that made him such a good match with Morris.

Clinton ran his 1978 gubernatorial campaign on three main issues: Raising teachers' salaries. Bringing in new industry. And preserving the environment. His first ad was a biographical one meant to introduce him to the voters. It featured his mother and his first-grade teacher, talking about his childhood. Both his message and his ads were positive and visionary, just like Morris coached.

His opponents tried to use his Ivy League education against him, trying to paint Clinton as an elitist, far removed from the everyday lives of ordinary people in Arkansas. Morris countered with ads that told the story of how Clinton had decided to come back to Arkansas after leaving Yale to seek public service. The message: He was one of them! One long-time political observer explained: "We're the lowest state in terms of education, and we're mighty proud of those who do get a good education."[79]

The gubernatorial primary ended with Clinton getting 60 percent of the vote, with the runner up receiving less than 22 percent. In a strong democratic state like Arkansas, this was as good as a victory in the general election. Clinton would be the next governor. Morris was not only about to get a victory in a gubernatorial race, he did so with his very first paying client.

But primary election night also brought a challenge. Pryor barely won the Senate primary, and was forced into a runoff with another Democrat, Jim Guy Tucker. This was a problem for Clinton. He wanted Governor Pryor to get the Senate seat and move on to Washington. So, Clinton went to work for the outgoing governor – and he brought Morris along.

Tucker was hammering Pryor for being too soft and lacking leadership skills. Tucker's slogan was "The Difference is Leadership." So, Clinton and Morris wrote a couple of ads to boost Pryor's credentials on that issue. The first ad depicted Pryor as a strong governor who had stood up to special interests when the security of the state was at hand. The second ad was written by Morris after his wife had noticed in the Congressional Quarterly that Tucker had a poor attendance in Congress, most probably because he had been out running for the US Senate seat. The ad featured a dull-voiced clerk calling the names of Arkansas congressmen:

> How does the House vote? Congressman Thornton? - Aye. - Congressman Hammerschmidt? - Aye. - Congressman Alexander? - Aye. - Congressman Tucker? ...Congressman Tucker? ...Is Jim Guy Tucker here? ...Will someone please check the cloakroom. ...Mr. Tucker? ...Mr. Tucker?

While continuing his frantic search, the announcer explained how often Tucker was absent and concluded by turning the Tucker slogan on its head, saying, "You can't lead if you're not there."

With the help of Clinton and Morris, Pryor went on to win the nomination, setting him on his path to Washington. The ads had made the needed impact on the electorate. But even if Pryor had Morris to thank for his victory, he didn't show much gratitude. Morris hadn't made a favorable impression on neither the outgoing governor nor his wife. On the contrary, Pryor felt "uneasy" about Morris, while his wife found him "especially disagreeable" and far too negative a presence. She even banned him from the Governor's Mansion.[80]

Clinton had no such qualms about Dick. He had found his very own master of strategy. After having secured the nomination, few were surprised when his first race for governor ended exactly like Morris had predicted. On election night, Bill Clinton won a handedly 64 percent of the vote and was elected the youngest governor in the country. Morris was elated. His first serious client had just been elected governor at the age of only 32. It was quite a start to his career as a political consultant.

Defeat and Resurrection

Clinton had won, but during the long race, he had also built up huge expectations.

"We've got to allow him time to make mistakes, like all young men will," one veteran statehouse official declared after his victory. "Our leaders are just human beings, after all."[81] It was a nice sentiment, but a sentiment far removed from reality.

The newly elected governor and his entourage immediately went to work, bubbling over with progressive ideas and initiatives.

He launched an ambitious agenda. Clinton wanted to create new state departments in energy and economic development, reorganize school districts, lift the standards of schools, and revamp the rural health care system. All this was to be achieved in his first two-year term, and most of the programs had to be crammed into the first budget as mere demonstration projects, with little money behind them.

Morris made a survey of Arkansas voters on the ideas Clinton had put into the budget, so they could be ranked in popularity and projected under some sort of overall theme. Combing through the poll answers, Morris had a hard time finding any such overall theme.

"He was left with a program that was thoroughly admirable but indescribable," Morris said. "There was a bit of everything. Like a kid in a candy store, he wanted to do it all." [82]

Clinton chose one large issue to define himself – building better roads. Good transportation infrastructure was important to the future of the state. In private, Clinton also expressed the belief that a major roads program would show that he was no Yale and Oxford elitist but had a deep understanding of rural Arkansas. Before presenting his highway proposal, Clinton asked Morris to conduct a poll on the voters' willingness to finance the initiative through an increase in the car license fee. [83]

Morris strongly advised against raising the fees. He warned that the increase in fees was one of those issues that could be felt by every single voter, especially by the voters in poorer rural areas that Clinton so badly needed for his reelection campaign. A campaign, that was only two years ahead. An increase in the car fees, Morris warned, could kill Clinton's chances of getting reelected. [84]

But the newly elected governor wanted the program and couldn't make himself believe Morris was right. The suggested fee-raises consisted of relatively small individual amount. Besides, it was a pledge he had made during the campaign, and it would win him favor with the highway contractors who were big contributors to political campaigns in Arkansas. So, he pushed on.

As soon as he presented the proposal, Clinton got in trouble with both the trucking industry and the poultry industry – two powerful lobbies in the legislature. To save his bill, the young governor signed off on a compromise that ended up angering everyone. The major burden of the increases was shifted from trucks to cars and pickups. And heavy pickups, mostly used in the rural areas, got the biggest increase. Now people got angry. Really angry.

There were people who had driven two hours over bad roads to bring their license plates for renewal. Many of them from experience carried the exact amount in their pocketbooks and no more. This was before the spread of ATMs, so when they got to the Department of Motor Vehicles and were charged twice their usual fee, they had to drive all the way back home to get more money, and then go back to the DMV again. This gave them exactly six long hours in which to decide just how much they hated the boy governor from Yale. In the press, Clinton went from being depicted as the Arkansas Wonder Boy, to being drawn as a child governor riding around on a tricycle. He should have listened to Morris.

Morris always felt Clinton had two different frames of minds. One was Clinton the savvy politician, always searching for a way to avoid defeat and come out on top, willing to embrace a host of new or controversial ideas to achieve victory. The other was Clinton the boy-scout, the idealist that wanted to stay above the fray, who didn't want to be attached to negative campaigning and saw himself mainly as a tool for good. Now, he felt, Clinton had gone all boy-scout on him.[85]

The frustration was mutual. After their disagreement on how the car fees would play out, Clinton thought Morris was just too negative. Listening to complaints from his entourage, he fired the strategist. Hillary later wrote, "...no one on Bill's staff or in his office could stand working with Morris, so they persuaded Bill to use a different team [for the 1980 election]."[86] Having Morris on the team was controversial, so Clinton simply cut him loose. It would prove to be the costliest mistake in the young governor's career.

Entering the reelection-campaign in 1980, Clinton met fierce opposition. He had a firm enough grip on the Democratic nomination, but this time around, that wasn't going to be enough. Frank White, a jovial savings and loans executive who had served under the former Democratic governor, switched parties and announced he would challenge Clinton as a Republican. After the car fees debacle and a handful of other political controversies, the young governor's electoral base was shrinking rapidly. This came at a time when President Carter was doing such a poor job, the Democratic Party was struggling all over. Still, the Arkansas polls weren't all that bad, and Clinton's team didn't perceive that they were about to lose.

But Hillary had a bad felling. She sensed something was amiss and called Morris to ask what he thought was happening. The strategist didn't mince his words. "He told me Bill was in real trouble and probably would lose unless he made some kind of dramatic gesture, like repealing the car tag tax or repudiating Carter," she recalled. But Hillary couldn't persuade anyone else in the Clinton entourage to ignore the polls that showed Clinton was winning.[87]

Towards the end of the '80 campaign, it became clearer to all that Clinton was in deep trouble. One day after campaigning, he returned to the office staggering from the negative reactions he was getting from voters.

"They're killing me out there," he said. "They hate my guts!"[88]

As White pounded Clinton with negative ads, the young governor's numbers went steadily down. Clinton didn't return fire. He was bewildered and didn't know what to do. Finally, Hillary called Morris again, begging for his help in the last days before the election. He got on a plane and hastened to Arkansas. But it was too late. His polling showed that few voters actually thought that Bill Clinton would lose, but at the same time, they felt he had ignored them and wanted to teach him a lesson. Six weeks before the election, Clinton had enjoyed a 41-point lead over his challenger, who entered the race with only 2 percent of the public knowing who he was. Even on Election Day, the exit polls showed Clinton winning by a wide margin.[89] But the polls hadn't picked up on the animosity Morris knew was out there.

The voters wanted to teach the Boy Governor a lesson, and Frank White ended up beating Bill Clinton, 52 to 48 percent. Morris had been right all along – about the car tax, the need for a dramatic gesture to remake the campaign, and about the deeper movements in the electorate that the polls didn't pick up on. But he had been ignored. And just like that, Clinton was no longer the youngest governor in America. He was now *the youngest ex-governor* in America.

After the 1980 defeat, Hillary called Morris to enlist his help in saving Bill's career. Putting the strategist back on their payroll, Clinton was eyeing a comeback in '82. Clinton listened to Morris now, and he had learned three important lessons through his defeat. The first was not to let an attack go unanswered. Or as he put it; "When someone is beating you over the head with a hammer, don't sit there and take it, take out a meat cleaver and cut off their hand!"[90] The second lesson was the need for a permanent campaign and continuous fundraising. In the 1980 campaign, he had lacked both money and volunteers; that wouldn't happen again. The third lesson was that the peddlers of conventional wisdom he had surrounded himself with didn't cut it. He needed Dick Morris' exceptional strategic skills, even if that came with the price of internal squabbling and controversy.

In addition to convincing Morris to climb back onboard, Hillary also reached out to her old friend Betsey Wright and got her to manage Clinton's '82 campaign. Wright would stay with Clinton for the next six years, restoring order and discipline to his life, organizing the Clinton machine. She also built a tremendous voter database that they could use to target voters.

Now Clinton and Morris were doing what they did best together – strategizing and finding new ways to communicate with the voters. Clinton knew he needed to raise money. The loss against White had partly been caused by the Arkansas press losing faith in Clinton. They had built him up, and now they wanted to tear him down – in their perception, he went from a Wonder Boy to a flawed, arrogant failure from an elite school. It seemed like every time he tried something new, they went for the negative angle. And this was the filter through which all of Clinton's statements, initiatives, and proposed programs now had to pass before reaching the voters.

Clinton, like Morris, understood that depending on the media to get their message across was nothing more than a recipe for defeat. They realized that they had to bypass the press and go straight to the people. That meant a lot of paid media time, which would cost loads and loads of money. It changed Clinton's whole approach to politics. From now on, he would continually be raising money to pay for political advertising – not just for the '82 election campaign, but for the rest of his political career. To Morris' delight Clinton was a natural at fundraising. This gave them the opportunity to always use television ads and other paid media to get his views out to voters, without the distorting filter of the press.

Clinton wasn't Morris' only client, of course. As his reputation grew, so did his client portfolio. And while most political consulting firms tend to stick to candidates from one party, that just wasn't in Morris' character. He jumped party lines without second thought and got criticized for it by both Democrats and Republicans. He shrugged of the criticism and defended his firm's political neutrality.

"We're not a political club, we're a business," he pointed out in an interview with *The New York Times* in 1982.[91]

Clinton certainly had no problem using a consultant that had a foot in both camps. In his eyes, it gave Morris the ability to see issues from both sides and to better understand the strategic thinking of his opponents. And that was the reason Clinton was such a good match with the strategist – he was more interested in actually winning than in the optics.

The two created a strategy and a game plan for Clinton's comeback as governor. Morris told Clinton straight up that he needed to apologize to the people of Arkansas. They had voted him out of office to teach him a lesson, and now he needed to let them know that he had heard them, that he had understood the message they had wanted to send him.

In December of '81, Clinton traveled to New York to meet up with Morris and shoot the first ad for the campaign. Just as prescribed by Morris, Clinton looked straight into the camera and said:

> In a few days I will formally announce my candidacy for gov- ernor. But before I do, I want to speak directly to you to share some of what I learned not only as governor but from my de- feat in the last election. All across this state, many of you have told me you were proud of some things I did as governor. But you also think I made some big mistakes, especially in increas- ing the car-license and title-transfer fee. When I became gov- ernor, we had serious problems with our streets and roads, and I did support those increases to try to solve the problems. But it was a mistake because so many of you were hurt by it... And I'm really sorry for that. When I was a boy growing up my daddy never had to whip me twice for the same thing. And now I hope you'll give me another chance... If you do, I assure you I won't raise the car licenses again."

It was the first ad of its kind. Paying for airtime to rekindle the memories of the things people didn't like about him in the first place had never been done before. It was an apology to the voters before the campaign had even begun.

When the ads started running in February 1982, it took people completely by surprise and got a lot of attention. But if he had hoped for a sudden jump in the polls, Clinton was disappointed. The effect wasn't a sudden outpour of support from the people of Arkansas. On the contrary, in the next poll, Clinton's ratings actually went down 10 points. Still, Morris wasn't breaking a sweat. He argued this was merely a temporary effect.

"It's like getting a smallpox shot," he explained, "You get a little sick, but you don't get the disease when you are exposed to it for real."[92]

Morris' logic was that Clinton would soon be immune to new attacks – especially attacks on his raising of the car fees, but also on other issues relating to his former term as governor – because he had apologized for his past mistakes and promised to do better in the future. By listening to Morris, Clinton had just made a huge gamble. Deep down, even Morris wasn't a hundred percent sure it would work out the way he hoped. After all, no one had ever done anything like this before.

By now, Clinton was deep in a heavily contested primary with Jim Guy Tucker as his main adversary – the man Clinton and Morris had helped defeat in the Senate race two years earlier. And this time, Clinton wasn't going to simply sit back and take his opponent's attacks. The two candidates went after each other from day one. Morris attacked Tucker as a tool of special interests, as someone too liberal for Arkansas. Clinton was seeking the middle ground and had no qualms about attacking Tucker as a bleeding heart on welfare issues. Tucker hit back, portraying himself as a though conservative democrat, attacking Clinton on car-tag fees, taxes, schools, and for commuting or cutting the sentences of 38 convicted murderers during the final weeks of his term.

But while Clinton's attacks sent Tucker tumbling down in the polls, Tucker's attacks on Clinton simply weren't working. On the contrary, Clinton's numbers rose steadily. It seemed Morris's strategy really had left Clinton immune.

"The polls showed a tremendous backlash of sympathy for Clinton because he had already apologized," Morris recalled. "People said, 'What's Tucker dumping on him for? He already apologized.'"[93]

After a runoff, Clinton won the primary with 54 percent of the vote. Now he just needed to unseat Governor White, who had beaten him two years earlier. If his campaign organization had been lacking money and structure two years earlier, his '82 campaign machine was its complete opposite. They had built an energetic volunteer apparatus, a large voter database, a dedicated staff, and the biggest war chest Arkansas had ever seen – the result of endless fundraising. And he had a solid strategy, developed by Morris.

White was beating Clinton over the head with a massive barrage of negative attacks. He attacked Clinton on issue after issue. But just like in the primary, the attacks didn't stick. Clinton lived by his new rule: When someone is beating you over the head with a hammer, don't sit there and take it, take out a meat cleaver and cut off their hand. Morris wrote one though ad after the other. With Morris' guidance, Clinton countered, ducked, and always hit back – hard.

The airwaves and the press were filled to the brim with the political war between White and Clinton. And, just like in the primary, Clinton's numbers went up while his opponents went down.

"We felt like we were behind bulletproof glass watching somebody aim at us and pull the trigger and the bullets splattered harmlessly," Morris recalled.[94]

Like Morris had predicted, Clinton had become immune. On election night, he won with 55 percent to White's 45. Bill Clinton had embraced Morris and risked his whole political career on one last daring campaign to retake the Governor's Mansion, and Arkansas had made him the Comeback Kid.

The Breakup

With Morris' help, Clinton went on to win reelection campaigns in 1984, 1986, and 1988. Then came 1990. Eyeing a bigger prize, Clinton struggled with whether he should run for reelection as governor or not. He had already held the job for 10 years, and he was considering running for president in 1992. But he feared leaving the Governor's Mansion could leave him with nothing, ending his political career if a presidential run didn't pan out. He discussed his dilemma with Morris. The strategist wasn't in any doubt. Clinton should definitely run for reelection. In the Democratic Primary, Clinton faced Tom McRae, who had hooked up with a savvy consultant named Mike Shannon. Shannon used very effective negative ads to suggest Clinton had overstayed his tenure and that Arkansas "deserved a leader that wouldn't just use the governorship to run for president." One ad showed Salvador Dalí clocks stretching out time surrealistically. In another ad, you could see Clinton supporters at the airport waving goodbye to Clinton, leaving on his presidential pursuit. It was symbolic that McRae had announced his candidacy carrying a broom with him on stage, declaring he was going to sweep clean Arkansas government and get rid of old ideas and career politicians.

Morris's polls found McRae gaining ground, and he reported to Clinton, "Your favorability is going up each week, but your vote share is going down. They're ready to give you a gold watch for your retirement, but they want a new governor. They think you've served them well, but that you've been in office too long."[95] Morris stressed the need to change the agenda from a referendum on Clinton's tenure, back to an election between the two candidates on the issues.

Hillary suggested she go to a McRae press conference and challenge him in person for misstating her husband's record and not presenting solutions of his own. All agreed. Ron Fournier of *The Atlantic*, who was covering the press conference, later described the confrontation:

> The sound of Hillary Clinton's low-heeled shoes on the marble hallway jarred McRae... The first lady of Arkansas rounded the corner and stormed his news conference. "Tom!" she shouted. "I think we oughta get the record straight!" Waving a sheaf of papers, Hillary Clinton undercut McRae's criticism of her husband's record by pointing to McRae's past praise of the governor. It was a brutal sandbagging. "Many of the reports you issued not only praise the governor on his environmental record," she said, "but his education and his economic record."[96]

It was a smart move which got a lot of press, changed the story, and broke McRae's momentum.[97]

Morris also made an ad to defend Clinton's many trips outside of Arkansas. During many of these trips, Clinton had not only been giving speeches, he had also brought back new business to the state. The ad showed workmen building a brick wall that rose higher and higher as the announcer spoke of Clinton's success in bringing jobs to Arkansas when on out-of-state trips. Citing McRae's criticism of these trips, the ad concluded, "Don't let McRae build a wall around Arkansas."

The Clinton race was not the only election Morris was handling in Arkansas. Betsey Wright, who now was state Democratic chairman, had asked Morris to work on several key state legislative races as well, to strong up Clinton's support in the legislature – a move intended to protect Clinton's home base if he was later to run for president. These races naturally took some of Morris's attention away from Clinton's own race.

Before the new ad and Hillary's stunt had taken full effect, Bill, Hillary, Morris, and Clinton's campaign manager were surveying a poll in a late-night strategy meeting that had McRae leading Clinton by 50 to 43 percent. Exhausted, angry and afraid for his career, Clinton finally lost his temper.

"You got me into this race," he screamed at Morris, "so you could make some extra money off me. That was the only reason!" By now his blood was pumping, his face was all red, and he shouted:

I'm about to lose this election, lose this primary, against a nobody, and you're too busy with the little legislative races that Betsey got you, to give me any attention at all. I pay your expenses and you come down here and you work on Betsey's

races, not mine. You've forgotten me. You've dismissed me.
You don't care about me. You've turned your back on me I
don't get shit from you anymore. You're screwing me! You're
screwing me!

Morris looked at him in amazed bewilderment. He too was tired and overworked. He was already taking major heat from his Republican clients for working for Clinton. For 12 years, he had worked for Clinton. He had even been fired but had come back when he was needed. In campaign after campaign, his advice, his strategies, and his ads had been a vital part of the Governor's path to victory. And now *he* was to blame for Clinton meeting some hard opposition?!

Morris couldn't take it anymore. He snapped, shouting back at Clinton, "Thank you. You've just solved my problem. I'm getting shit from [RNC Chairman Lee] Atwater...for working for you, and now I can solve my problem. Go fuck yourself! I'm quitting your goddamn campaign!"

As Morris got up and started to leave, Clinton charged up behind him, grabbed him and wrapped his arms around him to stop him from leaving. As they wrestled, Morris fell to the floor. Hillary helped him up. Bill became apologetic, saying he was sorry, asking Morris to please stay. But Morris charged out the door slamming it behind him.[98] As he sat in his hotel room calming down, he knew he needed to protect his own reputation. That meant not quitting the race after all. Morris stayed with Clinton throughout the campaign. But for now, their relationship had turned as sour as an unripe lemon.

In the end, the Morris-Clinton strategy, coupled with Hillary's ambush on McRae, saved the day. Clinton won the primary and would face Republican candidate Sheffield Nelson in November. Nelson used his huge personal wealth too fuel his campaign, which made him a formidable opponent. And even worse for Clinton, the chief Republican strategist, RNC Chairman Lee Atwater, had set his aim at the Arkansas Governor.

Atwater recognized that Clinton could pose a serious threat against Bush in the presidential elections two years down the line. So, he contributed significantly to the Nelson campaign. His logic was, if they could beat Clinton now, there was no way he could run in for president in '92. They would rather run against some other democrat. In the words of Atwater friend and RNC staffer Rich Petersen, "Lee recognized the threat of Bill Clinton and the quality of the candidate and tried to take him out of the game as early as possible."[99]

Atwater's contributions certainly helped Nelson. But taking down the Arkansas governor wouldn't be as easy as he thought. Clinton had enforced his campaign, soliciting talent from around the country, like the media consultant Frank Greer and pollster Stanley Greenberg. And Clinton's organization was a formidable campaign machine.

Throughout the race, Clinton was polling at around 55 percent of the vote. But as the race grew to a close, Nelson put out a surprisingly effective ad featuring Governor Clinton's own voice saying, "raise and spend."

The ad had the announcer saying: "What did Clinton do to us in 1979?"

Clinton's voice: "Raise and spend."
Announcer: "And what did he do to us in 1983?"

Clinton's voice: "Raise and spend."

Announcer: "And what did he do to us last year?"

Clinton's voice: "Raise and spend."

Announcer: "And what will he do to us next year if we reelect him?"

Clinton's voice: "Raise and spend."

The ad was catchy and aimed at Clinton's achilleas heel in conservative Arkansas. It was a possible game changer.

There was only one problem with the ad. It wasn't true. The Nelson campaign had cut Clinton's "raise and spend"-line from another speech where Clinton actually advocated economic prudency. However, the viewers didn't know that, and the ad started raising fears that Clinton would raise taxes if he was reelected. With Election Day fast approaching, Morris did another poll. As he got the results late one evening, he started going over them. The more he read, the worse he felt. In spite of the late hour, he decided he had to call the Governor. Clinton picked up the phone in the middle of the night to have Morris tell him he was down to 45 percent, and the answers in the poll clearly pointed to the "raise and spend"-issue as the major cause for the drop. The Governor was in deep trouble. And they had very little time to repair the damage.

Clinton and Morris reacted swiftly. Clinton got out of bed and drove straight to the television studio to shoot a rebuttal. There was no time for discussion, no testing of the message, no new poll. Morris – relying purely on his instincts – quickly wrote out a reply ad, which Clinton made a few changes to and then shot on the spot. Clinton looked straight into the camera and said:

This is Bill Clinton. You've probably seen Sheffield Nelson's negative ad using my own voice saying the words "raise and spend." But here's what I actually said in my speech to the legislature three years ago. "Unlike our friends in Washington, who can write a check on an account that is overdrawn, we can't. We can't just spend; we have to raise and spend." I was fighting for a balanced budget, not pushing higher taxes. But Nelson got out his scissors and edited the tape to give you the wrong impression. You can't trust Sheffield Nelson.

By dawn, the campaign had dozens of drivers ready to pick up the tapes and drive them to television stations throughout Arkansas. The Clintons even took out another personal bank loan to pay for airing the rebuttal ad. On Election Night, Clinton beat Nelson by 57 to 43 percent. Calling Morris afterwards, he thanked him for saving him, yet again.

Their last-minute action had saved Clinton's career. But later, when he asked Morris to come on board his 1992 presidential campaign, Morris turned him down. He wasn't over their quarrel yet. He still felt Clinton had let him down and taken him for granted. Morris said no, and recommended James "the Ragin' Cajun" Carville to run Clinton's '92 campaign. The Governor didn't know Carville, but Morris was sure he would do a great job. He thought that the Cajun's energy and passion were just what Clinton needed. As usual, his hunch was to prove absolutely correct. With Carville's help, Clinton went on to win the presidency, running as a "New Democrat" (chapter 4). In January 1993, Clinton moved into the White House.

Learning from Defeat - Again

With Morris on the sidelines, Clinton's first years as president were marked by several controversies and downturns. His big health care initiative, led by the First Lady, crashed and burned. Clinton had a Democratic majority in Congress, which pushed him to the left on a number of issues. The voters no longer saw the "New Democrat" they had voted for; instead, the President now seemed very much like an old-fashioned liberal.

While the White House went from one crisis to another, Republican House Minority Whip Newt Gingrich created "The Contract with America." The Contract laid out 10 policies that Republicans promised to bring to a vote on the House floor during the first 100 days of the new Congress, if they won the election. It brought a sense of national unity and clarity to the Republican election effort – in stark contrast to what the voters saw in the Democratic field.

Clinton knew that his party was struggling and that he was partly to blame for not being able to provide it with new energy and the needed focus. Even so, he still couldn't quite wrap his head around just how bad it could turn out. As so often when the Clintons struggled with understanding the mood of the country, they reached out to Morris. In the early fall of 1994, the First Lady put in a call to Dick.

"Bill and I considered Morris a creative pollster and a brilliant strategist," Hillary later explained in her autobiography. "I thought Morris's analysis might be instructive, if we could involve him carefully and quietly. With his skeptical views about politics and people, Morris served as a counterweight to the ever-optimistic Bill Clinton." Hillary felt the positive polls were wrong, that something was going on in the electorate that the polls didn't pick up. "Dick," she said, "this election doesn't seem right to me."[100]

So, Morris did a poll to tap the national mood. The results were highly discouraging. Most voters simply didn't believe President Clinton's biggest achievements – creating jobs, getting the deficit under control, getting the economy back on track. Obviously, this was bad news. But, as Morris pointed out, there were some good news as well. While voters didn't give Clinton credit for big achievements, they did give him credit for smaller victories, like the Brady Bill, the assault rifle ban, family leave, and AmeriCorps.

Morris told the President that the voters:

> ...are prepared to believe in your smaller achievements, and these are enough, more than enough, to move their votes back to you. They believe you delivered family and medical leave, and they love you for it. They believe you named pro-choice judges to the Court. They buy that you set up direct student lending and that this is lowering rent.[101]

It was something to build a competitive strategy on for the '96 reelection campaign. But it was far too late to salvage the '94 midterms, Morris said.

Speaking again on the phone just four days before Election Day in 1994, Morris told Clinton that the Democrats were going to lose their majorities in both the House of Representatives and in the Senate. He was sure of it. Clinton refused to believe such a bleak prediction. Maybe it was just Morris being his usual negative self again, he thought. Yes, maybe he would lose the Senate, the President said, but not the House. No way.

But yet again, Morris had gotten it right. 1994 became the year of the Republican Revolution, the Democrats suffering their biggest defeat in any midterm election in 50 years, losing both the House and the Senate. The morning after Election Day, Morris' phone rang early. It was Clinton.

"You were right," he said.

He understood now that he was in deeper trouble than he had thought. And that he needed Morris' help.

After the horrifying midterm defeat, Clinton hired him as his chief strategist for the '96 reelection campaign. They had less than two years to salvage the President's second term. Morris had helped him rescue his withering career back in 1982. Time and time again, when other pollsters and strategists had failed to read the electorate correctly, he had gotten it right. Now, for one last time, Clinton needed Morris' help to rescue the presidency and his legacy. He needed it badly.

They started having weekly meetings in December '94, which soon developed into the central forum for campaign strategy. Since Morris was such a controversial figure, Clinton at first gave him an alias and made sure most of the top staff didn't know about his central role. It didn't take long before people started to suspect that there was a hidden force behind the presidents new strategic thinking. Someone working in the shadows. Someone who had more influence over the President than the rest of his inner circle combined. They just couldn't figure out who it was.

Eventually, Clinton had to let the cat out of the bag. He included most of his central campaign staff in their strategy meetings.

Though there were a lot of huffs and puffs, the President had clearly made up his mind. Morris was there to stay. They might just as well make the best of it.

Morris prepared a document outlining a series of principles that would serve as the basis of their strategy. He made the case for letting the Republicans fast-forward the Gingrich agenda, most notably cutting the deficit, cutting taxes and cutting the overall size of the federal government. By letting the Republicans move ahead with the most popular issues that the voters had embraced in '94, these issues would make less of an impact in '96 since they would be on their way to be enacted. The Democrats, he argued, should present their own road to achieving the same overall goals, but without cutting programs that people needed the most.

By following this strategy, Morris said, they could move the public discourse from disagreement between Clinton and the Republican Congress on fiscal responsibility and tax cuts, to disagreement between them on important programs for the elderly and the poor. This would highlight Clinton's values. At the same time, the President should use executive branch action to show leadership in a positive direction, and foreign policy situations to demonstrate strength. Obviously, it was a daring strategy, sure to anger many Democrats in Congress. But Morris was sure it was the only clear path to victory.[102]

Morris saw himself as a new type of strategist, not merely packaging the message but actually crafting overall policy on major issues.

"Reporters like to use the word 'spin' to describe what political consultants do," he complained, "but the word implies no change in the substance, just in the rotation or presentation of the issue or the candidate. That is the exact opposite of what I do. I don't 'spin' anything, I put new substance and ideas before the voters."[103]

This had been Morris' mantra throughout his career. His first move was to change the White House message. Statements and speeches stopped being about the largest issues such as job creation and reducing the deficit, and instead began focusing on the smaller specific issues. The pre-election poll of '94 had shown that the voters trusted Clinton had delivered on these issues, like the Brady Bill, the assault rifle ban, and family leave, among others. Now Morris made sure the White House started pushing such smaller but tangible achievements into the press every day.

He also persuaded the President to run on a centrist platform, consisting of popular policies from both the blue and the red side of the aisle. Morris dubbed this tactic "Triangulation."

"Triangulate, create a third position, not just between the old positions of the two parties but above them as well. Identify a new course that accommodates the needs the Republicans address, but does it in a way that is uniquely yours," Morris advocated.[104]

Triangulation represented a bold move, as it meant the President challenging his own party base even as he would not be gaining support from the Republican side. He needed to take his case directly to the people and let them decide. It was a big gamble. If it failed, it would leave him weak and in a bad state – most probably it would entail defeat. But still, it was an approach that Clinton felt comfortable with. He had done this before, back home in Arkansas, with Morris at his side.

They started using the triangulation-approach in a televised speech Clinton gave in December 1994. In the speech, Clinton talked about rewarding those who took personal responsibility for creating new opportunities for themselves. Labor Secretary Robert Reich had suggested letting people deduct college tuition from their income tax. Polls showed that the approach resonated deeply with the public, with as many as 80 percent saying they supported the initiative, far more than any other tax cut suggestion that was tested. Clinton made it part of his speech and part of his new platform. In addition, the President proposed that those who saved for retirement or for a first home could do so tax free.

Getting rewarded for taking personal responsibility – this emerged as a new overall theme from the White House. When Morris discussed it with his wife, she came up with a slogan for the speech. Clinton liked it. They called it "The Middle-Class Bill of Rights." As many as 40 percent of Americans watched the speech, and among those watching, the President received a nine-point increase in his approval rating.[105] It was a sign that they were on the right track. And it bolstered the President's faith in Morris' strategy.

The Secret Ad Campaign

Back in Arkansas in the '80s, Clinton had built a formidable war chest to take his message directly to the voters through paid media, circumventing the media-filters and opinionated commentators. He did so by running a never-ending campaign, always fundraising and using paid media to push his views and initiatives, even in non-election years. Ever since the grisly attacks he had endured during the 1980-campaign, Clinton had a strained relationship with the press.

"He really believes there is this kind of 'got you'-mentality in the press, and he once told me 'The press destroys people. It's how they get their rocks off. It's how they enjoy themselves'," Morris explained.[106]

Using paid media to connect directly with the voters had been a necessity back in Arkansas. Morris and Clinton felt it was even more of a necessity now.

The campaign was to spend upwards of $85 million on ads, about as much as Clinton and Bush had spent on ads in the presidential campaign four years earlier put together. This would take a tremendous amount of fundraising, and Clinton complained bitterly to Morris; "You don't know, you don't have any remote idea how hard I have to work, Hillary has to work, how hard Al [Gore] has to work to raise this much money."

Night after night, the President had to meet hundreds of people at massive fundraisers, shake everyone's hand, chat with each of them, pose for photographs – for hours at end. Giving all those people his focus and attention took a lot of time and a tremendous amount of energy. The handshaking was the worst part of it. After shaking hundreds of hands, day in and day out, his hands hurt bad.

He might complain, but the truth was that Clinton was a master of donor maintenance. An expert reader of men, he intuitively grasped the deep-pocketeds' need for recognition and respect – and he massaged those feelings. He listened to them intently. He made them feel esteemed. Anyone hosting a fundraiser for Clinton would get a personal thank-you call or a handwritten letter from the President.[107] All that hard work paid off, and the money started flowing in. Soon Morris was ready to put their plan into action.

The idea behind the ad-campaign was to build Clinton's standing among the electorate, bit by bit, starting early. Conventional wisdom dictated the direct opposite – that you should hold your powder dry until the last months of the election and then overwhelm the voters with your ads. Using a huge chunk of your war chest early on left you much more vulnerable as the election grew closer, when you could end up outspent by your opponent. But Morris was convinced they needed to start early, had to start early, even if that entailed a huge risk. The Republican landslide in '94 had been a result of perceptions forming in the public's minds over time, and the President needed to change that before the big battle commenced.

From early July 1995 and more or less continually until Election Day 16 months later, the Clinton campaign bombarded the public with ads. During this period, television viewers in the key swing states saw on average 150 to 180 airings of spots paid by Clinton or the Democratic Party.[108] Morris's ad-strategy was dependent on the press not criticizing the ads, which could critically undermine their effect on the electorate. But how could the Clinton ads reach 130 million Americans without being picked up by the press? Morris had the answer. His team bought ad time three times a week for 18 months in media markets all over the country, but never in three specific cities: New York, Washington, or Los Angeles.

"We figured everybody that worked for the national media lived in one of those three cities, and if we were in any other city we could get away with it, without [the press] writing about it," Morris said.[109]

The prediction wasn't far off. Few newspapers ran articles, much less front-page articles, on the massive ad campaign. Before the Democratic Convention was even held, in a non-contested Democratic Primary, they had burned off a lot of money. It was an unprecedented amount to be used so early on by an incumbent president. But it proved a great investment. Morris' prediction had been right; getting a head start on your opponent was well worth the risk.

The stealth campaign allowed Morris to redefine Clinton in the eyes of the American public, before anyone on the other side really understood what was going on. And more importantly, this below-the-radar strategy allowed Morris to redefine Clinton's opponent, Republican nominee Bob Dole, tying him firmly to the increasingly unpopular Speaker of the House Newt Gingrich, without any Republican counterattacks. Morris concluded:

> *By the end of 1995, the Clinton and DNC ads had run unopposed by any Republican paid media for most of six months. The effect was devastating. In swing states like Michigan and Wisconsin, where our ads had run, Clinton's lead over Dole was actually larger than in core Democratic states, like Rhode Island and New York. On the issues, the Republicans had let us convert their majority to our side.*[110]

It had been a gamble. A huge gamble. The Republicans could easily have hit back. But they didn't. Instead, they decided to keep their ammunition in storage, planning to overwhelm the Democrats in the last months of the campaign. But as they were to find out, by then the game had tilted so heavily in favor of Clinton, they had no way of catching up. Morris describes the Republican decision not to strike back early as their biggest strategic mistake.

> The republicans had endless amounts of money on hand. ...
> they could easily have beaten our advertising. Every day
> Clinton would say to me "Are they on? Are they advertising?
> They have twice the money we do, how come they're not?"
> ...And there is some guy or woman, over there in the Repub-
> lican Party that said "No, let's not spend this money now, it
> doesn't matter." And that's the person that lost the election
> for them in '96.[III]

The ads helped Morris rebuild Clinton's image and tear down his Republican counterparts, all in one single swoop. The candidate got heavily involved, personally working on each of the ads before signing off on them. Morris also worked closely with Mark Penn in testing the ads. Each ad was made in several different rough versions, and Penn would test each version in 15 shopping malls around the nation. Clinton gave his team a virtually unlimited budget for polling and mall testing.

The first ads ran in July 1995, 16 months before Election Day. They told the story of President Clinton's refusal to give into congressional Republicans who wanted to repeal the ban on assault rifles. These featured a police officer describing how his partner had been gunned down by an assault weapon, and another officer talking about how he had been shot during a routine traffic stop. As a result, Clinton's ratings on "fighting crime" came to equal those of the Republicans, nullifying their historic advantage on this issue.

In August of '95, Morris released new ads hitting Republican budget cuts and promoting the President's own plan for a balanced budget. The spots told the viewers that Clinton had an alternative, a better way of balancing the budget and cutting taxes than the Republicans. One ad featured an EKG machine monitoring a patient's heartbeat as the announcer describes the premium increases and benefit cuts the Republicans planned for Medicare. At the end, the comforting beeps stop, and we hear the terrifying, continuous monotone and see the flat line on the screen – indicating the death of Medicare.

As the ads ran their course, voters began preferring Clinton's budget plan to the Republican plan by a margin of two to one. Women over 65 were especially outraged at the Medicare cuts, and Morris saw a huge swing in favor of Clinton in this demographic.

Many of the spots linked Clinton's opponent, Republican Senator Bob Dole, with the Speaker of the House Newt Gingrich. The speaker was becoming more and more unpopular, as the effects of the Republican Revolution became apparent to the voters. Eight years earlier, Lee Atwater had tied Willie Horton so close to the Democratic nominee that he almost looked like Dukakis' running mate. Now Morris stole a page from that playbook, portraying Gingrich as Dole's running mate. This placed Dole in the difficult position of being seen as a cold ideological warrior, intent on cutting care for the elderly and school subsidies for children. In movies, it is said, the story is only as good as it's villain. No less so in politics. Dick Morris made Newt Gingrich the villain of the '96 election.

Ads with a positive message, that also contained a negative differentiator between his candidate and the opponent had been a Morris trademark for years. As the award-winning journalist Joe Klein saw it, the whole '96 campaign could be summarized by one of these remarkable ads. Wrote Klein:

The woman is not a "soccer mom." She is, clearly, less affluent than that. She has short brown hair, a mild Texas accent. Her husband has a mustache and a stomach; he looks like someone who works with his hands. We see them speaking about the death of their daughter. We see them walking hand in hand along a country road at dusk. We see a picture of the girl, wan and thin and smiling. Then an announcer – a female announcer – says, "President Clinton signed the Family and Medical Leave law so parents can be with a...sick child and not lose their job." And then we find out that this is not just a political ad, but a negative one: "Bob Dole led a six-year fight against family leave," the announcer continues as a black-and-white shot of Dole appears. Then the mother again, saying that Clinton understands the struggles of families. And, finally, an almost painterly shot of the president sitting in the White House garden with a little girl in a wheelchair, golden light streaming to the left.

Klein continued,

This 30-second ad, which can only be described as an Empathic Negative, is a masterpiece. It may be all you need to know about the presidential campaign of 1996. It is subtle, personal, moving, manipulative and incredibly effective.[112]

This ad shows how Morris combined triangulation with a new values agenda that was incorporated into all the ads and speeches held by the President in '96. Traditionally, the Republicans were the ones known for their values agenda, but Morris thought theirs was largely a negative one – anti-gay, anti-single mothers, anti-abortion, and so on. Morris wanted a positive values agenda.

Penn polled to ask people whom they trusted more in different values areas, Clinton or Dole. They found five value-areas where the voters favored Clinton over Dole. The first was "providing opportunity to all," the second "carrying out our duty to our parents," the third "standing up for our country," the fourth "doing what's right even if it's unpopular," and the fifth "respecting the common ground of America's values." Rather than focusing on the traditional Democratic economic language of subsidizing those in dire need, Morris made sure these values were now fitted into all the ads and speeches of the campaign.

The ad about the family and medical leave law was just one example of how the values agenda became the core of the campaign's message. When speaking about providing funds for Head Start, the President spoke of "providing opportunities for young children." When speaking about Medicare, the President spoke of carrying out "our duty to our parents" by protecting Medicare. Morris made sure every such issue was framed in this context.

The values agenda emerged fully in the president's 1996 State of the Union address. Morris saw this as the real turning point – the speech that irreversibly tipped the scale in Clinton's advantage.

"Before the speech, Clinton's rating was 50 percent favorable; after, it was 60 percent, and his job approval rating rose from 55 percent to 60 percent. He moved from 47 percent of the vote and a five-point margin, to 53 percent of the vote and a nine-point margin," Morris remembered, adding:

And the changes lasted. Thereafter, until just before the election ten months later, the president never lost more than a

few points of the share of his vote, his lead over Dole, his fa-
vorability rating, or his job-approval percentage. ...In the end,
the values agenda succeeded in laying out a new plan of ac-
tion for the country, one that America focused on during the
months before the election.[113]

The Most Influential Private Citizen in America

On Election Day, November 5, 1996, Bill Clinton became the
first Democratic president to win a second term since Franklin
Delano Roosevelt. Dick Morris had brought Clinton's presidency
back from the dead. Through a new values agenda, triangulation,
and a bold and risky ad strategy, they had made history together.
As *The New York Times* wrote, "With the president's close and
sometimes solitary cooperation, Morris has overseen the virtual
remaking of the Clinton presidency."

Morris' close and long-lasting relationship with Clinton was
undoubtedly crucial to his success. The two men knew each other
well; they knew how to maximize each other's strengths. Clinton
said of Morris, "We've been together so long that he not only understands me, I understand him."

Morris was really enjoying himself in the role of special adviser and chief strategist to the President. He told reporter Alison
Mitchell:

> I was sitting with the President one night and we were working
> on some speech or other, and it was getting kind of late. We
> were alone. And I looked at him and I said, "You know Mr. Pres-
> ident, ever since I was 8 years old, I dreamed of doing exactly

this in exactly this way." And he looked back at me and he smiled and he said, "So did I."[114]

For his historic turn-around of Clinton's chances, and the huge influence he was given in policy crafting at the White House after the '94 midterms, *Time* magazine proclaimed Morris "the most influential private citizen in America." It was an accurate description. The strategist had challenged conventional wisdom time and time again, and succeeded. Not only had he saved Clinton. He handled the winning campaigns for more than 30 senators or governors, before becoming an author and political commentator.

After the '96 campaign, he drifted farther and farther to the right. Ousted from the Democrats after his sex scandal, Morris eventually started denouncing the Clintons in books, columns, blogs, and television appearances. He helped orchestrate Vicente Fox's presidential campaign in Mexico in 2000, masterminding yet another victory. Morris also chose to work for Victor Orban, the controversial autocratic leader of Hungary, who declared his goal was to create an "illiberal democracy." And he has worked for the former leader of the British UKIP-party, Nigel Farage, who led the charge against British membership in the European Union.

The editor of *The Weekly Standard* concluded that Morris is "Perfect for the age of Trump!" Morris himself stated, "I believe politics is increasingly not left versus right, but insider versus outsider."[115] In this one sentence, he summed up the wave of populism that has swept across the American and European political landscape. But it was also, in many ways, a suitable description of his own political journey.

The political gunslinger is still for hire.

CHAPTER 3

THE ULTIMATE POLITICAL HITMAN

Roger Ailes

"If you have two guys on a stage and one guy says 'I have a solution to the Middle East problem' and the other guy falls in the orchestra pit, who do you think is going to be on the evening news?"

- Roger Ailes

Just an Average Guy from Flyover Country

Roger Ailes was a remarkable man – for better and worse. If not a genius in the art of political communication, he was certainly the closest you'll ever get. He wielded his magic for decades, changing the world along the way – making America more divided. He was crucial to the GOP, as he helped bring the Nixon presidency into life in 1968, boosted Ronald Reagan's reelection campaign in 1984, and was – together with Lee Atwater and James Baker – one of the masterminds behind George Bush's successful 1988 presidential campaign.

Along the way he got countless Republican senators elected and went on to shape the new right-wing media, as creator and president of Fox News. Eventually, he was ousted from Fox after several allegations of sexual misconduct. He died a year later. By then, he had changed America profoundly. He was, and still is, a source of both pure hatred and deep admiration. Movies have been made portraying him as a depraved evil genius. Books have been written exalting his achievements. Hate him or love him, Ailes always was one of a kind.

The political world he grew up in was the world of Eisenhower, Kennedy, and Nixon. Born in 1940 in Warren, Ohio, his childhood shaped his world views in a profound way. His father worked as a maintenance foreman at General Motors' Packard plant. From this blue-collar environment, Roger gained a deep understanding of the emotional levers that move ordinary Americans. Later in life, he would say, "Growing up in Ohio and just being kind of an average guy from flyover country – my dad was a factory guy – I try to put things on a screen that reflect reality. ...it's more common sense than anything else."[116] To him it surely was. His upbringing not only defined where Ailes felt he belonged, it also defined where he *didn't* belong. To Roger, his world was the real world, and everything else was bullshit.

His world was the world of conservatism, and Ailes felt it was under constant attack from the mainstream liberal media. "See, the mainstream media thinks conservatives are nuts," Ailes explained. "They deeply fear conservative thought because it's too common sense, too pedestrian, it's not intellectual enough, it's not university talk. It's not Columbia Journalism bullshit. It's real stuff."[117] Blue collar traditions became his emotional platform and they would remain so throughout his life. "I like the traditions, so I tend to try to keep them alive. ...I'm more comfortable with the traditional stuff," he told a reporter from *Esquire* in 2011. He couldn't stand the way America changed into a more culturally liberal society.

The young Roger suffered from ill-health. As a hemophiliac, he always had to careful. But that was easier said than done for a young boy. There were incidents in his youth when he almost didn't survive even smaller injuries. After one serious accident, his father in desperation had to get some men from the plant to come in and give blood directly to the young boy, helping him survive a severe bleeding.

His father, like many of his generation, would discipline his sons, hitting them with his belt when he felt they had overstepped. And there were always strict demands. When he had finished high school, his father told Roger in no uncertain terms it was time to move out and make a living on his own. Later in life, he describes his dad as "a tough guy."

It could not have been an entirely happy childhood. Even so, Ailes loved his father. One incident in particular left a deep impression. His father had dropped him off at the bus station and gone to park his car. Entering the station, Roger walked past three shabby homeless men, begging for money. He went inside to purchase his ticket, but afterwards couldn't find his father. Looking around, he finally spotted him through a glass frame, sitting in the adjacent coffee shop. Ailes later recalled:

> My dad was sitting with one of the bums on one side of him and two on the other side of him. And he was buying them food. And he was talking with them like he knew them. And I remember looking through the frame glass, it was almost like a television frame, and seeing my dad with these homeless guys and he's...buying them coffee. And it made a major impression on me. I still have that scene, that frame in my mind that I can't lose, that's who he was.[118]

It was a complex image of a strict authoritarian father, who also embodied kindness and personal responsibility. It was a dualism that Ailes would carry with him his whole life. It is telling that he experienced this moment like a scene observed through a frame, "like a television frame." It was how Ailes would connect with lower- and middle-class voters later on in life. To him, they were not just consumers or voters, they were real people with very real emotions. He had grown up amongst them. He shared their traditions and many of their views. He knew what made them proud, angry, and engaged. He knew how to press those buttons and he could do so in the form of emotional television scenes. It was exactly what would make his political communication skills so effective.

After he went to college, his parents split up, and Roger's mother moved on to California. Having no idea of the breakup, he returned that Christmas only to find his childhood home and all of his belongings sold off. "All my stuff was gone. I never found my stamp collection. I never found anything. Everything was gone," Ailes remembered vividly. "My father was depressed — sitting at his mother's house in a chair, going to work every day, but not really communicating. And I went over to my buddy's house to stay for a couple days. Then I went back to college."[119] At Ohio University, Ailes managed the student radio station and graduated with a degree in broadcasting in 1962.

He found a job as a prop boy on the local *Mike Douglas Show*.[120] The hard working and intelligent young man rose rapidly through the ranks. When the station, and the program, moved to Philadelphia three years later, he had become its producer. A further two years on, Ailes was made executive producer. He understood the product better than most and spent his years on the show tuning his craftsmanship on the exact triggers that attracted and moved audiences. He was tremendously good at it. By 1967, the show was available in 171 media markets and had over six million viewers a day.

That same year, Ailes, who by now was largely responsible for the show's success, won an Emmy Award for his achievement.

It also opened a door to the world of celebrities for its ambitious executive producer. The affable Mike Douglas would chat with his guests much like Johnny Carson did on *The Tonight Show*. One of the show's signatures, Douglas's use of cohosts, was actually an Ailes invention.[121] Backstage, he would rub elbows with the likes of Bob Hope, Marlon Brando, Ray Charles, John Lennon and Yoko Ono, as well as some of the most famous politicians of the time.

One day, former Vice President Richard Nixon walked in.

The Man in the Arena

The '60s were a tumultuous decade for America. It was also the decade when television became the most important tool for political communication with the voters. The 1960 presidential election was one of the closest in US history, and it's fair to say it was won by John F. Kennedy partly because of his energetic television charisma. It's also fair to say it was lost by Richard Nixon partly because of his lack of understanding of this new powerful medium.

Back in 1952, Nixon had been in the middle of a controversy. There were allegations of improprieties relating to a fund established by his backers to reimburse him for his political expenses. Then vice presidential candidate Nixon was in danger of being dropped from the Eisenhower ticket over the debacle. So, he flew to Los Angeles and delivered a sensational half-hour television address in which he defended himself directly to the American people.

Looking straight into the camera, Nixon went through his finances, then declared:

> *Well, that's about it. That's what we have. And that's what we owe. It isn't very much. ...One other thing I probably should tell you, because if I don't, they'll probably be saying this about me, too. We did get something, a gift, after the election. A man down in Texas heard Pat on the radio mention the fact that our two youngsters would like to have a dog. And believe it or not, the day before we left on this campaign trip we got a message from Union Station in Baltimore, saying they had a package for us. We went down to get it. You know what it was? It was a little cocker spaniel dog in a crate that he'd sent all the way from Texas, black and white, spotted. And our little girl Tricia, the six-year-old, named it 'Checkers.' And you know, the kids, like all kids, love the dog, and I just want to say this, right now, that regardless of what they say about it, we're going to keep it.*

It was an impressive piece of television performance that secured Nixon's place on the Republican ticket in 1952.

However, the episode left him feeling a little too cocky about his own abilities when it came to the new medium. That is why he, as the Republican presidential nominee, said yes to debate Kennedy in what would become the first ever televised presidential debates in 1960. He didn't have to; in fact, he had little to gain from it. He was considered the front runner, the one with experience in governing, while Kennedy lacked comparable credentials. Even President Eisenhower advised Nixon not to debate Kennedy on television. But Nixon was too sure of himself.

Arriving at the studio, he looked pale and a bit listless. He had just gotten out of the hospital, where he had lost weight after a knee injury. Nixon wore a gray, ill-fitting suit that seemed to blend with the studio background and hastily added cheap makeup. Kennedy on the other hand, looked to be radiating health. He wore a dark suit, a wide smile, and showed off a vivid tan. The difference in their appearances was so striking, Chicago mayor Richard Daley on seeing the Republican candidate, exclaimed, "My God, they've embalmed him before he even died." Henry Cabot Lodge, Nixon's running mate, said, "That son of a bitch just cost us the election."[122] Lodge wasn't far from the truth. The election was among the closest ever fought, and Kennedy won the national popular vote by a margin of just 0.17 percent. There can be little doubt Nixon's dreadful television appearance helped tip the scale in Kennedys favor.

The debate had such a devastating effect on the Nixon campaign that it scared subsequent candidates and consultants alike. No more televised debates between the top presidential candidates were held after 1960, not until Jimmy Carter ran against Gerald Ford in 1976. It also left a personal mark on Nixon, who in his hatred for the medium convinced himself that television was a sideshow, no more than a passing fad.

In fact, Nixon's relationship with the media in general was bordering on abysmal. After his defeat against Kennedy, the beaten presidential candidate went home to run for governor of California. And lost. Again blaming the media for his defeat, Nixon held a press conference where he began his remarks with, "Now that all the members of the press are so delighted that I have lost, I'd like to make a statement of my own."[123]

By 1967, Nixon was running for the Republican presidential nomination again – with his sights set on conquering the White House in '68. And part of that meant he had to make his rounds on the popular television talk shows, like *The Mike Douglas Show*. He simply hated it. Nixon was offended by television's role in politics.

"It had not been part of the game when he learned to play. And he could see no reason to bring it in now," concluded author Joe McGinnis. "He half suspected it was an eastern liberal trick: One more way to make him look silly." [124]

Backstage at The Mike Douglas Show, Nixon struck up a conversation with the 28-year-old Ailes and made his views on the new medium perfectly clear "It's a shame a man has to use gimmicks like this to get elected," the presidential hopeful said. Ailes just looked at him, not believing what he heard.

"Television is not a gimmick," he brashly snapped back.[125] He explained to the former Vice President why he would lose the election if he didn't adopt television as a political tool. Nixon was impressed, and some weeks later, his staff called Ailes with a job offer – as Nixon's chief media consultant. Ailes accepted the challenge and jumped into his new job with the same energy and intensity he had shown in building *The Mike Douglas Show*.

His task was huge. He understood that in order for Nixon to succeed, he would have to reinvent his image completely. The grumpy, self-centered Nixon of old had to be erased from the public's mind. He was to be replaced by a positive, confident and jovial "New Nixon." Luckily, the candidate himself also understood the necessity of such a makeover, and he was willing to go to great lengths to win. More important, he had great respect for Ailes.

So, Nixon, who only months before had viewed television as nothing but a nuisance, now told his staff, "We are going to build this whole campaign around television. You fellows just tell me what you want me to do, and I'll do it."[126] Ailes created a game plan for how they would sell "New Nixon." He trained with the candidate, to show him how to act and behave in a way that played well with television audiences. The "New Nixon" that met the voters in 1968 was in large part molded by Roger Ailes.

This time around, there would be no televised debates between the presidential candidates. Instead, Nixon toured the news programs like *Face the Nation* and *Meet the Press*. But their format and appeal were limited. Survey research showed that there existed a perceived "personality gap" between Nixon and the Democratic candidate Hubert Humphrey. Nixon was perceived by most voters as cold, while more voters perceived Humphrey as warm.[127]

Ailes understood that he had to invent a totally new setting for Nixon to appear in. Somewhere he could show more emotion and connect with the television audiences on a more personal level. He came up with a brand-new concept, that he called "Man in the Arena." He would shield Nixon from the press, and instead use the programs to sell New Nixon directly to the electorate.

"Let's face it, a lot of people think Nixon is dull. They think he's a bore, a pain in the ass," Ailes told his staff frankly, continuing:

> They look at him as the kind of kid who always carried a book-bag... They figure other kids got footballs for Christmas, Nixon got a briefcase and he loved it. He'd always have his homework done and he'd never let you copy. Now you put him on television and you've got a problem right away. He's a funny looking

guy. He looks like someone hung him in a closet overnight and he jumps out in the morning with his suit all bunched up and starts running around saying, "I want to be president." I mean this is how he strikes some people. That's why these shows are important. To make them forget all that.[128]

Ailes produced 10 one-hour long "Man in the Arena" programs, as well as Nixon's election eve telecast. The programs ran from September to October in 10 big cities selected for maximum electoral impact. Ailes filled a studio with voters. But contrary to what the public might believe, these were not just ordinary people. In fact, the audiences of about 300 were recruited from local Republican Party organizations, so as to manufacture a friendly and emotionally supportive environment for the candidate.

To make them seem as authentic as possible, the shows were taped live, depicting the energy and enthusiasm for the candidate among the audiences. A panel of citizens would ask Nixon questions to provide a sense of authenticity. The panelists were all handpicked and screened before getting on the show. This way, Ailes could also compose a panel that looked representative in terms of gender, race, occupation, and so on. The audience was heavily coached before the taping started. They were told how to behave, when to applaud, and to rush the stage at the end of the show – depicting Nixon like something of a rock star. Meanwhile, the press that was part of the presidential candidate's entourage were put in an adjacent studio, seeing no more and no less than the average voter viewing from any living room.

The duplicity of it didn't bother Ailes at all. He brushed off journalists that wanted a closer view, who wanted to be in the main studio where the meeting actually took place. "Fuck 'em," he told his staff, "It's not a press conference." He had no more respect for the audience, concerned only about getting the right amount of applause from them. "That's all they are," he said, "an applause machine."[129] To Ailes, the presentation of a political candidate was a mere performance. And he knew better than anyone how to cast, design, and produce a show.

Always the perfectionist, Ailes craved control over every part of the production. The camera should zoom in close on the candidate, the candidate would be lighted more than his surroundings, a rear camera, placed behind the candidate, would show how the audience looked from his perspective, and so on. It might not sound very different from how such shows are done today, but at the time, it was revolutionary. Few in televised entertainment, and certainly no one in politics, had created anything like this, until Ailes produced the "Man in the Arena" shows for Nixon in '68.[130]

Ailes had a commitment to detail that bordered on the extreme. At one point, he ran up and tore down big curtains that had been put up as backdrop, then put up plain stark wooden panels instead. "The wood has clean, solid, masculine lines," he declared.[131] During the taping of the program in Philadelphia, he got so angry at the floor director because he didn't get the right close-ups of Nixon, that he fired him, right there on the spot. From then on, he directed the last five programs himself.[132]

Each program was shown in the region where it had been taped. This way, Ailes could tailor his approach more specifically for each different region. Bud Wilkinson, a successful football coach of the time, served as the host. He assured the viewers that "the gloves are really coming off this time."[133] But the questions from the panelists were mostly friendly. Moreover, the questioners could not follow up, so if Nixon didn't like the question, he could give a general reply and quickly move on. The fact that the shows were run regionally rather than nationally, also meant that Nixon would get many of the same questions in front of the different audiences and could hone his answers accordingly.

The work Ailes did in training Nixon for television, as well as building a new image for the candidate through the "Man in the Arena" programs, was of immense value to the candidate. On Election Day, Nixon received 43.4 percent of the vote, just irking past Humprey who captured 42.7 percent. (Independent candidate George Wallace captured 13.5 percent.) Nixon knew well just how important Ailes had been to his success, and the rest of the country were also about to find out.

In the book *The Selling of the President* published in 1969, author Joe McGinnis told America the story of how Roger Ailes had been absolutely critical to the success of the Nixon campaign. The book made Ailes an overnight celebrity in the political world. At the age of only 28, he had played a crucial role in electing the next president of the United States. His work was a huge success; he had reinvented televised political communication. Amazingly, it was also Ailes first political gig. It would definitely not be his last.

Juggling Show Business and Politics

After the inauguration, Ailes started consulting for the Nixon White House. But, as with most perfectionistic strong-willed strategists, there were soon clashes between him and the rest of the President's entourage. Ailes was flying high. His lack of respect for the top brass in the administration reached a peak. In 1970, Nixon's chief of staff Bob Haldeman let Ailes know that his services would no longer be needed.

But the young man didn't despair. He founded Ailes & Associates and signed up several campaigns, did some productions for television, and began selling strategic communication advice to corporations. In the early '70s, he worked for both the Republican nominee for governor of Florida, Jack Eckerd, and senatorial candidate Robert Taft Jr. from Ohio. Eckerd lost the primary, Taft Jr. won his race.

When he wasn't working in television or producing plays, most of Ailes time was used on his many corporate clients. He provided them mostly with media training and communication counseling. American Express, AT&T, General Electric, and Polaroid were just a few of the many huge companies whose executives sought out the services of Ailes & Associates. From the 1970s to the 1990s, it is fair to say that Ailes cultivated long-term relationships with some of America's largest, most influential and powerful corporations.

In 1977, he won another Emmy for a television special about the great Italian movie director Frederico Fellini, whose work include the classics "La Strada," "La Dolche Vita," and "Amacord." For a short while, Ailes even worked as an off-Broadway producer. He had met the Broadway producer Kermit Bloomgarden at a party, and they started talking. Soon they were partners. Throughout his life, Ailes would meet people randomly, and following short conversations, they would start working together. Nixon and Bloomgarden were among the first in a long series of such remarkable encounters. Ailes wasn't afraid to say whatever he meant; he was brash, direct, and intelligent. He knew who he was and what he wanted and wasn't shy about telling other people. This obviously made a very strong first impression.

In the '78 election cycle, Ailes worked for the US Senate campaigns of William Armstrong of Colorado and David Durenberger of Minnesota. The Colorado race turned into a regular political war, with the Democratic incumbent Floyd Haskell and Republican challenger Armstrong going after each other's jugulars. It was a familiar ideological battle and turned into a nasty, negative campaign. Haskell, a 62-year-old attorney, was a true liberal. Armstrong, a 41-year-old radio station owner, focused on free enterprise and tax cuts.

Much of the attacking was made by Haskell, who tried to paint Armstrong as too conservative for the people of Colorado.

"As far as we're concerned, Armstrong is the issue in the campaign," Haskell told the press. The Democrat accused his opponent of being "on the fringe, a minority of a minority." He said Armstrong opposed legislation to help older Americans, the handicapped, and Nicaraguan earthquake victims while favoring big oil.[134]

Ailes wasn't about to take such an onslaught lying down. He hit back hard, in what was to become a typical Ailes tactic – not going after his opponent's stands on the issues, but rather assailing his opponent's character. He charged that Haskell had broken Senate rules in his use of Senate staff and that he had misused taxpayer's money by abusing the Senate mail system. He also accused Haskell of consistently voting against weapons systems needed to stand up to the Soviet Union, painting him as somewhat of an appeaser.

Armstrong had a focused, well-organized, heavily funded campaign. He spent nearly $1 million, twice as much as Haskell. And he had Roger Ailes on his team. Soon Ailes was flooding the airwaves with attacks on Haskell's character. Outspent and out-organized, Haskell was fighting an uphill battle against the Republican candidate and his strategist. On Election Day, Armstrong was elected by a huge margin, defeating Haskell by 59 to 40 percent of the vote. Another notch in Roger's belt.

Ailes also prevailed in Minnesota, where David Durenberger was elected in a special election to complete the unexpired term of Senator Humphrey who had died earlier that year. Durenberger faced off with former Texas Rangers owner, Bob Short. It was a strange situation, where the liberal Republican Durenberger was positioned to the left of the conservative Democrat Short on many of the major issues. In liberal Minnesota, Ailes made sure this became a huge problem for Short, whose conservative stand on hot button issues such as abortion and government spending led to Democratic voters crossing party lines to vote Republican.[135] With Ailes' help Durenberger won with a whopping 61 percent of the vote. Ailes would continue to work for David Durenberger in both his 1982 and 1988 successful reelection campaigns, producing television ads and supplying strategic advice.[136]

In a memo to the executive director of the National Republican Senatorial Committee (NRSC) after the election, assistant Larry McCarthy wrote, "I watched several cassettes of [Ailes'] campaign material and found them to be well-crafted and professional, but lacking in imagination and pizzazz."[137] McCarthy couldn't have found the ads all bad, because two years later, he joined Ailes' company as a senior executive. He would retain this position until leaving to play a central part in the 1988 presidential election, producing the infamous Willie Horton ad.

Connally, Reagan, and Mama D'Amato

Entering the Republican nomination for president in 1979, Texas governor John Connally was seen by many as the most probable candidate. One of those who believed the Texan had good odds was Roger Ailes, who decided to go to work for him. Like Connally's opponent Ronald Reagan, the governor was a man of national fame. He had become a household name back in 1963, riding in the front seat of President Kennedy's car when the assassin Lee Harvey Oswald shot Kennedy and wounded Connally. A Democrat who had switched teams in '73 when he felt the Democrats had gotten too liberal, Connally was seen as a moderate. Unlike Reagan, Connally was expected to have a strong appeal among the important centrist swing voters. The Connally campaign also raised more money than any other Republican candidate in the field.[138]

John Connally wasn't a typical politician. He spoke his mind and didn't pull his punches. In 1968, responding to criticism of the Vietnam War, he would use words like "treason" and "appeasement" to characterize then fellow Democrats Robert Kennedy, George McGovern, and Eugene McCarthy. As a Democratic governor he had even branded his Republican opponent Jack Cox – who had switched from the Democratic party to the Republican Party – as a "renegade, turncoat opportunist" –

something of an irony considering he made the same switch himself a few years later.

Connally was just as plainspoken on the issues. His campaign statements scrubbed of the qualifiers that mark most political rhetoric. In a speech that drew a lot of flak, he said that the United States should push Israel to withdraw from all the territories gained in the 1967 war in return for an Arab guarantee of Israeli security, a radical suggestion to say the least. Later, after being pressed by his staff to be careful on commenting the subject of nuclear power, he simply told a crowd in New Hampshire that he had been cautioned not to speak his mind, adding "OK. I'll be real careful of what I say. I'm for it, period."[139]

This was a man Roger Ailes felt he could sell to the public. Connally hired John Mahe and Roger Ailes to run his campaign and communications, and they went straight to work. They mostly produced positive and issue-related ads. Connally, as Ailes himself would acknowledge in his 1995 book, *You are the Message*, could come across as arrogant and a little pompous. That was an image the Ailes wanted to change, and he masterminded an ad campaign aimed at showing Connally's gentler side.[140] The strategy was to advertise nationally and build Connally as the alternative to Reagan early on. Connally was the first Republican candidate to run an ad for the 1980 campaign. It started in the fall of '79, when Ailes bought five minutes of airtime on the CBS network that kicked off a three-week ad blitz. One typical ad showed Connally as a Texas rancher and dotting grandfather.[141]

But all of their efforts were in vain. As the primary progressed, it soon became clear that the Reagan campaign machine had too much speed, too much publicity, and too much momentum for anyone to overtake. Reagan also had Lee Atwater masterminding the South Carolina primary. Connally had to face reality and pulled out of the race. The author of the book *Rendezvous with Destiny – Ronald Reagan and the Campaign That Changed America* dryly observed that "…even Ailes's powers could not stop the runaway train of Ronald Reagan." Alas, Ailes had bet on the wrong horse. After using more than $2 million on ads alone, they were out. But Ailes' efforts hadn't gone unnoticed. The head honchos in the Reagan campaign were impressed by his work. They put his name in their files, ready for their 1984 re-election campaign.

Ailes wasn't out of work for long. In New York, a young Republican named Alfonse D'Amato was to go up against Democrat Elizabeth Holtzman in the Senate race. D'Amato had defeated the incumbent, Senator Jacob Javits, for the Republican nomination. Right after the primary, the polls showed Holtzman clearly ahead of D'Amato. All things being equal, she would have won on a landslide. But in the fairly liberal state of New York, Javits decided to run on the established Liberal Party's ticket. He raised money, kept his union endorsements, and never withdrew, knowing he would receive a substantial number of votes – enough he hoped to have a shot at reelection. Most of these votes would have gone to Holtzman, had Javits not stayed in the race.[142] The election was suddenly wide open.

Ailes could make devastating negative attack ads, but he also knew exactly when to build positive image ads. The ones he made for D'Amato would become famous, part of New York folklore. D'Amato was a conservative Republican, anti-choice, anti-gun control, and anti-environment. He had beaten Javits in the primary partly by attacking his age.[143] He most definitely wasn't viewed by most voters as a warm or likeable person. This was a man badly in need of a makeover. Luckily for him, Ailes was just the man to give him one.

Ailes understood he couldn't just start selling D'Amato as a nice guy per se. No one would believe that. He needed another angle. So, Ailes produced heartfelt ads that didn't feature the candidate, but his mother. In one, "Mama D'Amato" was seen carrying grocery bags while walking home, as she talked genuinely about the problems facing the middle class. She would then, in the way only a mother can, urge viewers to "vote for my son Al. He'll be a good senator."

D'Amato himself described Ailes's ads as "short, simple and brilliant." The ads did wonders for D'Amato. "I was no longer the evil ogre from Long Island. I was somebody's son, a human being again." It was such a hit that "Mama D'Amato" was made an overnight celebrity in New York, and she soon began campaigning on her own.[144] On Election Day, D'Amato beat Holtzman by a margin of just 1 percent of the vote. Ailes's ads had clearly tipped the election in D'Amato's favor. The newly elected senator knew as well as anyone that Ailes had helped him over the top. Their friendship was to last a lifetime. D'Amato would introduce Ailes to many of his future political clients, among them Rudy Giuliani.

But there was another Big Apple candidate who was about to boost Ailes' ever-growing reputation as one of the best political consultants of the eighties; Republican nominee for New York governor, Lew Lehrman.

Holy Mackerel!

From the start, the "Lehrman for Governor" campaign of 1982 seemed doomed. New York is a solid democratic state, with Republicans winning only the odd race. The Republican Party was having a hard time across the nation in these midterm elections. Besides, Lehrman, a millionaire businessman, was relatively unknown to most New Yorkers. And now he was taking on the popular, well-funded Democratic candidate, Lieutenant Governor Mario Cuomo. Cuomo had real momentum. He had beaten New York mayor, Ed Koch, in the Democratic Primary. The extremely popular Koch had won reelection as mayor with 75 percent of the vote only a few years earlier, which made Cuomo's achievement all the more impressive.

Even so, Lehrman would astonish everyone with his surprisingly good showing on Election Day. This was a result mainly of two things; Lehrman's huge personal fortune – from which he was willing to spend millions on his own campaign – and Ailes' excellent strategy and game plan execution. Under slogans like "It's time to take the handcuffs off the police," Ailes and Lehrman ran an anti-crime campaign that had strong appeal among New Yorkers tired of seeing rising crime rates.[145] Most of the ads were positive. Ailes wanted to reshape the tough businessman image of Lehrman into a family man with humor, a regular guy who didn't take himself too seriously.

One of the spots called "Outtakes" began with Lehrman seated on a stool in his shirt sleeves, addressing the camera about taxes. He flubs a line and giggles – normally an outtake. But Lehrman continues: "That one blew me right off the chair. Holy mackerel! Too much energy." Then the frame freezes, and the camera pulls back to show the candidate sitting, watching himself on a monitor, a spot within a spot. Lehrman turns and addresses the camera. "Hey, I made some mistakes when taping my commercials. I'll make mistakes as governor. But I'll try new ideas and make tough decisions."

When Ailes decided to use the outtake as a spot, he at first had a problem persuading the campaign.

"People said it was undignified," Ailes remembered, but he believed the voters "want their elected officials to show a wide range of emotion."[146] Using his mistakes and admitting he would make new ones, Ailes showed the candidate's human side. And Lehrman gave him thumbs up:

"He really was able to laugh at himself," Ailes remembered.

The ad he had conceived was refreshing and started pushing Lehrman's numbers up in the polls.

Copying the approach he had used so successfully in other races, Ailes also made several "though on crime" spots. Wrote journalist Michael Kramer:

> *Lehrman's commercials have made their mark. A recent Associated Press/NBC News poll confirms what money can buy. One question, for example, asked which candidate would do a better job reducing crime, ...Lehrman led Koch by five points and Cuomo by thirteen - despite the mayor's years of public exposure and the fact that crime fighting is the centerpiece of the Koch campaign. Since he's never held public office, Lehrman's showing can only be attributed to his "Crime Program," a series of vague proposals enunciated in 30-second television commercials.*[147]

Lehrman didn't win. But everyone had expected him to lose to Cuomo by a landslide. He didn't. His very decent showing on election night was widely attributed to the strategy laid out by Ailes. The rumor spread. It cemented Ailes's already strong reputation as one of the top Republican strategists and imagemakers in the country. By now, he had become a sizzling hot commodity, and he would play a critical role in the two most prominent campaigns of the decade. The first was President Ronald Reagan's '84 reelection campaign, the other was George H. W. Bush's '88 presidential campaign.

I Will Not Make Age an Issue of This Campaign

The last month of the 1984 election was supposed to be a smooth ride for Ronald Reagan. But the President was about to have such a dismal, confused debate performance that the election would suddenly be in full play. It started on October 7 on the stage in Louisville, Kentucky, with Election Day just four weeks away. Only minutes into the debate, everyone could see that the Gipper was in trouble. It made a huge impact because Reagan, who had long seduced the nation with his master performances, was considered "the Great Communicator." The man up on stage this night seemed a completely different person.

It was his first debate against Democratic nominee Walter Mondale, and the aging president sounded like a rambling out-of-place amateur. He seemed unsure, even admitting before his closing statement that he was "confused." The impression left on the American people wasn't that of the Leader of the Free World, rather that of an old man who was wandering around in the streets, not remembering his way home. It was an absolutely abysmal performance, raising immediate questions of Reagan's age and ability. The press was all over in. Even *The Wall Street Journal*, a staunch supporter of the president, asked, "Is oldest U.S. President now showing his age? Reagan debate performance invites open Speculation on his ability to serve."[148]

After the debate, the campaign went into full crisis mode. Reagan's friends complained that the President had been brutalized by his team, whom were supposed to be there to coach and help the President. It was an assessment shared by the First Lady.[149] There could be little doubt the President's advisors had him overreaching – they would drill him on tons of specifics, drown him in facts and minutia. That worked poorly for Reagan. He had always been the visionary, conceiving folksy ways to explain his ideology and world views, often with the help of humor. The First Lady was obviously right; Reagan didn't function well when treated like a databank.

Something had to be done, and the Reagan campaign had someone in mind to help them deal with the emergency; Roger Ailes.[150] He requested some private meetings with the President, without all the other advisors around. He urged the Gipper to be more thematic in his answers in the second debate. Reagan should reconnect to the images and themes that had gotten him elected in the first place. Ailes started training with the President, firing questions at him and helping him to go with his gut feeling. "What do the instincts tell you about this issue?" he asked him, "Forget the details of issues, why are they important to you?"[151] He was trying to help him regain his confidence, but also get him into a positive mindset, and start a certain rhythm and beat going. To achieve this, he wanted Reagan to forget about all the details, reset his mind, and then write easy overall messages that were both easier to remember and more appealing to the voters.

The rest of the President's team wanted age to be a non-issue. At this point, they were scared. Really scared. So, they strongly advised against bringing it up. But Ailes thought they were out of their minds if they believed that the issue would just fade away. He talked it over with Reagan, who answered with a humorous line. Ailes told him to forget everything else and just go with his quip. "That's perfect. Just use that line and don't say anything else," he advised.

Ailes' magic worked wonders. In the next debate, in Kansas City on October 21, Reagan had gotten a lot of his swagger back. Watching the debate we can see him smiling, giving straightforward answers, speaking from his gut, not diving into complexities. Then came the moment the brass at the White House had feared. One of the panelists, Henry Trewhitt of *The Baltimore Sun*, asked Reagan the dreaded age-question; "You already are the oldest president in history. ...I recall how President Kennedy had to go for days on end with very little sleep during the Cuban missile crisis. Is there any doubt in your mind that you would be able to function under such circumstances?"

The President's team were huddled together around a television set. As the age question came up, they all groaned.

"Don't worry," Ailes said confidently. "Here comes a home run."

Up on stage, the President smiled easily and answered emphatically, "Not at all!" Then came the line he and Ailes had rehearsed; "And Mr. Trewhitt, I also want you to know that I will not make age an issue of this campaign. I am not going to exploit, for political purposes, my opponent's youth and inexperience."

The audience burst out in a mixture of awe and laughter. Even Mondale couldn't hold back a broad smile. In one single stroke, the age-issue was laid to rest.

"As far as I was concerned the debate was over," Ailes later wrote. "The public had the reassurance they were looking for, and Reagan had the election won."[152] He could sit back and enjoy the rest of the show. His magic touch had helped the President deliver a strong comeback, essentially saving his reelection campaign.

Ailes also worked for Mitch McConnell during the '84 election cycle. McConnell is the longest-serving US senator for Kentucky in history, and the longest-serving leader of US Senate Republicans. Back then, he was a county judge trying to unseat incumbent Democrat Walter Huddleston for a seat in the Kentucky Senate. Ailes and his associate Larry McCarthy put together a series of humorous but deadly ads against Huddleston, where they criticized him for missing too many important votes in the state senate while he was out collecting speaking fees at luxury venues.

In one of the ads they made, a guy in a plaid flannel shirt, pulling on the leashes of a pack of sniffing bloodhounds, goes looking for the missing senator. In another, the chaser and his dogs have finally found Huddleston and are chasing him around trying to "pin him to his record". Both ads ended with the tag line "Switch to Mitch". The very funny ads made the Republican challenger a household name in Kentucky. Mitch McConnell won with the slender margin of 0.4 percent of the vote. The "Hound Dog" ads, simple, humorous and effective, soon became famous in the political advertising world. And with Ailes' help McConnell had managed to cross the finishing line first.

Saving a Doomed Campaign

Roger Ailes worked closely with Lee Atwater developing and executing campaign-strategy for George H. W. Bush's 1988 presidential campaign. Entering the campaign, Bush was trailing behind his opponent, Governor Michael Dukakis, by as much as 17 points. Many felt the election was as good as over already. But together Atwater and Ailes produced the "Revolving Doors" ad for the Bush campaign. This ad, coupled with the Willie Horton spot produced by Ailes former employee McCarthy, drastically hurt Dukakis in the polls (more in chapter 1). The two ads have since become part of political folklore, and more than any other of his achievements they cemented the public perception of Roger Ailes and Lee Atwater as masters of the dark arts of politics.

There were other effective negative spots running in the '88 presidential election, courtesy of Roger Ailes, as well. In one, "The Harbor," Ailes practiced some political aikido – not attacking his opponent's weaknesses, but rather his strengths. The Democrats were viewed as more concerned about environmental issues than the Republicans, and Dukakis had made it a central part of his platform. Everyone had expected the Republicans to steer clear of the issue, and the Dukakis campaign was completely taken aback by the attack.

Ailes' spot begins with the narrator saying, "As a candidate Michael Dukakis called the Boston harbor an open sewer." As he talked, the screen is filled with footage from of the harbor, garbage, sewage and spilled oil floating in the water. "As Governor he had the opportunity to do something about it but chose not to. The environmental protection agency called his lack of action the most expensive public policy mistake in the history of New England," the narrator continued, as the camera zoomed in on a sign from the harbor saying, "Danger Radiation Hazard – No Swimming." Then, in a stern voice the ad closes with the narrator warning, "Now Boston harbor, the dirtiest harbor in America, will cost residents six billion dollars to clean. And Michael Dukakis promises to do for America what he's done for Massachusetts."

It was a hard kick in Dukakis' stomach, an ad clearly meant to demobilize the environmental voters of the Democratic Party. It didn't bother Ailes at all that it told a half-truth at best. Dukakis had in fact tried to get federal funding to clean up the harbor but hadn't succeeded. However, such semantics mattered little in the hustle and bustle of a presidential race. The ad was highly effective, and that was all that mattered to a political hit man like Roger Ailes. He was in it to win. Period.

Like four years earlier with Reagan, Ailes in '88 also helped reshape Bush's public image and boost his performance in difficult media situations. Bush had a serious image problem, mainly because he was perceived by many voters as something of a wimp. Newsweek magazine even put picture of Bush on its cover under the headline "Fighting the Wimp Factor." Ailes decided they needed to show the world just how though Bush really was.

In 1944, 20-year-old Lieutenant Pilot Bush was among nine airmen who escaped from their planes after being shot down during a bombing raid. Bush ditched his plane and managed to scramble on to a life raft. American planes launched a hail of fire at Japanese boats which set out to capture him, driving them back, and he was eventually rescued by a US submarine. Ailes got a hold of some old raw film taken by one of the submarine crew which showed Bush being rescued from the raft, and he made it into an ad.

The spot showed Bush as a courageous and forceful military hero, climbing out of the sea, on board the submarine in his flyer's jacket. The ad worked well, partly because they simultaneously made a negative ad showing Dukakis driving around in a tank with a funny looking helmet, still wearing his business suit and tie, smiling sheepishly, while a long list of weapon programs Dukakis had opposed ran across the screen. The differences between the two candidates portrayed in Ailes' ads were stunning – even if they created an image that was unfair to Dukakis, who on his own accord had enlisted in the military, serving two years in South Korea. Fair or not, the Ailes ads had the intended effect.

The Iran-Contras affair was another big problem for Bush. The Bush campaign kept insisting that the Vice President had been "out of the loop" on the issue, and therefore could not be blamed for what had happened. But the media wouldn't back down. CBS News had scheduled a live interview with the Vice President, supposedly as a nice profile interview. However, the campaign was tipped off that the interviewer, CBS News anchor Dan Rather, was about to ambush Bush on the Iran-Contra affair. Ailes trained with Bush, urging him to go on the offensive with Rather, putting himself on the attacking side rather than the receiving end.

CBS News began its segment on the VP with a five-minute taped report that suggested the Vice President had played a greater role in the Iran-Contra affair than Bush has acknowledged. The 10-minute live interview soon became somewhat of a shouting match, with Bush showing viewers a much tougher side than they'd seen of him before – just as Ailes and Atwater had coached. The VP accused Rather and CBS of misrepresenting themselves in obtaining the interview. Bush said that CBS had promised that his appearance would be for a political profile, not a "rehash" of the arms-for-hostages issue. In the most memorable moment of the interview – which Ailes later admitted had been written and rehearsed beforehand – the VP seemed to stun Rather by referring to the anchor's well-known walkout from the set of *The Evening News* the year before, which caused CBS to transmit a blank signal for nearly seven minutes.

"I want to talk about why I want to be President," Bush said, his voice rising. "It's not fair to judge my whole career by a rehash on Iran. How would you like it if I judged your career by those seven minutes when you walked off the set in New York?"[153]

Today it is not all that uncommon if a politician gets into explicitly heated arguments with journalists on national television. In '88, it was a memorable stand-out moment. The confrontational interview was widely seen as a strong performance by the VP – and a victory for Ailes. As CNN/*Time* journalist Richard Stengel later wrote:

> *Ailes has been the unseen hand behind Bush's best moments...[among them] the on-air pummeling of CBS's Dan*

Rather last January. ...The tactic illustrates an Ailes axiom: when attacked, hit back so hard your opponent rues the day he got nasty. ...Ailes' involvement has been crucial to Bush's candidacy.[154]

Ailes became the go-to man on the Bush campaign when it came to taking down the opposition.

"In any campaign you have a small table of inside advisers," said top GOP consultant Mary Matalin, who also worked on Bush's campaign, adding:

Roger always had the clearest vision. The most robust, synthesized, advanced thinking on things political. When you came to a strategy impasse, he'd be the first among equals. I can't remember a single incident where he lost a fight.[155]

With the help of Ailes, Bush had reinvented himself in the public eye.

The campaign's "Double-A Team" (Ailes and Atwater) kept hammering away on Dukakis until the Democrat's strong lead evaporated. They understood early on that they could not win on the merits of their candidate alone. They needed to destroy Dukakis, a task in which they were highly successful. Their work certainly accelerated the increasingly negative tone of the national debate, but it did get Bush elected. And in the end, that was all that mattered to Ailes. On Election Day, Bush won 426 of the electoral votes to Dukakis' 111.

First Nixon, then Reagan, and now Bush. For the third time in Ailes' extraordinary political career, he had contributed significantly to the election of a Republican president.

The next year, he helped orchestrate the reelection of Republican Governor Thomas Kean in the governor's race in New Jersey. Kean won by the largest margin of victory ever recorded for a gubernatorial race in New Jersey, defeating Democrat Peter Shapiro with a whopping 71 to 24 percent.

A Smorgasbord of Negative Charges and Personal Insults

Ailes also played a crucial role in the political career of Rudolph Giuliani. After 9/11, Giuliani became "America's Major" for the way he handled the terrorist attacks in New York, and later he became famously embroiled in President Trump's attempts to overturn the 2020 election. But at the time Ailes started working for him, back in 1989, he was still relatively unknown to most Americans outside of New York. The voters in the Big Apple knew him only as the tough US Attorney for the Southern District of New York – a position he fearlessly used to prosecute cases against the mafia and corrupt corporate financiers.

In a bold move, Giuliani charged the dons of the five major Mafia families that dominated the East Coast with operating a "ruling council." This council controlled a variety of illegal enterprises. According to *Time Magazine*, it was perhaps the most significant assault on the infrastructure of organized crime since the high command of the Chicago Mafia was swept away in the 1940s.

Monopolizing the spotlight, Giuliani tried the case himself, declaring that his goal was to "wipe out the five families."[156] All eight defendants in the dramatic trial were convicted and the judge gave 100-year sentences to seven of the defendants. So by the time Rudy Giuliani decided to run for mayor in 1989, few New Yorkers doubted he was a serious contender that would go to great lengths to win. They were about to find out just how far he'd go. [157]

When the race started, Giuliani was far behind the known and beloved Democratic mayor David Dinkins in the polls, and he made notable gains during the campaign. In the end, Giuliani would lose to Dinkins by a margin of just 47,080 votes out of 1,899,845 votes cast, in what was the closest election in New York City's history. In a city that had not elected a Republican mayor in more than a generation, this was no small feat, and a large part of the credit for the Republicans' showing belonged to Ailes.[158] The strong result enforced Giuliani's brand and secured him the Republican nomination four years later, when he would go on to beat Dinkins.

At the very start of the 1989 campaign, Giuliani seemed to struggle. He had made few substantive speeches. He also muddied his image by straddling such sensitive issues as abortion and gay rights, displeasing people on both sides. So, in an effort to revive his campaign, he made changes to his team.[159] Most significantly, he hired Ailes for "that extra punch."[160]

Ailes was itching for a fight. In an interview with *The New York Times*, he said "Now I am poised to strike. I've been an underdog all my life. It gives me a feeling of security." [161] With Giuliani teaming up with Ailes, the campaign was about to become one of the most negative the city of New York had ever seen.

In that same interview, Ailes said of Dinkins, "'He's not a bad guy; he's a nice fellow. You don't run against Dinkins as a man. You run against his record." Then, without blinking an eye, he moved on to attack, "I think his public performance has been disgraceful. David Dinkins was a financial disaster personally – and as an administrator. That is what the record shows."

Beside his financial record, the other main point of attack for the Giuliani campaign was painting a picture of Dinkins as too soft on crime. Ailes dug up the case of Robert "Sonny" Carson. In 1974, Carson and several other people were convicted of kidnapping a man whom they suspected of stealing money and artifacts from a small museum in Brooklyn. Carson was acquitted of murder but served 15 months in prison.[162] Now Carson had been retained by the Dinkins campaign, who had paid him $9,500 in what Ailes claimed was "walking around money," money to be used for buying votes. The attack threw the Dinkins campaign on the defensive, and they could produce few receipts showing how the cash was spent. Ailes charged it was just another example of Dinkins being too soft on crime.

To most, the attacks linking Dinkins with Carson looked a lot like the attacks linking Willie Horton with Dukakis that Ailes had been involved in just a year earlier. *The Washington Post* ran a story with the headline "With Ailes's Aid, Convict becomes 'Willie Horton' of N.Y. Campaign"[163] Obviously, the Carson case had some similarities to the Horton case; they were both convicted felons, and they were both black. But unlike Horton, Carson had not been convicted of murder. The Dinkins campaign disavowed Carson and hoped it would all blow over. But Carson didn't make things easier for the Dinkins campaign, giving an interview where he described himself as a black nationalist and denied accusations that he was anti-Semitic by saying, "I'm anti-white! Don't just limit me to a little group of people."[164]

Ailes even got his former employer, the newly elected President Bush to travel to New York to give a speech supporting Giuliani. Calling Giuliani "America's greatest crime fighter" Bush told the crowd, "don't postpone your return to good government, your return to greatness. Don't wait another four years." The President heaped praise on Giuliani, comparing him to Eliot Ness, who led the famous team of law enforcement agents nicknamed "The Untouchables."[165]

In the hope of tarnishing his opponents' credibility further, Ailes also claimed that Dinkins had broken the law in personal financial transactions. He told *The New York Times* that Dinkins was guilty of 33 "clear violations of the law" – ranging from a stock transfer to his failure to file income tax returns in the 1960s and 1970s. Giuliani followed Ailes' lead, saying that "there are an awful lot of situations where David's conduct raises a lot of legal questions."[166]

Ailes kept up the pressure, telling *The Washington Post*, "If [Dinkins] breaks the law and hires a kidnapper and pays him secretly, I would be remiss if I didn't make it an issue. We have at least six cases where he has broken the law. He apparently feels stealing a little bit is okay."[167]

For Dinkins, enough was enough. He issued an ultimatum to "stop the gutter politics" within 24 hours, or else. In a public letter to Giuliani, he threatened to retaliate if Ailes's attacks did not end; "If you persist on your present course, you will learn something I learned in the Marine Corps. Marines aren't very good at picking fights, but they certainly know how to end them." Both Ailes and Giuliani scoffed at the ultimatum, with the candidate calling the letter "silly" and "a ploy, adding in a public statement, "I really feel sorry for David. He's got a lot of problems. They're mounting. The questions are becoming more serious every day."[168]

But Dinkins' warning wasn't a hollow threat. The Democrat changed strategy and set his aim for Giuliani and Ailes. For the duration of the race, both campaigns were in a "take no prisoners" mode. The insults and allegations piled up. To some New Yorkers, it felt more like a soap opera than a political contest.

Ailes and Giuliani knew they were fighting an uphill battle. As the results ticked in on Election Night, no one were surprised that they lost. The big surprise was that they had come so close to the prize. Ailes had built a rock-solid platform for Giuliani's rematch. He had positioned Giuliani as *the* tough-on-crime candidate, ready to brush all opposition aside in the ensuing race four years later, in which he would succeed.

The New York mayoral campaign of 1989 was, to put it mildly, a smorgasbord of negative charges and personal insults. This was familiar waters to Ailes, an environment in which he thrived. He knew what made the electorate both angry and engaged. He knew how to press those buttons, and he did do so in the form of emotional television scenes and intense personal attacks. When he had located the jugular of his opponent, he bit down and never let go. It was raw and dirty and real – it was pure Ailes.

The Ultimate Political Hitman

Roger Ailes masterminded a range of political campaigns. In all, he wielded his powers for three presidents and 15 United State senators, as well as several gubernatorial candidates. Remarkably, today most people do not remember him for these impressive political campaigns, but rather for what he did next.

In 1993, Ailes became president of CNBC and later created the "America's Talking" channel, which would eventually become MSNBC. Three years later, in 1996, he was commissioned by Rupert Murdoch to build the Fox News Channel. He not only succeeded in creating a news channel, he built a news media juggernaut. Under his leadership, Fox News became the most important right-wing media force in American politics. Without Ailes and his ability to fire up the conservative right, without the strong ideological force he let lose through Fox, Donald Trump would most probably never have been elected president in 2016.

Ailes was the ideological force behind Fox for two decades, until he had to resign in 2016 after accusations of sexual harassment. He died less than a year later. What you think of Roger Ailes might depend on your affiliation. In the Trump camp, many see him as a brilliant political strategist, a fighter for the good cause. On the other side of the aisle, many saw him as nothing but a wielder of the dark arts, playing on racism and fear, leaving democracy tainted in his never ending quest to win. No matter what camp you belong to, is certainly fair to say that Roger Ailes at times played dirty. He was highly controversial, unquestionably brilliant, and extremely effective.

Ailes was a Master of Political Communication – the ultimate political hitman.

CHAPTER 4

THE RAGIN' CAJUN

James Carville

"Anybody who's been on a battlefield, whether it's a real battlefield or a political battlefield...will know this: There's the smell, the odor, the feel that draws you back after it's done."

- James Carville

Crying on the Sidewalk

By the summer of 1991, Arkansas governor, Bill Clinton, had decided to pursue the Democratic nomination for president. He had been planning this move for years, and his guts told him this was the right time. It was a feeling contrary to all conventional wisdom. The sitting president, George H. W. Bush, was flying sky high in the polls, and most of the prominent Democratic leaders had bowed out of the contest, leaving the Arkansas governor a perceived front runner for the Democratic nomination. But Clinton was sure the country was about to turn on Bush, mainly because more and more people in the middle class were struggling to make ends meet.

Bill Clinton might have been a relatively young governor from a small southern state, but he was no novice. He had spent a decade building a vast network of supporters and contributors across the whole country. He had a large rolodex of old friends – a small army known as FOB (Friends of Bill) – who were loyal to a fault and eager to assist his national ambitions. He had built a solid platform as a New Democrat, more centrist and pragmatic than the Democratic Party's more liberal candidates of the '80s. He was an expert fundraiser, who knew exactly how to acquire the necessary resources needed for a money-gorging presidential campaign.

What Clinton *didn't* have was a master strategist. After a quarrel during the governor race the year before, he had fallen out with his old friend and strategist Dick Morris. For more than a decade Clinton had relied on Morris for important strategy decisions. But during the 1990 campaign, they had a fierce quarrel. When he had tried to mend fences and get his old friend to join the presidential bid, Morris turned him down. But he did offer a suggestion: James Carville – the Louisianan known as the Ragin' Cajun – who's energy and passion would be a perfect match for Clinton.

Carville is a tightly wound man, tall and bald, with a sharply angled face. He speaks with a Southern drawl and has a propensity for the lively quote. An intense political genius, Carville shows no pretensions and creates a down-to-earth and energetic first impression. He was born in 1994, as the eldest son of Lucille and Chester Carville. His mother was Cajun, descended from the Acadians who settled in Louisiana.[169] She was a schoolteacher and a door-to-door encyclopedia saleswoman. His father was a postmaster who also owned a general store. These were hard-working people.

He has seven younger siblings, all raised in Carville, Louisiana, just south of Baton Rouge. The town was given its name in the late 1800s in honor of James Carville's paternal grandfather, who was postmaster. It wasn't a terribly exciting place to grow up. In Carville's own words, "It was barely a blip on the map back then, and the only thing that stopped folks passing straight through was the stop sign in the middle of town."[170]

James loved his parents and had "…a remarkably happy childhood. Whatever scars I have are self-inflicted," he remembered.[171] His high school teachers described him as "a handful." If there was trouble, he would seek it out. Drinking and gambling were simply more exciting to the young man than dusty old books of wisdom. He still jokes that he graduated with a 4.0 – not grade point but blood alcohol level.[172]

James' early fascination for the machinery of politics stems from his experiences at the Louisiana state legislature in Baton Rouge. He had a summer job running checks around town for a local bank and would jump at the opportunity to get assigned a delivery to the legislature, which was part theater and part circus. One day, he saw Governor Earl Long marching down the halls, trailing cops, reporters, and functionaries behind him like he was the most important man in the world. It was the coolest thing James had ever seen.[173] Years later, he described it vividly, "There was a commotion in the capital halls, hard shoe leather on marble, echoing, and it was coming right at me. I looked up and he was there… It took my breath away… I was fifteen, and it was like I was staring at a naked woman."[174]

The encounter set off a spark in the young man. From that moment on, he wanted to become part of the political world. That same year, he used his newly minted driver's license to motor around Iberville Parish, stumping for Price LeBlanc, a car dealer and unsuccessful state legislative candidate who ran under the Elvis-inspired slogan, "I want you, I need you, and I'll fight for you."[175] He knocked on doors and spent a lot of time putting up signs and tearing the opponent's signs down. But his efforts and hard work were all in vain. LeBlanc lost.

"It broke my heart," Carville remembered.[176]

After graduation, he went off to Louisiana State University but struggled with his motivation.

"I was something less than an attentive scholar," he admitted, in something of an understatement.[177] After eventually flunking out, he enlisted in the Marine Corps. He served two years and reached the rank of corporal. His time as a Marine brought a new kind of discipline and structure to his life, and he returned to LSU where he earned his undergraduate and Juris Doctor degrees.[178] He campaigned for Hubert Humphrey in 1964 – his fascination for the craftmanship of politics growing steadily each passing year.

For a while he practiced law in Baton Rouge, in the firm of McKernnan, Beychock, Screen, and Pierson. He helped Jerry McKernnan run for the public service commission. He lost. Then he worked for Mary Olive Pierson, who ran for city judge. She lost. In 1979, he worked for "Bubba" Henry who ran for governor of Louisiana. He lost. Carville was 36 and had never worked on a winning campaign. But that didn't deter him. On the contrary:

"I knew I liked it. I liked the excitement," he said.

Finally, he realized his heart was in politics, not the law. Sitting at his desk one day in 1980 he told himself, "If I had to hire a lawyer, I wouldn't hire me."[179] So he quit. He was out of a job, but he had a dream. He knew what he wanted to do. He got a job as a consultant under the tutelage of Gus Weill in 1980. Weill, who is considered the father of modern political public relations work in Louisiana, was a colorful personality who was constantly telling tales. He had served as a US Army Counterintelligence Special Agent in Germany in the 1950s. Now he ran a political consulting firm together with Raymond Strother, another famous Democratic consultant.

"Our national pastime isn't baseball; it's politics," Weill used to say, "where every little boy in other states wants to be Joe DiMaggio or Willie Mays, here he wants to be Huey Long." Carville was certainly inspired by the Kingfish. Years later, behind his desk in the Clinton campaign War Room he had pictures of the Louisiana's populist dynamo brothers Huey and Earl Long hanging from the blinds.[180] The appeal of the economic populism of the Long brothers was to stay with him for the rest of his life.

Working for Weill and Strother gave him new opportunities to learn the craft. Carville assisted on the campaign of Billy Tauzin, who was elected to the US House of Representatives in 1980. He managed the campaign of Baton Rouge mayor Pat Screen, picking up a lot of the planning, detailed work and minutia that goes into the building and running of a political campaign. After his victory, Screen got Carville a job as the number two guy in the mayor's office. But a city bureaucrat job was too slow and unexciting for Carville. In the spring of 1981, he left city hall.

A friend got him a job running the Senate campaign of Virginia lieutenant governor Richard Davis. For a while, he did a terrific job. Then, with just one week left of the campaign, his candidate made a big gaffe at a public event. But they still had a small lead in the polls and virtually no money left, so Carville got cautious and tried to sit on the lead.

"It was a major mistake. ...I let the opposition be more aggressive than me," he admitted. Davis lost the race by just 1 percent. The loss provided several valuable lessons for Carville, the most important being "...don't let the other guy outraise you by two to one, no matter what. Money talks."[181]

After Davis' loss, Carville wasn't exactly flying high. He had lost the very first campaign he had managed on his own. He was 38 years old. He had no job, no prospects, and he was sleeping on a rollaway bed at his girlfriend's house. He even hung out in the public library every day just to have a place to go. Professional politics can be a harsh world, and Carville was struggling at the bottom of the ladder. He felt depressed and dejected.

Flat broke and in real despair, Carville got a tentative assignment from Gary Hart to go organize the South. One rainy day in April, he went to Washington DC to get his marching orders. Leaving the Hart campaign HQ, trudging toward Union Station in the cold April rain, he had nothing more than $47 in his jeans and everything else he owned in a garment bag over his shoulder. He was walking along Massachusetts Avenue when the shoulder strap broke, and the bag hit the wet pavement. So did Carville – he sat down on the sidewalk and started to sob.[182]

The Guru and the Alley Cat

The gig for Hart didn't last long. They had little money and Carville left in July. Then a friend helped him land a job managing the Senate campaign of Texas state senator Lloyd Doggett. In Carville's words, Dogget was "a gazillion points back in the polls, and didn't have many prospects, but I wasn't about to turn down a job that was offered to me, even if it was a looser."[183] But something was happening to him. He was slowly evolving. It was the first campaign where Carville really found his footing and started to wield his political magic.

Through hard work and pure resolve, they changed the game, created a runoff in the heavily contested primary, and then won the Democratic nomination. It was during this race that Carville earned the now famous nickname, "the Ragin' Cajun." It was also were he met and befriended fellow southerner Paul Begala, who would later become his partner. On primary night, they celebrated hard. But winning the Democratic Primary was one thing, beating their Republican opponent another. Doggett went on to get slaughtered by Phil Gramm in the general election. Yet another loss.

Carville scratched out a living in Louisiana for a couple of years. He was about as low as you could get, skating on the edge of oblivion, when he was hired by Bob Casey in 1986. Casey was running for Pennsylvania governor against Bill Scranton. Teaming up with Paul Begala, Carville engineered the whole campaign. Casey was known as "the Three-Time Loss from Holy Cross" on account of having lost the race for governor in 1966, 1970, and 1978. While he was pro-life and socially conservative, he was also a strong union supporter and very liberal in economic matters. This mix was a good match for Carville.

Their Republican opponent, Bill Scranton, was the son of the late Pennsylvania Governor William Scranton. He had started his life on a conservative path, graduating from Yale and then working as editor for some of his family-owned newspapers. But when the papers failed, his life took a more unusual turn – Scranton went to Europe to study Maharishi Mahesh Yogi's transcendental meditation. Later, he returned to America to enter politics, serving as lieutenant governor of Pennsylvania from 1978 to 1986. Then he used his strong brand name to square off with Carville's candidate for what he perceived to be his rightful political inheritance – the governorship.

To most, Scranton seemed a sure winner. At the start of the race, he was 18 points ahead of Casey. But the Democrat had a silver bullet; James Carville.

"I was totally invested in the race," Carville recalled. "I had to win. I was broke."[184]

This was the first campaign where his special brand started emerging to the outside world. Like most brilliant people, James Carville is a high maintenance personality. He isn't shy about showing his emotions. To those around him, his passion, anger, and raw energy comes across as intensely personal and real.

He is a man without pretensions. While many political consultants make sure to be seen at the hot spots, fine downtown restaurants, and other gathering spots for the rich and mighty, he would have none of it, mostly dressing in ordinary jeans and a T-shirt. He has never toned down his southern dialect. On the contrary, Carville have always used his roots as a branding tool.

"I reek of Louisiana," he once boasted. "You can smell it all over me."[185]

Carville projects the image of a man obsessed only with politics. He is convinced that an unrelenting focus on strategy, combined with fierce message discipline, is the key to victory. And that in the end, winning is all that really matters. In the words of *New York Times*' Peter Applebome, "beneath [Carville's] wild-man image is a shrewd, sophisticated marketer who has crafted a deceptively rough-hewn image for himself as skillfully as he runs campaigns."[186]

That might well be, but some of those who are close to the Ragin' Cajun seem to be of the opinion that his image is mainly just James Carville being himself – an authentic political genius. Said Hillary Clinton, "A lot of people think James is a normal person trying to be eccentric. The truth is he is actually desperately trying to be normal."[187]

Carville was right. He was broke, and he had to win. But they started far behind. That meant full war mode. So, the Pennsylvania governor race quickly went negative. Carville had the campaign produce a spot criticizing Scranton's poor attendance record.

"We gave him a job because of his father's name," the voiceover said. "The least he could do is show up for work."

The attacks worked. Carville watched as the Republican's lead grew smaller. In frustration, Scranton held a press conference where he declared he was ending all his negative attacks.

"Clearly what happened was that Scranton's people had gotten into a pissing contest with a skunk and saw that they couldn't win," Carville wrote. "It was the Persian cat against the alley cat."[188]

Scranton's pledge made it extremely difficult for Carville to keep up the heat without tainting his own candidate. The move was intended to stop Scranton's bleeding while he still had a solid lead in the polls. That was smart politics. Or rather, it would have been if the Scranton campaign had possessed the discipline to actually halt their own attacks. They didn't. Carville got hold of a new Scranton mailing that labeled Casey a crook. He seized on it, making sure Scranton's hypocrisy got maximum attention. In desperation, Scranton claimed he hadn't known about the flyer. So, Carville ordered 600,000 empty envelopes to be delivered on the pavement outside Scranton's campaign headquarters, where his candidate held an impromptu press conference.

Standing in front of the mountain of envelopes, Cassey said, "This is six hundred thousand envelopes, the same number Bill Scranton mailed out about me... But Scranton wants you to believe that he sent out six hundred thousand of these and had no idea what was going on." [189]

Carville's commitment to winning the race went a lot further than clean stunts. He wanted to run an ad where they criticized Scranton for his earlier known drug use, but he knew they couldn't get away with that after all the opprobrium around Scranton's stunt with the mailing. Still, something had to be done. They were still eight points down with only 10 days to go. Carville ordered his deputies to get the word out, through a third party, that they were about to run an ad on the drug issue. The rumor was spread that, "The Cajun's lost his mind. He's going to put this drug spot up on Scranton. Casey knows nothing about it."

Predictably, the press went wild, demanding answers on whether the rumor was true. At a campaign rally, Carville strolled over to the press and told them, "Mr. Casey said no, that he'd given his word. So we are not going to run a spot attacking Bill Scranton for using drugs." The cameras rolled and journalists printed every word. It was a dirty trick, and Carville gladly took the heat. Now every voter in the state had heard that Scranton had used drugs, while Cassey's hands stayed clean.

With just a few days left in the race, Carville launched the now infamous "guru ad"; a television spot attacking Scranton's practice of transcendental meditation, depicting him as something of a loony. The ad mixed old and new pictures of Scranton as well as of the guru Yogi. With flaky Indian sitar music playing in the background the narrator asks:

> *Is Bill Scranton qualified to be governor? After College he bought three papers with his family money, but he stopped going to work when the papers failed. Scranton joined transcendental meditation and became a disciple of the Maharishi Mahesh Yogi. Time Magazine said Scranton traveled the world evangelizing for transcendental meditation, and he said his goal was to bring transcendental meditation to state government. His only real job was Lieutenant Governor, and they gave him that because of his father's name.[190]*

In what had up to then been a very close race, the effect of Carville's drug rumor and the "guru ad" was exactly what was needed to deliver a win. Casey defeated Scranton by a margin of 79,000 votes. The final tally showed Casey with 50.4 percent of the vote to Scranton's 48.4 percent. Carville's candidate, who had been eight points behind going into the last week, won by 2. That was an impressive 10-point jump in a mere seven days. Most remarkably, the ad helped Casey garner a surprisingly high vote total in the more conservative rural regions of the state.

In a campaign where both sides had gone negative, the Ragin' Cajun had unscrupulously assailed his opponent's character to secure victory. The man who four years earlier had sat on the sidewalk in the pouring rain crying out of desperation and hopelessness, could finally carve a big notch in his belt. He had managed a winning campaign for governor in an unexpected upset.

A Lottery or a Tax Raise?

There wasn't much time to savor his victory. Carville was already busy strategizing for his newest candidate, Wallace Wilkinson. Wilkinson had grown up on a farm in Kentucky, dropping out of college at the University of Kentucky in 1962 to attend to a book retail business he started, which soon developed into a chain of bookstores. Wilkinson re-invested his profits in real estate, farming, transportation, banking, and other businesses, becoming a wealthy man. In the 1980s, he went into politics as a Democrat, declaring himself a candidate for the Democratic nomination for governor of Kentucky in 1987. He was one among a wide field of strong candidates, among them two previous Kentucky governors, John Brown Jr. and Julian Carroll, and the sitting lieutenant governor, Steve Beshear.

Wilkinson used his own large fortune to finance his campaign, but he was relatively unknown throughout the state. From the get-go, Brown and Beshear were considered the two front runners. Wilkinson was trailing fifth in the race, with less than 1 percent in the early polls. Obviously, it would require some political magic for him to succeed, and his campaign manager had a novel idea on where they could get their hands on some. They called James Carville.

While the two front runners were busy bashing each other – overlooking the rest of the field – Carville made sure Wilkinson attacked all his opponents in a loud way creating maximize attention. At the same time, his candidate kept touting his own rise from a man of humble beginnings to a successful business leader. His main theme was as simple as it was popular; he vowed to increase the state's income to reform education, without raising taxes. This, he promised, could be done by instituting a state lottery, which he claimed would generate $70 million annually for the state's coffers.

Having made his case, Wilkinson and Carville went on the attack against both Brown and Beshear for wanting to raise taxes. It was a clever set up. It appealed both to supporters of education reform and to opponents of tax increases. In addition, it harvested many voters in Northern Kentucky, where residents had to travel to neighboring Ohio to play that state's lottery.

Wilkinson bombarded the state with ads, winning the primary with 36 percent of the vote. The nomination didn't come cheap. In total, he spent a record $4 million during the primary campaign. They still had the general election to win, but the Democrats enjoyed a three-to-one voter registration advantage in Kentucky. This was a disadvantage his Republican opponent John Harper wasn't able to overcome, though he tried his best.

Harper attacked Wilkinson's lottery proposal as "Alice in Wonderland" economics, and he raised a number of ethical issues with regard to Wilkinson's business dealings. Wilkinson's brother-in-law, who was serving as president of one of his companies, pleaded guilty to illegal wiretapping and rolling back the odometers on company vehicles. The company was also forced to pay back-taxes. It all became campaign fodder. Carville wasn't one to take such attack laying down. He returned fire at every opportunity. Both campaigns ran investigations on its opponent and planted several controversial rumors.

With the help of some Ragin' Cajun magic, Wilkinson eventually carried 115 of Kentucky's 120 counties and captured

65 percent of the vote. Carville had taken Wilkinson, an unexperienced candidate who had started out with less than 1 percent of the vote, and guided him to victory. This he had succeeded to do in spite of a massive barrage of critique concerning his candidate's business dealings. That he had helped Wilkinson capture the governorship under such dire circumstances was a feat that impressed even the most experienced political operators across the country. He had finally made it. He was now in the big leagues.

In the late '80s, Carville moved to Washington DC.

"I think at some point if you are a country-music singer you end up in Nashville; if you are a playwright or a stockbroker you end up in New York; if you're an actor you end up in LA," Carville mused. "If you are a political consultant, sooner or later you wash up in Washington."

In 1988, Carville helped New Jersey's Frank Lautenberg win a US Senate seat, and in 1990, he led the gubernatorial campaign of Georgia's Lt. Governor Zell Miller, winning by a six-point margin. Carville was fast becoming a very hot commodity in Democratic politics.

It was in Washington DC that he teamed up with his old friend to form the Carville & Begala political consulting firm. They specialized in strategy, message development, earned media, and – of course – winning elections. The brilliant Begala, who was the more reserved and coolheaded of the two southerners, was 17 years younger than Carville. But the Ragin' Cajun still seemed the more energetic.

Hitting the Right Nerve at Just the Right Time

In the summer of 1990, Republican operative Mary Matalin, then the deputy chairman of the RNC under Lee Atwater, read an article in *The Wall Street Journal* about the meaner and tougher "new breed" of political consultants. She knew most of them, but one was new to her; Democrat James Carville. Remembered Matalin years later, "He was quoted saying, 'It's hard for somebody to hit you when you've got your fist in their face.'" It made a lasting impression. They had a mutual friend who kept pushing them to meet, and they finally did in January of '91.

If Matalin had been fascinated by the Ragin' Cajun before their meeting, she wasn't any less intrigued after getting the Carville treatment.

> *He was clearly a bad boy, and funny. And interesting. We agreed on practically nothing but we had a good time barking at each other. We sat at the bar and ate greasy fried zucchini and french-fries for dinner. It didn't take long before we were fighting... I don't remember what we were shouting about, just that he was so intense... I really liked him.[191]*

From that moment on, the two were a couple. They didn't know it yet, but in less than a year, they would be at the head of two opposing presidential campaigns. But first, Carville had a mission to accomplish in Pennsylvania.

The Pennsylvania US Senate race of 1991 became a memorable showdown between Democrat Harris Wofford and Republican Dick Thornburgh; an intense race that Carville once more entered on the side of the underdog. Pennsylvania's senior senator had died in an aviation accident in April that year, leaving his seat open. By law, governor Bob Casey – whom Carville had helped elect five years earlier – was required to appoint a replacement until a special election could be held. After considering several potential candidates, he appointed Harris Wofford to the seat.

Wofford had an impressive CV. He had served in the Army during the Second World War, been on the United States Commission on Civil Rights, worked as a law professor at the University of Notre Dame, worked for John F. Kennedy, been a friend and unofficial advisor to Martin Luther King Jr., chairman of the Pennsylvania Democratic Party, and the state's Secretary of Labor and Industry. Still, he had a relatively low name recognition in a state that hadn't sent a Democrat to the US Senate for 22 years.[192]

His opponent, Dick Thornburgh, was a national republican celebrity. Serving as the US Attorney General under Presidents Ronald Reagan and George H. W. Bush, his candidacy got a lot of attention. This was a seat President Bush could hardly afford to lose. Therefore, Thornburgh had the full backing of the Republican National Party and the funding that came with it. He seemed invincible. But for all his advantages, there was one that Thornburgh lacked; James Carville. The Ragin' Cajun liked Wofford and his history of fighting for civil rights and liberal economic ideas. He was a candidate worth fighting for. Carville and Begala mounted their horses and rode into battle.

It certainly looked like a fight they would lose, no matter how motivated and clever they were. Wofford began the campaign so far behind in the polls that the pundits assumed he had no chance of winning. No chance at all. Even his own internal polls showed him losing by over 40 points. Because Wofford was not widely known outside the state's political establishment, his candidacy excited few. Many felt the governor had squandered a golden opportunity by picking him. Even within the Democratic Party, Wofford was viewed as a caretaker, an interim senator holding the seat until Thornburgh could legally assume it.[193]

But Carville was undeterred. He felt the mood of the country had changed during the last part of the '80s. Middle class families were struggling, and the promised trickle-down effect from 12 years of Republican tax cuts for the rich was nowhere to be seen. The Reagan revolution – dismissing government not as the solution but as the problem – had fallen out of demand among most of the middle class, many of whom were struggling to make ends meet. Carville recognized this shift long before most others, giving him a competitive edge. He had a knack for tapping into the gut of the electorate.

Under Carville's stewardship Wofford generated a strong message focused on the need for a middle-class tax cut to ease the plight of the middle class, more affordable education and national health insurance. Their prime target became President Bush and what they saw as his failed economic leadership. They wanted to attack his Reaganesque "government is the problem" message and fight for a new "we need government to step up when we're struggling" platform. Carville had first embraced this kind of economic populism in his youth, through his admiration of Huey and Earl Long. Now he honed the message to resonate in a powerful way with the modern electorate. He didn't know it yet, but he was, in fact, shaping the fundamental principles of what would become the Democrat's main message in the crucial '92 presidential election.

Because it was a special election, the campaign lasted only six months. With his substantial lead in the polls, Thornburgh lay low from the start, to avoid gaffes or miscalculations. This was a strategic mistake because it allowed Carville and Begala to go on the offensive without countering much resistance, and Wofford soon started gaining traction. Later, Thornburgh's media consultant Greg Stevens admitted, "The major thing I would do differently is to have defined Wofford earlier and not let him get up a head of steam."[194]

But at the time, they did little, which left plenty of room for Carville to wield his magic. Building on the populist economic theme, Wofford connected well with working class voters and the struggling middle class. Their campaign kept pounding away on Thornburgh for his close connection to Bush, who even came to the state to campaign for Thornburgh. For Carville, this just made it easier to portray Thornburgh as an out-of-touch creature of Washington, with the recession growing worse by the day.

At their final debate, a well-coached Wofford aggressively attacked Thornburgh with charges that his opponent was out of touch. He hammered his opponent on education, tax cuts for the middle class, and affordable health care. They had crafted the classic line, "If criminals are entitled to a lawyer, working people should be entitled to a doctor."[195] It might seem unlikely that a man like Wofford, an Ivy League man with an elite background, was serving as a vehicle for such a populist message, but Carville and Begala made it work. They had hit the right nerve in the electorate, at just the right time.

They also had a detailed plan for building a majority. They made sure the campaign touted Wofford's liberal credentials to the social liberal voters in the eastern part of the state, which boosted Wofford's appeal there. But it was the populist economic message which unlocked the Democratic votes in southwestern Pennsylvania that really held the key to victory. It played exceptionally well in the economically distressed towns of that area. The message also resonated well in the blue-collar towns of the northeast.

The battle plan proved unbeatable. Wofford surged forward in the polls. Carville being Carville, wore the same underwear all through the campaign's final week, rather than break up his favorable karma. If there was any chance at all that a little superstition could help, he reasoned, then why not?

When the votes were counted, they had delivered a knockout blow to Thornburgh, winning by 338,000 votes statewide for a solid 10-point victory. In his victory speech, Wofford said of his election, "I thank Pennsylvania for sending me as its messenger, and the message is it's time for change!"[196]

Once again, Carville and Begala had taken a candidate no one else had believed in – that from the onset of the race was far behind in the polls – and delivered a decisive victory. Thornburgh, the President's knight in shining armor – who only a few months earlier had seemed destined to succeed – now lay beaten on the battlefield. The Ragin' Cajun left Pennsylvania with another victory and, just as important, with a new populist "economy first" message he had articulated. It was a message that resonated deeply with the voters. The outcome of the race was a clear premonition of the nation's mood entering the next year's presidential contest.

Clinton Wins the Carville Primary

And so it was, that in the summer of 1991 Carville and Begala found themselves being courted by Arkansas governor Bill Clinton. The two consultants were hot commodities, and several of the presidential hopefuls tried to persuade them to get on board. But Carville felt that Clinton would be a more natural fit for his message and temperament than the others.

"When I pick a candidate I've got to live in the same foxhole with him for a year," he said. "You've got to smell their breath a lot."[197]

He had become a savvy political operator, and for his first swing at a presidential race, he wanted a candidate who understood both policy and the game as well as he did. He wanted someone real, someone he could feel good fighting for. Now he found that someone.

Their first meeting was casual. Carville, Begala, and Clinton sat chatting over beers on the sofa in the bar of a Capitol Hill hotel. Clinton talked about his political passion, about how he wanted to change the country for his daughter. He was charming, intelligent, and obviously passionate. Incredibly knowledgeable on the issues, he also had an obvious talent for the mechanics of the game.

"However smart and whatever ability to connect with people you think Bill Clinton has, you have no idea. He's so much better in person than you think he is," Carville concluded.[198] Begala was blown away.[199] The two operators had never met anybody like Clinton in politics. Leaving their first encounter, Carville's only question was, "Is this guy too good to be true?"[200] They decided to find out.

Closing the deal with the consultant superstars was a major move for Clinton. The headline of *The Washington Post* on December 3, 1991 summed it up; "Clinton wins the Carville primary!"[201] It gave the Arkansas governor extra credibility as a front runner. The rest of Clinton's newly assembled team were almost as impressive; Rahm Emanuel came in to run the fundraising operation, succeeding in building a war chest that by far outdid Clinton's competitors; the highly respected Frank Greer became Clinton's ad man; the sought-after Stan Greenberg his pollster. This group of elite political mercenaries became a billboard projecting Clinton's strength. The governor chose the charismatic George Stephanopoulos as his communication director.

Clinton's main rivals for the Democratic nomination were former Senator Paul Tsongas of Massachusetts and Senator Bob Kerrey of Nebraska. Senator Tom Harkin of Iowa had also entered the race, making the rest of the field ignore the state, which was expected to go overwhelmingly to its favorite son. So, all eyes were focused on New Hampshire. Clinton was perceived to be one of the strongest contenders for the nomination, which meant he needed to deliver in the Granite State if he was to keep up his momentum.

At a meeting of state party chair-people in Chicago in the fall of 1991, all the candidates were put on display. Clinton used the opportunity well, giving the first clear hints of how anti-establishment his message actually was.

"Washington DC has become a city of irresponsibility," he told the crowd – and made it clear he wasn't speaking just about the Republicans. Voters didn't care much about politicians of either party, he said. "The American people have lost faith in the political process, and they have ample reason!"[202]

It was a clear and simple message that left the rest of the contenders seeming rather bland. Clinton's presentation of himself as a new kind of Democrat – someone who wanted the nation to throw of the yoke of old stringent party ideology, stop partisan fighting, and embrace new solutions for a new age – put him front and center. He was the first to formulate a clear message, he had attracted an array of impressive political operators, and he had the largest war chest.

On January 19, a poll in the Boston Globe put Clinton ahead of the field with 29 percent. Tsongas got 17 and Kerrey 16. In any campaign, being the frontrunner puts you in an extraordinarily exposed situation. With all eyes on his candidate, Carville knew they had to be expecting both harsh attacks and fierce scrutiny. Still, he was expecting a storm, not the tsunami that was on its way.

For years, rumors had circulated that Clinton was something of a ladies' man. There had even been some specific allegations that had been covered by the press back home in Arkansas, but none of it had stuck to the Governor. In mid-January 1992, the tabloid *Star* magazine ran a story about those earlier allegations. The rumors grew, and the press started smelling blood. In an instant, they shifted their focus away from policy onto Clintons sex life. Soon enough, the press was writing stories about old rumors and inuendoes. The issue grew in strength, becoming a real headache.

At a rally in New Hampshire, Hillary was confronted by a voter asking whether the candidate's fidelity to his wife was a relevant issue for voters to ask about. Hillary didn't even flinch.

"From my perspective, our marriage is a strong marriage," she answered confidently. Sure, there had been some issues, as in most marriages. But they were nobody else's business. "Is anything about our marriage as important to the people of New Hampshire as whether or not they will have a chance to keep their own families together..."

The rest of the answer was drowned out in an explosion of cheers. In the back of the hall, Carville whooped and clapped his hands. In his view, Hillary had knocked the ball out of the park.[203] Getting such a strong response from the crowd in front of their press entourage, he hoped the incident would dampen the pressure. It didn't. The next days, the heat just increased.

Even if Carville hadn't told his candidate to put on his game face, Clinton did. He was a natural. At every campaign stop, he kept smiling.

"I knew they would try to do this," he told reporters, "it's flattering that they think I'm gonna win, I guess. They don't think they can beat me on the issues."

The press was all over it now. Carville knew they would leave no stone unturned. A distressed single mother from Arkansas even called Clinton's office in tears, reporting how she had been offered money to come forward with sex stories about herself and Clinton.

"You're trying to raise your kids," a stranger had told her. "We can make it a lot easier on you." She turned them down. But not everyone reacted the same way.

Amongst the old rumors was the story of Gennifer Flowers, a night club singer seeking fame and fortune but not doing very well in the entertainment industry. Now, *Star* had paid her a six-figure number to come forward with her allegations. "My 12-year affair with Bill Clinton," the headline shouted. She even had some tapes of conversations between herself and Clinton. Clinton told Carville that he hadn't had intercourse with Flowers. Carville believed him, but that didn't really matter. The media didn't care much about the accuracy of the allegations. To them, Clinton was a man of fame and power, which meant they could throw whatever they liked at him. The ensuing media coverage blocked out the sun, making it impossible for Carville to get attention back on Clinton's message, tarnishing his image. There was no way the campaign could survive this storm without a bold tactical step. But what was the right move?

Popular talk show host Ted Koppel had invited Clinton to his show *Nightline*, and some in the campaign liked the idea. But Carville, who was following Clinton around the state to be as close as possible to the candidate, was dead set against it. He thought Clinton wasn't ready – neither physically nor psychologically – to go rushing into a high-pressure, high-stakes televised interview. They didn't even know how the story was going to unfold in the days ahead. Instead, they sent Mandy Grunwald from the campaign as a surrogate. The tough and intelligent Grunwald, described by one acquaintance as "Lee Atwater in a Chanel suit," turned the attack right back on Koppel for embracing trash journalism. This at least bought them some time.

As the mainstream media coverage on the Flowers case settled into a pattern and no more women came forward, Carville and the rest of the team found their footing. Finally able to see the whole landscape, they developed a strategy on how Clinton should deal with the story. It was clear to all that the story wasn't going away until Clinton had properly addressed it.

"When the story hit, the option was, what is the most vigorous response that we can give to deal with this? You knew you had to be aggressive," Carville later stated.[204]

They had also been offered an interview on a prime-time edition of *60 Minutes*, and Carville was sure this was their make-or-break opportunity. "Do *60 Minutes*," he advised the Clintons, "and then shut up."[205] If they performed well, it would let Clinton brush of further questions from the press on the issue until they grew tired and moved on. It was the only safe way out of the raging storm that surrounded them. Of course, it was a huge risk. One slip-up, and the whole campaign would go down in flames. But with few other choices available, the Clintons decided to go for it.

Carville was sure it was the right decision. But that didn't mean he had to like it. As a matter of fact, he loathed it. At one point, alone in his hotel room, he felt totally overcome by embarrassment for Bill and Hillary. They were only human, like the rest of us, and now they had to be interrogated about the most private part of their marriage on national television. He started to weep and couldn't stop for a half-hour. The next day, he kept getting emotional outbursts.

"Have you lost your mind?" he would yell at reporters and network executives, "you people are goddamn amazing. You went to college, you got a degree, you are a professional journalist, and you are letting someone like Gennifer Flowers dictate your coverage. What are you doing? This is crack cocaine of journalism!"[206]

Carville and Begala wrote a memo to Clinton outlining a strategy for the *60 Minutes* interview. The memo dated January

24, 1992, started with a quote from Hemmingway's book *A Fare-well to Arms*: "The world breaks everyone and afterwards many are stronger in the broken places." They urged Clinton to make a virtue out of the fact that his relationship had been tested, but that the couple had overcome their problems and had emerged stronger. Pinpointing just how important Hillary was to Bill's survival, they wrote: "Hillary's the best thing you've got going for you. ...she's our ace in the hole. Like you, she needs to be calm and confident, unlike you she can leap to your defense and more importantly your family's defense."[207]

Clinton did great on the show, answering difficult questions about Flowers and the state of his marriage. He admitted having caused pain in his marriage. He was sorry. He defended Hillary. When the interviewer, Steve Kroft, suggested that most people would find it admirable that the Clintons had worked through their problems and found some sort of understanding, Bill cut him short.

"Now wait a minute, you're looking at two people who love each other. This is not an arrangement or an understanding. This is a marriage. And that's a very different thing," he said in a firm, emotional voice.

Hillary did even better than her husband, coming across as both honest and genuine. She was fighting for her family. Looking straight at Kroft, she said:

> *You know, I'm not sitting here like some little woman, standing by my man like Tammy Wynette. I'm sitting here because I love him, and I respect him, and I honor what he's been through and what we've been through together. And you know, if that's not enough for people - then, heck, don't vote for him.*

Both Bill and Hillary came across as people you could relate to, respect and sympathize with.

Wrapping up, Kroft asked Bill why he wanted to be president. He gave a forceful answer, talking emotionally about his call to public service and how he wanted to help change people's lives for the better. Watching on monitors in the adjacent room, the Ragin' Cajun started to cry again, this time out of pride and relief.

On the flight back to Arkansas, his mood was up. Drinking bourbon and playing cards with the Governor, he said, "We may go down, but at least this thing is behind us."

Clinton sighed. He knew how much was at stake once the interview ran on national television. He felt they had done well, but they had no control over the editing.

"This thing could go down like a turd in a punch bowl," he whispered quietly.

Even though *60 Minutes* cut out some of Clinton's best moments before it ran the interview, it still worked out like Carville had predicted. Now that the candidate and his wife had responded, they hammered home the point that the election should be about the lives of the voter, not the life of Bill Clinton. A counteroffensive was mobilized to achieve exactly that, with Carville out in front leading the charge.

Too often, the media and the pundits live in their own bubble, misinterpreting what's important and not, underestimating the common voters' ability to see through the commotion and make up their own minds. The Gennifer Flower circus was such a moment. Back in New Hampshire, most primary voters agreed with Carville. They wanted the media to focus more on the issues that made a real difference in *their* lives, not keep wallow in the past sex life of the candidates. An ABC News poll found that as many as four out of five Americans said Clinton should stay in the race.[208] Carville had made the right strategic call; Clinton would live to fight another day.

Ill-luck Seldom Comes Alone

The Ragin' Cajun had been in desperate situations before, and he knew that ill-luck seldom comes alone. The campaign had barely finished with Flowers when a new scandal broke. Again, it was a well-known story which had been fought over in an old Arkansas campaign that came back to haunt Clinton. Back in his college days, while hundreds of thousands of youths from his generation were shipped off to Vietnam, he had escaped the draft. His account of what had happened seemed innocent enough on the surface, but the media had sources alleging that he had been given special treatment. Had he schemed to dodge the draft?

The story became extra damaging because Clinton's character had already been put under so much scrutiny by the Flowers debacle. The draft story added fuel to a fire that was still smoldering. Carville saw just how dangerous this was. Surviving one scandal so early in the primary season was hard enough, surviving two would be nearly impossible. At this point, the campaign really had just two alternatives; either they had to declare defeat, or they had to go into an all-out war mode. For an old Marine like Carville, defeat simply wasn't an option. So they suited up for the battle ahead. The tactic was simple; they would vehemently deny

that Clinton had dodged the draft and keep talking about the issues, even if the journalists didn't listen.

Sensing the drama, the press was all over his candidate now,
literally questioning everything he had ever said and done.

"I think it is almost blood lust," Clinton said wearily, continuing:

> I think it's an insatiable desire on the part of the press to build
> up and tear down. And they think that is their job - and not
> only that, their divine right. ... You're dealing with a group of
> people that basically believes that, for whatever reason, they
> ought to have the right to determine the outcome of this elec-
> tion. And they can justify anything, anything, under the guise
> of the First Amendment.

Clinton wasn't the only one frustrated by how the media so
often stepped over ethical boundaries in their eternal quest for "the
story". Carville and Begala nicknamed the press pool "the Beast."

"You can just see the media in a pack, howling for red meat,"
Carville asserted.[209]

In many respects they had a fair point. As soon as the press
had gotten the scent of blood, most of them had lost sight of the
big picture, burying themselves in the dirt. The truth, often filled
with ambiguities, mattered less than creating a scandal. And almost any fact, not matter how innocent, could be fashioned into
a story that at least left an impression of a scandal. It was obvious
the press wouldn't let go. If he was to survive, Clinton needed to
get out there to win over some voters, while his generals fought
back the media.

With the New Hampshire primary just nine days away, they
have very little time. Their internal polls showed them plummet-

ing toward the abyss. They had lost 20 points in a matter of days.[210] Carville and the rest of the campaign leadership knew that their road to victory had to go through New Hampshire. At this point, they didn't even need to beat Tsongas. After all, everybody knew he practically lived within an hour's drive of a majority of New Hampshire voters and was considered a favorite son. But they did need Clinton to at least finish second. If he didn't, some other strong Democrat – one of those famous popular ones who had declined to run so far – might be enticed to enter the race from the sidelines to "save the day for the Party," and that was the last thing they wanted.

To finishing second, they would have to recapture most of the votes they had lost. But in the polls, both Tsongas and Kerrey were by now far ahead of Carville's candidate, who had plunged into the single digits. Could they turn it all around in just one week? It seemed impossible. But the candidate himself, who was caught in the midst of the storm, the man who had spent most of his adult life working toward this very moment, didn't intend to go down now. Clinton was no less of a fighter than the Ragin' Cajun, and he worked just as hard. Perhaps harder, which was incredible considering the enormous pressure he was under. Clinton walked in front of the cameras and said, "I just have one thing to say about the next eight days: I'm going to fight like hell!"[211]

Barely getting any rest and very little sleep, Clinton started a personal blitzkrieg, meeting as many voters face to face as humanly possible. He went anywhere, to small bowling alleys, restaurants, cafés, fast food joints, shopping malls, small stores – just any place where he could shake the hand of a voter. He was like the Duracell Bunny, when everybody around him collapsed out of exhaustion, he just kept going, kept shaking hands, kept smiling, kept asking people for their support. From dawn to dusk, day after day after day. It was impressive by any standard, even more so when you saw the press tearing into his flesh like jackals, while he just kept smiling and shaking hands.

"The strategy really was, be everywhere. Shake every hand," said Carville.[212] "It was the most remarkable thing that I have seen in politics. You were watching a guy literally fighting for his life, his political life."[213]

Carville wanted to use ads to hit the media for how they didn't focus on the issues that really mattered in ordinary people's lives. He wanted the campaign to be on a constant offensive.

"I was the most hawkish in the group," he said. "You know, aggressively pushing back."[214]

He was joined by Hillary in their take-no-prisoners approach. He advocated digging deep into their war chest to add a television advertising-barrage to the candidate's handshaking offensive. Some in the campaign wanted to save the money for later, but the Ragin' Cajun bulldozed over them.

"This week is life or death!" he shouted. "If we have to spend an extra $200,000 to take a chance, let's take a chance."[215]

On February 18, 1992, as the votes were counted across New Hampshire, Carville was as tense as his candidate. No one knew for sure if their last dash had given them enough of a boost to survive. Then the exit polls came out, and a silence fell over the room. People were shocked. They didn't know whether to believe what they read. Instead of the expected 8-9 percent, Clinton got close to 25. He finished a strong second, with Tsongas just eight points ahead and Kerrey lagging far behind. It was a dramatic, spectacular comeback. The generals in the Clinton campaign knew it gave them a great opportunity to boost their momentum. While Tsongas lingered, awaiting the final tallies before giving his victory speech, Clinton rushed to the podium.

"I think we know enough to say with some certainty," he told his followers and millions watching at home, "that New Hampshire tonight has made Bill Clinton 'the Comeback Kid'."

It was one of those memorable lines you never forget. It got repeated a thousand times on all the news networks and in all the national newspapers. Most Americans barely noticed that Tsongas had beaten Clinton.

"One of Clinton's greatest strengths was his ability to take the spotlight that shone on him because of his personal adversity and shine it on the problems of the country and the things he wanted to change," Carville recalled. Now Clinton did exactly that.

Having declared himself the Comeback Kid, he went on, "I've taken some hard knocks in this state but they are nothing compared to the knocks that I've seen people take here in New Hampshire, back home in Arkansas, all across the country."[216]

Carville was as elated as the rest of the team. They had done the impossible. They had survived two scandals in a row. They had stolen Tsongas's victory right from under his nose. But both the candidate and his chief strategist knew that they hadn't really won New Hampshire. They had simply survived. They still needed to take down Tsongas.

Georgia was one of the upcoming primaries. It was the state were Carville had helped elect his client Zell Miller as governor. Now Miller returned the favor. He had moved up his state's primary date, and now he let Carville use his many influential statewide connections to secure a win. Even Carville's girlfriend, Bush campaign operator Mary Matalin, was impressed:

> *James delivering the Georgia primary panicked me early. ...*
> *Lee Atwater got his home-state political pals to move the*
> *South Carolina primary up before Super Tuesday because we*
> *knew we would win there and it would catapult us into the*
> *cluster of primaries... I knew Zell Miller was Carville's client*
> *and when I saw him move up his primary before the campaign*
> *started I presumed it was Carville's doing. Clinton could use*
> *it as the same launching pad into Super Tuesday that we had*
> *used South Carolina for. Manipulating the primary system so*
> *a specific candidate can get an advantage is a smart thing to*
> *do, and often not easy. Carville was better than I thought.*[217]

Governor Miller also went after Tsongas, so that Clinton didn't have to dirty his hands.

"The truth is that Paul Tsongas will lead the party we love right down that well-worn path of defeat," the Governor told the crowd at a Clinton rally in Atlanta. Another Clinton surrogate, Georgia Lt. Governor Pierre Howard, explained to *The Atlanta Journal* that Tsongas just didn't connect with ordinary people, saying, "Tsongas is not Greek for Bubba."

They continued hitting Tsongas, but that wasn't enough. Their polls showed they had a problem getting through with their message. In one of their strategy sessions, Carville summed up their biggest challenge: "Strategy is not a priority in this campaign. In fact, we have bad strategy. This campaign works too hard and thinks too little." He searched frantically for a new overall strategy and a new theme.[218]

In their meetings, Carville would get up from his chair and pace restlessly back and forth. He had little patience for beating around the bush, and when the discussion left strategy or tactics and drifted into logistics or practical issues, he would most often just leave the room. He always pushed hard for the campaign to focus on a simple message, and to implement relentless message discipline.

The first big hurdle they faced now was getting through Junior Tuesday. On March 3, seven states and 380 delegates were in play. Carville had been dispatched to Atlanta, where he worked with his old friends from the Miller campaign to deliver a decisive victory. In terms of the total delegate count of the day, Tsongas was the undisputed victor. He won three states, did well in several others, and racked up more delegates than any of the other contenders. Trying to copy Clinton, he declared himself the Breakthrough Kid. It didn't stick. Jerry Brown, the former governor of California, also did better than predicted and was fast becoming a contender to be taken seriously. He won Colorado and did well in several other states. In fact, Clinton won only one of the seven states: Georgia.

One would think that winning just one state out of seven was a pretty bad showing for the self-declared Comeback Kid. But again, Carville and the team proved that none of the other campaigns came close to their ability to spin even a disappointing outcome as a victory. The result Carville had delivered in the one state they won was by all means impressive – with a whopping 57 percent of the vote, Clinton beat Tsongas in Georgia by more than two to one. So, they made the most of it, working practically every news outlet with the story. As a result, the victory in Georgia got as much attention from the national media as all of Tsongas combined victories did. Tsongas may have had the best numbers on the scoreboard, but with Carville's help and an exceptional team, Clinton was winning the perception game.

This helped sustain Clinton's momentum going into the immensely important Super Tuesday seven days later. There were other advantages too; Tsongas's campaign had focused too much on the early states, while Clinton's generals had been busy building local campaigns in states that held later contests. The Clinton team also beat Tsongas in the most critical primary: Money. Clinton himself was already a master money raiser, a skill he had nourished and grown for more than a decade, and his chief money guy Rahm Emanuel was unmatched. In this crucial area, Tsongas had neither the personal skill to match Clinton, nor a money man to match Emanuel.

Beneath the surface, Tsongas was running out of money. Trying to win a presidential campaign without money is like trying to win the Daytona 500 in a Volkswagen Beetle. The resource deficit meant he couldn't get the best people, couldn't buy enough ads, couldn't do the necessary polling, couldn't build the grassroot organizations he needed – simply couldn't get his message across.

While Team Clinton kept hitting him in paid media, Tsongas simply didn't have the capacity to strike back through ads and professional spin. So, he lost his focus and strayed of his message like someone waving of a swarm of mosquitos. In the last days before Super Tuesday, his polling showed that the large states he had counted on to carry him through were all slipping away.

Carville's numbers showed it, too, and he allowed himself a rare moment of optimism. What he didn't know was that another bad story was about to hit his candidate right in the face. As in New Hampshire, it turned out that the Clinton campaigns biggest challenger wasn't his opponents, but the candidate's own history. *The New York Times* was still digging into his past and had come over a land-development deal that the Clintons had entered into with some old friends back when he was Attorney General in Arkansas.

The deal was pretty straight forward. The Clintons and their friends Jim and Susan McDougal had entered into a 50/50 partnership called Whitewater Development. They had bought 230 acres of land in the Ozark Mountains and divided them up into 42 lots that they tried to sell off to customers who wanted to build vacation homes. As the market crashed, so did the project.

Both the Clintons and their partners ended up losing money on the venture. It shouldn't have been an issue at all, but the campaign added to the problems by simply not having done their homework. The way they communicated on the issue was clumsy and inept. When the *Times* asked for all the details, they were handed some of the relevant documents but told that many others had "disappeared." For scandal hungry journalists, that word was enough to get the blood rushing. Without further ado, the *Times* published a story that left the reader with a myriad of unanswered questions about possible conflicts of interest, sweetheart deals and ethical breaches.[219]

The campaign quickly set up a press conference, where Clinton went through the basic points of the Whitewater case, most importantly that the Clintons and their partners had all lost money on the venture. The campaign also, after some detective work, produced most of the documents that had been missing.

All this dampened the speculations. But the dynamics of the story showed how the press were devilishly eager to hunt down the Clintons. To Hillary, the whole episode was just one more example of the cynicism of modern reporting – the presumption of wrongdoing by anyone in public life.[220]

It was obvious that the old principle of being presumed innocent until proven guilty had been turned on its head. For some journalists, politicians were presumed guilty until they could prove their own innocence. So, if the press *thought* you were guilty of something, you *were* guilty of something. If it later turned out that you were only guilty of some bad judgement and no real wrongdoing, the press would just leave the issue hanging, leaving a smear on the person. The experience, and the cloud it left over the campaign, bothered both the Clintons and Carville immensely.

Luckily for Carville, they had managed to build such a powerful momentum, that even the Whitewater story couldn't derail them. On March 7, Clinton won South Carolina and Wyoming, while Tsongas only barely captured Arizona. Three days later, on Super Tuesday, Clinton won seven of the eight states, among them Florida, Louisiana, and Missouri. It was a slam dunk. Clinton's overnight lead in delegates now put him on a near certain track to become the Democratic nominee. Tsongas was simply overwhelmed.

In his own way, Carville rejoiced in every victory. But he wasn't one to be carefree and naively optimistic. What worried him most was something they had picked up in their polling. Two out of three voters harbored serious questions about Clinton's authenticity. They had much the same question as Carville had had after his first meeting with the candidate: Sure, he had bucketloads of charisma and intelligence, but was he too good to be true?

The stories about Flowers, Whitewater, and the draft stoked suspicions that underneath it all Clinton was perhaps just another sleazy politician. The voters didn't really know him yet, and in the midst of the primary race – moving their focus from state to state and answering new scandals by the day – there was neither time nor resources to go out to the American people and define who Clinton was. Building his image nationally was a major and costly move that would have to come later in the race.

Tsongas campaign had also picked up on the voter ambivalence against Clinton. In a last effort to shoot down his opponent – by now Tsongas' only realistic way to perhaps win the nomination – he launched ads that attacked the Arkansas governor for not being genuine. In one ad, the voice-over said, "He's no Bill Clinton, that's for sure. He's the exact opposite. Paul Tsongas – he's not afraid of the truth."

The charge that Clinton was nothing but a liar was a desperate move from a desperate candidate. But another bad story in the press was actually about to help Clinton show some of his real character. On the day of one of the televised debates for the Illinois-Michigan market, *The Washington Post* published a story about how Hillary's law firm had done significant work for the Arkansas government during Bill's tenure as governor.

The story left an impression that as governor, Clinton might have funneled business to the firm to help his wife, and it didn't take a rocket scientist to figure out that at least one of the other candidates would bring up the subject in that night's debate.

Coaching Clinton before the verbal exchange, Carville argued that his candidate shouldn't hold anything back, telling Clinton, "If he attack's Hillary, I would jump. You have the license to just jump on him."[221]

Carville had expected Tsongas to use the *Post* story against them in the debate. But it was former California Governor Jerry Brown that mounted the attack.

"I think he's got a big electability problem," Brown said of Clinton, cameras rolling, "He's funneling money to his wife's law firm for state business." The *Post* article hadn't actually said that, but instead of arguing the facts Clinton saw the opportunity Carville had prepared him for.

"Let me tell you something Jerry," he said in an emotional tone, "I don't care what you say about me…but you ought to be ashamed of yourself for jumping on my wife. You're not worthy of being on the same platform as my wife." Brown was taken aback, mumbling something about it being *The Washington Post* that had actually put forward the charges. "I never funneled any money to my wife's law firm," Clinton stated forcefully. "Never!"

The clip of Bill coming to Hillary's defense ran as a segment on all the mayor news networks. Carville was pleased. His candidate had been given a chance to defend his wife, and he had jumped at it. It showed the American people that even as Clinton seemed almost superhuman in his ability to take repeated blows and get up again, he wasn't going to let anyone attack those he loved most. To many voters, it seemed a cleansing moment, a testimony to his inner core, his real character.

Some days later, Hillary, who was more used to defending her husband than herself, made what seemed like a minor gaffe.

When pressed about the story at a news conference, she barked back, "I suppose I could have stayed home and baked cookies and had teas, but I decided to fulfill my profession..." In the atmosphere of the early '90s, many mistook her answer as a downgrading of homeworking moms. The Republicans made a note of her mishap. They would revive it, trying to make a major issue out of it, at their convention.

On March 17, Clinton won two more landslides, this time over Brown in Michigan and Tsongas in Illinois. For Tsongas, who had framed the Illinois primary as the first real showdown between himself and Clinton, it was a disaster. It didn't take long before he withdrew from the primary contest. The race between Tsongas and Clinton had been between two candidates who – even as they were directing fire at one another – actually had a profound respect for the other, for the rules of the game, and for their party. With Tsongas out of the race, the only one left with some credibility beside Clinton, was Jerry Brown. And unlike Tsongas, Brown had little respect for the rules of the game.

Brown saw his Democratic Party as rotted by money, drowned in cynicism, about to elect a deeply flawed candidate. He promised radical change and touted his campaign's $100 limit on contributions as a guarantee he couldn't be bought. While Tsongas and Clinton had mainly been dueling about their policy differences, Brown mounted a crusade against Clinton's character. Sure, Tsongas had tossed a few grenades out there. But Brown didn't mind going after Clinton with a full nuclear arsenal. Though Carville hadn't grasped it yet, the game had just changed.

Yes, the Real Bill Clinton

Jerry Brown's appeal was that he seemed so genuine. Many perceived his $100 donation limit as proof that he was the real deal. The limit meant his campaign had very little money, imposing a strong discipline on his followers.

"We couldn't spend any money," one aide said. "We had to create a myth."[222] And so they did.

Brown cast himself as the hero, the only pure candidate in a corrupted field. Those who knew him well described the ascetic former governor as brilliant, self-absorbed, friendless, idealistic, erratic, opportunistic, cold, and hypocritical.[223]

Of course, Brown understood that he had no clear path to the nomination on his own. Largely unnoticed by the press, he had been picking up some delegates by winning Maine, Colorado and Nevada, and he had done okay in several other states. His delegate count wasn't formidable by any standard, but he had enough delegates to carry on the fight, and if he won some more, he would have enough to make real noise at the convention.

Said Gray Davies, Brown's former chief of staff, "In a way he has already won the campaign. His real goal is to point the country in a different direction." It was a sentiment also echoed by one of his former appointees, Tom Quinn, who said of Brown, "He's had a drive in him for 20 years or more to reform the political process in America. ...He really wants to reform the system."[224]

An important part of Carville's strategy had been to position Clinton as the outsider, a candidate the voters would send to Washington to exact change. Now, with the fight being between

Clinton and Brown, Clinton was suddenly the insider. In an instance, it evaporated Clinton's most important strategic advantages – and a core part of Carville's strategy. Their late receptiveness to the major change that had just occurred, left them without a workable strategy in the midst of battle.

On March 24, the Clinton team gathered for a strategy session, when they got a fresh exit-poll from that days voting in Connecticut. The race would end with Brown winning with 37.2 percent of the vote to Clinton's 35.6 percent. Carville knew the result portrayed Clinton as vulnerable.

"We're damaged by our fuck-ups and our lack of strategy," Carville said. "Right now we're hemorrhaging. We better stop some bleeding. We have to define ourselves."[225]

They had only two weeks left until the April 7 primaries in Wisconsin, Kansas, and New York. New York alone was to elect 244 delegates. If Brown beat Clinton there the primary contest would be a whole other ball game. Wrote *The New York Times*:

> Despite his seven-to-one edge in delegates, Mr. Clinton finds himself confronted with an opponent who revels in probing his 'character issues' and delights in assaults on the Democratic establishment. Add to this the discontent among voters this year with politics-as-usual, and the movement of this two-man race into ever-volatile New York, and Mr. Clinton has major headaches.[226]

Carville offered only one solution to the campaign generals assembled at the meeting:

We have to knock Jerry off his game and off his message. To do that takes unbelievable focus and concentration. We are faced with a grave danger. This bastard's coming to New York with the kind of thing people like there: He's anti-this and anti-that. We have to fight that son of a bitch in the trenches.[227]

They decided to attack Brown on what they considered his weakest point; his proposal for a flat tax system.

The flat tax meant everybody would pay the exact same percentage, regardless of their income. This meant lowering the tax for the wealthy, while increasing it for the poor. Carville saw the flat tax as Brown's Achilles heel in the Democratic Primary contest, making it possible for his opponents to label him a relic of the '80s. Carville told the Times, "We're going to run against [Brown] the same way we'd run against any other candidate who wants to raise taxes on people making $50,000 a year and cut them on people making half a million."[228] They dubbed it "Jerry's Tax" and went for his throat.

Brown, of course, returned fire.

"Governor Clinton's Arkansas – a right-to-work-state that ranks dead last in worker safety," one ad proclaimed as a picture of Clinton playing golf came up on the screen, "Its wages amongst the lowest in the country, Arkansas remains one of only two states with no civil-rights act." Playing of the derogatory 'Slick Willie' nickname that Clinton's opponents had adopted to conjure up the image of a sleazy politician, the ad ended, "Now that's *slick*, but we want real change."

The attacks on Brown's flat tax proposal played well in the electorate. In a twist of irony, what ended up drowning out Brown's attacks wasn't what Clinton uttered, but what he inhaled

– or rather hadn't inhaled. Over the years, Clinton had repeatedly stated that he had never "violated the drug laws of my country." Now, in responding to questions at a candidates' forum on WCBS-TV in New York, he answered, "I've never broken a state law, but when I was in England, I experimented with marijuana a time or two, and I didn't like it. I didn't inhale it, and never tried it again."[229] It was too good of a soundbite not to be played over and over on every news outlet in the country. When comedian Billy Crystal, hosting the Oscar Night show that week, simply uttered the three words, "I didn't inhale"; he got the biggest laugh of the night.

Brown's campaign seized on the issue and produced an ad called "Man on the Street." It featured ordinary New Yorkers talking about Clinton's alleged private vices and public failings, some of them mentioning the sex and marijuana stories. The moment Brown saw it, he flew into a rage and demanded that the campaign pull it before it got aired. But it was too late. The press had already gotten a copy. The story gave Clinton a chance to act pious, calling the ad the sleaziest he had ever seen.[230] The incident hurt Brown, who had built his whole image as an opponent of "politics as usual." Now he seemed nothing more than a hypocrite.

The "didn't inhale" episode wasn't serious in terms of Clinton's electability; several other leading Democrats had already admitted to having smoked marijuana. Of course, it wasn't a plus that even when admitting to having tried weed, he at the same time sort of denied it with his "didn't inhale" comment. That affirmed the image of the slick politician. But still, there was a silver lining: For many New Yorkers, this was the moment they would remember, this was what they would attribute "Slick Willie" with, not Brown's more substantial attacks on policy and moral. Truth was, most Democratic voters didn't give a damn about whether Clinton had tried marijuana in his youth or not.

Going into the last week before the New York primary Carville and Grunwald made an ad that would serve as something of a closing statement in the Big Apple contest. It presented Clinton's plan for reinvigorating the economy and creating new jobs.

"Looking for a different kind of candidate? Someone who actually has a serious plan to move this country forward and put people first?" the voice-over asked, before ticking off some of Clinton's proposals on job-investment, upgrading schools, reforming health-care and moving people from welfare to work. "That's the plan of a different candidate," the voice continued. "His name? Bill Clinton. Yes, the *real* Bill Clinton."

The ad hit a nerve. Beneath the media frenzy something was stirring, and Carville had picked up on it. It could be seen when Clinton went on the Phil Donahue show that week. The host spent 25 minutes pelting him with hostile questions about his marriage, alleged infidelity, and belated admission of marijuana use. But then the audience got its chance. Melissa Roth, a Republican, raised her hand from her back-row seat. She immediately turned her wrath, not on the troubled candidate, but on Donahue.

"I think given the pathetic state of most of the United States at this point – Medicare, education, everything else – I can't believe you spent half an hour of air-time attacking this man's character," she nearly shouted. Her voice was almost drowned out as the studio erupted in applause. "I'm not even a Bill Clinton supporter," she continued, "but I think this is ridiculous."[231] People had had enough of the pummeling. The country was so eager for change, they were willing to look past a candidate's personal flaws if they believed that candidate could bring that change.

In politics, things change rapidly. Two weeks earlier Clinton and Brown had been running neck to neck in some New York polls. On election night, the Arkansas governor won New York with 41 percent of the vote. Brown didn't even manage to finish second. He came third with 26 percent, while Tsongas got 29. The same night, Clinton also won Kansas and Wisconsin. These were the last really contested primaries in the race. There was no way Clinton and his team could be derailed now. They even went on to win Brown's home state of California. Despite of a barrage of scandals and attacks, Carville's candidate had finally prevailed. Clinton was now the de facto nominee.

Carville was happy, but not jubilant. The state-by-state contests had consumed all their energy and focus, which meant they hadn't yet had the resources nor the time to create the overall picture of Bill Clinton they wanted. They had catered to each state with customized messages, which meant they lacked that one overreaching national message. Carville was the first to admit this, and to act on it.

"We went back and talked about how we'd worked in the beginning, with crispness and clarity," he remembered. "We had lost our clarity and we had to recapture it."[232]

They still desperately needed to redefine Clinton before the fall. They had to fill the public's perception of their candidate with associations other than those conjured up by the press in the Flowers, Whitewater, and draft scandals. They needed Clinton to stand out as the greatest symbol of change. Part of the change image was generational – if elected he would be the first baby-boomer to come into the highest office in the land.

On June 3, the 45-year-old Arkansas governor did a ground-breaking appearance on *The Arsenio Hall Show*, to chat with the host and wail on his saxophone for soulful renditions of Elvis's "Heartbreak Hotel." As Clinton, looking cool, wearing dark sun-glasses and riffing on his sax, made the audience jump to their feet in pure excitement, Carville and Begala watched from back-stage with broad smiles on their faces.

At Bush HQ, the mood was gloomy.

"Not only did we not see that coming – we couldn't compete with that," remembered Mary Matalin. "Could you imagine put-ting President Bush on Arsenio Hall? Young voters loved it. It spoke to change. It was really, really brilliant."[233]

Clinton looked like the future.

The Ragin' Cajun enjoyed the moment immensely. But he also knew the President wasn't their main headache. Leading both Bush and Clinton in the polls was the new kid on the block – Ross Perot.

The Perot Phenomenon

Unlike Bush and Clinton, Ross Perot had not spent half his life dreaming about becoming president. First and foremost, he was a strong-willed business entrepreneur. Born and raised in Texas, Perot went to the US Naval Academy and graduated a battalion commander. After serving four years at sea, he left the Navy, eventually getting a job as salesman at IBM. He did well, at one point even fulfilling his yearly sales quota in just two weeks. He quickly moved up in the company, but when he tried to pitch new ideas, he was largely ignored by his supervisors. Frustrated, Perot left IBM and founded his own company. In the mid-'80s, General Motors bought a controlling interest in his company for $2.5 billion, making him an extremely rich man.[234]

During his rise in business, Perot had cultivated an image as the ultimate self-made man; a though, intelligent, and determined billionaire. He stood up to business tycoons, politicians, and dictators alike. He had even conducted a dramatic and successful rescue mission to free two of his employees who had been taken hostage by the Iranian government in 1979. Over the years he got to be something of a myth, though that was not the first impression you got when you met him face to face.

Perot was, at 61, a small man with large ears and a Navy haircut, and his Texas drawl came out in a thin, shrill tone. He also came with some distinguishable quirks, many of them products of his struggles and successes in business: He most often viewed himself as the most intelligent person in the room, he was immensely stubborn, and he had a bit of a temper. In the words of author Gene Landrum, "When it came to conflict, Perot was often seen as a 'high testosterone' personality with a Machiavellian style of leadership."[235]

Perot had entered the race reluctantly. There were political operators that had been pushing him to run for some time. At first, he found the proposition preposterous, but after being worked on for a while, he came around to the idea. The myth surrounding him had already made him something of a national celebrity. On February 20, 1992, Perot was a guest at Larry King's talk show; when the host asked him whether he would consider running for president. Perot answered straight from his gut, "If you, the people, will on your own register me in 50 states, I'll promise you this: Between now and the convention, we'll get the parties' heads straight."[236]

Without a real plan or strategy, he had proclaimed his run for president on a live television show. But this only made him look more attractive to many voters, appearing like an independent leader that would enter the chaos from the sidelines and cure the ills of the nation with plain talk and some sound business sense. In a year when people craved change above everything else, Perot was exactly what many of them were looking for, and they responded to his challenge with unbridled enthusiasm. Soon his flock had grown to tens of thousands. They did indeed get Perot on the ballot in all 50 states. And just like that, Perot's independent campaign for the presidency had been born.

Perot wanted to keep the magic alive. He didn't want to run a professional campaign. He wanted the campaign to orbit around himself, supported by the people who had drafted him, whom he dubbed "Perot's Volunteers." He hired some big guns, but wasn't comfortable being handled by them, and mostly did whatever he wanted – which would prove to be a big mistake. Succeeding in politics, it turned out, wasn't like succeeding in business at all. You had to have a long-term strategy involving a myriad of operative tasks, and you had to stick to it. But at first glance, the Perot myth was all people saw. And alongside a tired president and the scandal smudged Arkansas governor, that myth didn't look bad at all. In the polls that spring, Perot climbed high, getting ahead of both Bush and Clinton.

As the weeks went by, the press started digging into Perot in the hopes of uncovering some scandal or another. They didn't find the a-bomb story they were looking for, but they did find and publish enough stories about "grey zone practices" in the Perot business empire to tear him down from his pedestal. Meanwhile, the Texan billionaire couldn't get his campaign off the ground. He despised his professional handlers, did little of what they asked, and couldn't make up his mind on how and when to run a major ad campaign to define himself and his candidacy. There was no real strategy. As a result, come summer, his numbers were crumbling, his negatives rising. He slipped back in second place. Then third.

The problem was neither money nor a lack of access to professional talent. The problem was the candidate's stubborn refusal to act like anything more than a political amateur. Perot's co-campaign managers – Republican Ed Rollins and Democrat Hamilton Jordan – eventually reached their Defcon-1 level of frustration. They found Perot unwilling and uninterested. When important tactical decisions had to be made, he demurred.

The Texan's disdain for the professionals of the trade was painted thick on his face; he just didn't trust their advice. He wanted to do what he did in his business dealings – go with his guts. Fed up, Rollins told Perot that he only had three options left: He could start listening to the pros and go for the win; he could get out of the race; or he could continue running as an amateur and maybe get 12 percent of the vote.

Perot still didn't know what to do. The resourceful business champion had always come up with a solution, but now he had tumbled down the rabbit's hole and was lost in the new and strange world of professional politics. The Democratic Convention was upon them, but they had nothing to answer with, no strategy, no tactics, no ads, no airtime. The result was inevitable.

On July 16, the very last day of the Democratic Convention, Perot stunned the world by dropping out of the race. The reason, he told the press, was the way Clinton and Gore had revitalized the Democratic Party. This created a situation where an outright Perot victory in the polls was highly unlikely. If none of the three candidates won a majority, the contest would be thrown into the House of Representatives. And he didn't want that neither for himself nor his country, Perot said.[237]

This was great news to Carville, of course. He needed the race to boil down to a simple choice between Clinton's message of change and Bush's message of more of the same. Perot's participation had thrown a giant monkey wrench into the mechanics of his strategy. The billionaire Texan had stolen the mantle of change from Clinton and had acted like a magnet for disillusioned voters, creating totally unpredictable swings in the electorate. No wonder Carville and Clinton were relieved that Perot was now out of the contest. And the reasons he had given for quitting – that Clinton had "revitalized the Democratic Party" – obviously helped bolster the public image of Clinton as a real agent of change.

Carville had other reasons to be happy as well. The choice of Senator Al Gore from Tennessee as Clinton's running mate had proved a formidable success. Conventional wisdom decreed a presidential candidate should pick someone different than himself as his running mate, someone who could broaden his electoral appeal, like an elderly, liberal easterner. But that would breach with their strategy. Clinton, Carville, and most of the higher echelons of the campaign understood that they needed this election to be about just one thing: Change! When Clinton picked Gore, they essentially proved just how committed they were to achieve that change.

Gore was a New Democrat like Clinton, focused on the middle class, the economy, and creating jobs. They were both in their mid-'40s. If elected, they would become the youngest combined ticket in history. Clinton himself would be the third youngest president, only John F Kennedy (inaugurated at 43) and Franklin D Roosevelt (inaugurated at 42) were younger. The crowning of the two young men at the democratic convention had been a success. The party was united and eager to take on the Republicans. The millions watching had seen an young, energized force for change from the convention hall in Madison Square Garden. Carville sat back in his chair. He savored the moment. Right now, he was content.

Don't Stop Thinking About Tomorrow

Like after most conventions, Clinton too got a boost from the prime-time televised speeches, the cheering and the issues presented. So had the Democratic nominee Michael Dukakis four years earlier. But Dukakis had left the convention, gone home, and stayed there for weeks, letting his 19-point lead dwindle away. The Clinton generals were adamant not to let the same happen to their candidate. As soon as the lights were switched off in the great convention hall in New York, Clinton and Gore boarded a campaign bus to embark on a tour of small-town USA.

The tour was a tremendous success. On the road, the two candidates shone in each other's company, talking, laughing, and energizing each other like a couple of newlyweds. The crowds were large and fawning, exploding of positive energy. Clinton and Gore delivered their stump speeches flanked by their two beautiful, smiling wives. At every stop they hammered in the Clinton-Carville message of investing in people and protecting the middle class, framed in attractive populist language.

From the speakers blared Fleetwood Mac's "Don't Stop Thinking About Tomorrow!" It was a show of youth, passion, and purpose, embraced by the people of the heartland. Kids and their parents stood by the road as they rolled by, everyone cheering and waving flags like they were witnessing a procession of royalty. It all seemed so natural, so hopeful. Unbeknownst to the adoring crowds, the tour was actually a professional six-day production, orchestrated by the Hollywood producer Mort Engelberg. It hit all the right buttons, and Carville knew it was a home run.[238]

With Perot out of the contest, Clinton dominated the field, trouncing Bush by 22 points, 56-34 percent in the polls. The convention and the tour helped his image significantly, changing the public perception of him from that of a professional politician riddled with scandals, to that of a passionate champion of ordinary Americans. He looked like someone who really cared. A young, energetic man from Hope.

All the while, the Bush campaign seemed bewildered on how to deal with it all. Rumors were swirling around Washington that the President was about to order his old friend Jim Baker to quit as Secretary of State and run his campaign. Most Democrats trembled a little when that name came up. Baker was a formidable tactician, a shrewd and ruthless operator. He was the Republican general who, working with Lee Atwater and Roger Ailes, had been one of the architects of Ronald Reagan's landslide victory in 1984.

Carville knew Baker was a formidable adversary. And he knew the killer instinct of the Republican Party. He felt his troops didn't yet get just what they were up against. Trying to jar his people back at campaign headquarters in Little Rock awake, the Ragin' Cajun threw one of his tantrums.

"Some of you think Republicans are just like us – that they just have a different philosophy. They're not," he shouted. "They're seasoned. They're professional. They're ruthless! And they're rotten!" As the message sank into the troops, he got up and left the room.[239]

They didn't have to wait long for the barrage of Republican attacks to start. But Carville was ready for it. He sat at the heart of their HQ, strategizing and giving commands. After the nomination contest was over, the Clinton campaign generals had all seen the need for a central command headquarter, and they agreed Carville was the right person to run it.

"It was a conspiracy by about ten or twelve people to create a power center," Carville remembered. "You couldn't call it anything less than a naked power grab."[240]

To Carville's delight, Hillary had dubbed their HQ "the War Room," and the name stuck. He surrounded himself with the most central deputies: the pollster Stan Greenberg; the tactician Mandy Grunwald; Clinton loyalist Mickey Cantor; top shelf operators Mike Donilon, Eli Segal and David Wilhelm; longtime Clinton-staffer Betsey Wright; and the young George Stephanopoulos – among others. His old friend and partner Paul Begala was traveling with the candidate, always just a phone call away.

With Carville firmly installed as the captain of the ship, few of the staff ever doubted the urgency of their work. He treated it like a military campaign. He ruled with firm orders, threats, insults, and the occasional sermon. Carville had reduced the campaign's core message to three sentences written on the blackboard of the War Room: "Change versus more of the same. The economy stupid. Don't forget healthcare."[241]

He made sure everyone knew they were not to yield even a foot of ground. All attacks from the Republicans were promptly answered with counterattacks, directed from the War Room. And every counterattack contained some version of the core message. The central buzzed with energy. Even in his calmest of moments, Carville could scarcely sit still. He had little patience with those who failed to step up to the level he expected. Yelling into his telephone receiver at an aide, he sputtered, "We haven't won this thing in 12 years. We're in a war here, you understand that?!"

He was running a campaign that often seemed more military than political, adept at the sort of warlike politics that at the time were generally thought of as the specialty of Republican operations.[242] Carville had the aggressiveness of Patton, pushing his team to stay on the offensive. After all, he knew by experience that the best defense was offense, and he lived by his old saying, "It's hard for someone to hit you when you have your fist in their face."

One day, a young War Room aide messed up. He had been away for a day, and as a result a Bush event had gone under the War Room's radar. The Ragin' Cajun went ballistic. In a meeting, he told the aide in front of everybody, "You no longer have a

name. From now on you're just 'you.' You let everybody down…
You're a nothing fuck-up, you ain't got a name." Carville was
merciless. (It turned out the aide had been away because it had
been a Jewish holiday, and Carville later apologized).[243]

The Republicans gathered for their convention in Houston,
Texas, where they lit up their arsenal, taking aim at the Clintons.
Bush's generals even allowed Pat Buchanan on the stage. Carville
thought Buchanan's speech, a call for a holy war for America's
soul, full of venom, would repel most moderates and work to the
democrat's advantage.

To his surprise, the GOP also let loose on Hillary. They
brought up her earlier gaffe from the campaign trail, when she
in frustration had blurted out, "I suppose I could have stayed
home and baked cookies and had teas, but I decided to fulfill my
profession…" Now they attacked her relentlessly from the podium for not valuing stay-at-home moms, for not respecting traditional family values.

"Do they talk about the problems of the country? No – they
attack the spouse," Carville fumed. He thought it projected weak-
ness. And what's more, he saw an opening in making the issue
about respect for women. He sent his team of spinmeisters into
action. They talked to every journalist and news outlet that would
listen, spinning their boss' message that the GOP had become an
intolerant, anti-women crowd.

Carville had not quite known how to sell Hillary to the public.
She was the poster girl of a modern woman, much more politically assertive than other candidate spouses, which could seem
intimidating to the older and more traditional part of the electorate. But he thought the Republicans had gone too far this time.

And he was right. The GOP attacks didn't turn out the way they had hoped. On the contrary, they did wonders for Hillary's image. Most voters balked at a political convention bullying the wife of a political opponent. You could see the immediate effect in the polls, where Hillary's favorable ratings got a sharp rise. Said one Clinton operator, "The Republicans did for us what we could never have done. They made her a sympathetic figure."[244]

100 Percent Negative

The Bush campaign had enlisted advice from England. They set up a meeting with a group of British Conservative party operators who had been central in getting the British prime minister John Major reelected in April of 1992. They too had gone to war with a weak candidate, a weak economy, and an electorate that had clamored for change – and now Bush's generals wanted to pick their brains.

"There were definite parallels to our situation," Mary Matalin remembered.[245] The Brits told them they had won by relentless daily assaults on their opposition. They had made taxes and trust their key issues, with fierce attacks on their opponent, the British Labour Party. The conclusion from the meeting was that the best, and maybe only, way to victory was to incinerate Clinton. The rationale was simple: It was obvious they couldn't move Bush's numbers much, so they needed Clinton's support to evaporate.

It wasn't a novel strategy; the GOP had done it in 1988 against Dukakis. But at least it was a strategy. "For the rest of the way, we're going 100 percent negative," one high ranking member of the Bush campaign concluded after the convention. They also came away from the meeting with some new ideas; a couple of Bush's attack ads on Clinton as a binge taxer and spender were borrowed almost frame for frame from the Major campaign.[246] "[We] quite consciously copied the British approach," Matalin later admitted.

The Bush campaign generals presided over a formidable arsenal of data they could use to build their attacks on Clinton. Their opposition research team consisted of more than 50 people, who had the latest technology and a huge budget at their disposal. The Bush ads focused on painting Clinton as untrustworthy – someone who would say or do anything to become president. One spot opened with a split screen of two candidates (both in jackets, one with a red tie and the other with a dark blue tie) speaking, gesturing, their faces obscured by gray dots. A voiceover spoke of their different stands on important issues. Then, as the dots disappeared to show that both candidates were actually Clinton, the voiceover concluded, "One of these candidates is Bill Clinton. Unfortunately, so is the other".[247]

In the War Room, Carville was prepared for the onslaught. They too had been meeting with someone familiar with the last campaign in Britain. The Labour Party's pollster Philip Gould had been invited to Arkansas. Gould stayed several weeks. Carville and Greenberg pumped him for all the information they could on the late-in-the-game tory strategy and how it had undermined confidence in Labour.[248] They analyzed the situation and decided that the oncoming attacks needed to be met head on.

Their main tactic was to call out the expected GOP attacks as mere copies stolen from the British race. War Room researcher

Bennet Freeman charged that such an imported copycat campaign "based on lies and distortions" just wouldn't work for the GOP. "They're exporting our jobs – but importing their campaign ads," he wrote. So when the Republicans started their barrage, the War Room immediately attacked its credibility. The spin worked, and the press started writing critical pieces of the new GOP ads, letting some of the air out of the balloon.

"But the biggest difference between us and the Labour party was that we responded," Carville concluded. "They never did, and they got beat."[249]

The War Room now kicked off their own ad blitz, linking the terrible state of the economy to President Bush. For anyone watching closely, it was obvious that Carville and his crew had grasped the publics doubts about Clinton as a "Slick Willie" politician. With this in mind, they framed the election as a referendum between change or more of the same, not a choice between the two candidates per se.

"Be aware of being too political," Carville told his ad team, "and be aware of overpromising, or being too slick, too good to be true... The advertising should always come back to, 'We can't afford four more years of Bush.'"[250]

They're Breaking for Us, Boys, They're Breaking for Us!

With only 11 weeks until the election, the Bush campaign got a new General Supreme. The rumors proved to be true; James Baker quit his dream job as Secretary of State to run the President's re-election campaign. He brought with him a more experienced staff and a new command structure. Begala admitted he was scared to death when he heard Baker had been drafted. Carville also understood what they were up against.

"In this business," he admitted, "Jim Baker is the gold standard."[251]

"James Baker knows how to parachute into chaos and bring focus, bring a strategy, and execute it," Mary Matalin concluded.[252] "Baker hit the ground running. He was better than we thought was possible, given the late start."[253]

The Bush campaign improved noticeably. Decisions that had taken weeks were now made in mere minutes. The attacks on Clinton became even crisper and more effective.

When Baker called the old GOP communication guru, Roger Ailes, for strategic advice, he got a straight and short answer.

"Politics is execution," Alies said. "Get off the fucking defensive!"[254] He also recommended they hire some of the old gunslingers in the Republican ad trade who had helped destroy Democratic candidates on the airwaves in the past. Baker agreed.

Almost overnight, the Bush campaign had gotten a crisper message, new energy, and a lot more engine power. Even so, at this late stage, there was a limit to what even General Baker and the Old Cavalry could do for a president that the majority of the people wanted to throw out of the White House. By the beginning of October, nearly half of the electorate said they would never vote for Bush. Clinton's lead was at 16 points, and Carville kept hammering their message home with the voters.

Under immense pressure, Bush and Baker decided to make it personal. The President started attacking Clinton ferociously on the draft issue. In effect calling out his opponent as a draft dodger,

Bush even questioned Clinton's ability to serve as president. His team joined in the attacks on Clinton's character. "It's pathological deception," Mary Matalin said of Clinton. "If we cannot believe what he says about the past, how can we believe anything he says about the future?"[255]

But even as his girlfriend fired away at his candidate, the polls told Carville to stay calm. The vast majority of the electorate didn't want to keep hearing about the draft issue. It was like your sister's sex life, Carville remarked dryly. You knew something was going on, but you didn't want to hear the details.

When the Clinton campaign showed a short film of their candidate telling his side of the draft story to two focus groups, the voters in the groups made it clear they long since had concluded that Clinton *had* dodged the draft and that he *was* lying about it. But they just didn't care.

"I don't care what he did," one woman said, "I want to know what he wants to do tomorrow."[256]

The President's attacks ended up not moving the numbers in any significant way.

Still frantically searching for a line of attack that could penetrate Clinton's armor, the Bush campaign decided to paint him as a traitor. In their view, he had been some sort of pawn for the Soviet Union in his days as student anti-war activist at Oxford. At the time, Clinton had taken a short tour of Moscow as well as some other European capitals. While he had spoken of the people with whom he met in other capitals, including Oslo, he has said he could not recall those he met in Moscow.[257] Beside Clinton opposing the war, there were no evidence to suggest something was amiss. But Roger Ailes urged Baker and Matalin to pursue the issue anyway. "Go for the red meat," he bellowed. "Get on the fucking offensive! This guy's hiding something."[258]

The President went on Larry King Live to get the ball rolling. When King asked about Clinton's trip to Moscow, he answered, "I don't want to tell you what I really think," he said, adding:

> But to go to Moscow one year after Russia crushed Czecho-slovakia, and not remember who you saw? ... You can remember who you saw in the airport in Oslo, but you can't remember who you saw in the airport in Moscow? I say level with the American people on the draft, whether you went to Moscow, how many demonstrations you led against this country from foreign soil.[259]

It was a harsh attack and certainly raised some eyebrows. But without a plan to follow up, without the rest of the party standing ready to bash Clinton on the issue, it was a strategic mistake. Carville saw it as an act of desperation and most pundits agreed.

"I can't tell you how silly I thought Bush looked in that whole thing, and I'll never understand why he let himself look that way," Carville wrote. "It was one of those times where you don't get in the way of an opponent who is self-destructing. We didn't say much about it unless we were asked."[260]

But that was about the only attack the War Room let slide. Carville and the rest of his team continued to treat all other Republican assaults like an existential threat. Every attack was answered by a counterattack. They had a solid lead and even Carville had to admit the numbers looked good. So, was he content? Not at all. Unbeknown to most, he was expecting something that would change the dynamics of the electorate and make the contest highly unpredictable again.

Ever since he had dropped out, Ross Perot had been contemplating getting back in. When he had exited the race in July, he had wanted the story to be about how he had affected the agenda and nudged American politics in a different direction. Instead, the media had labeled him a quitter.[261] He didn't like that one bit. Many of his Volunteers kept pushing him to reenter the race. Besides, he missed being the man of the hour.

In mid-September, Perot had a phone conversation with Clinton to see if the Governor could be willing to change some of his policies. The rationale was simple; it would give Perot the opportunity to project himself as an important and influential mover, while Clinton's upside was a possible endorsement from Perot. But neither was willing to give enough to satisfy the other. After their phone call, Clinton told Carville that the conversation had been strange. His guess was that Perot was about to make a comeback as a candidate.[262]

With only 33 days left until the election, that's exactly what happened. From the stage in Dallas, Perot declared that he was 'The One' the country needed, after all. Carville saw Perot's re-entering the race as a double-edged sword. On one hand, it would force the Republican camp to fight harder to maintain their support in the South – support Bush had to have if he was to have any chance of winning. On the other hand, Perot would steal a lot of voters from Clinton as well. What troubled Carville the most, was that Perot's reentry took away Clinton's biggest advantage; that he was the only alternative for those who wanted change. In the coming weeks the Texan businessman hacked away at both Bush and Clinton, and his new surge in the polls drew more supporters away from Clinton than from Bush.[263] He reestablished himself as a serious threat and rattled the crowd entrenched in the War Room.

Perot's reentry made the televised debates even more important. From the onset, there had been some haggling over the number of debates and the format. The Bush campaign had dragged its feet and been unwilling to commit. Carville had even ordered volunteers to show up at Bush's rallies dressed in chicken costumes to taunt the president. Though he acted irritated at Bush in public, Carville was in fact delighted the president seemed so unwilling to go face to face with his challenger. As time went by, the pressure on the incumbent increased. Carville thought Bush looked weak and afraid, which was just peach.

The bipartisan commission had originally suggested the first debate be held in East Lansing, Michigan, on September 22. When the day came and the President still hadn't agreed to a debate format, Carville sent Clinton there anyway. Speaking outdoors on the campus of Michigan State University, the Governor criticized Bush for failing to show up for the debate, and for spending his time attacking the Democrats instead of debating the issues. Behind him at the rally was a large sign stating, "Bill Clinton. There's no debate about it."[264]

Eventually, Bush caved. The two campaigns agreed to three presidential debates, all held in a nine-day period starting on October 11. The War Room knew these debates would be absolutely crucial. Before the first debate, Clinton underwent extensive preparations, going through a number of training sessions and a stack of briefs. Nothing was left to chance. Carville boiled down their message to, "Change versus More of the Same, and Bill Clinton is a Very Different Democrat." The first part to keep pounding Bush, and the second to beef up their armor against Perot.

The chief strategist's last words of advice before sending Clinton into battle was, "Don't lose your temper. And be ready for anything." The Bush camp had been spreading rumors that they were going to spring something big in the debate, a game changer. "They're signaling like crazy that they have something dramatic," Carville said. "But I think it's just a 75 percent chance they're playing a mind game with us."[265] He was right.

The first debate at Washington University unfolded without much drama. Bush never pulled anything remotely dramatic out of his sleeve. Clinton did well, executing Carville's strategy to a fault. Right of the bat, he challenged the president.

"Tonight I say to the President: Mr. Bush, for 12 years you've had it your way. You've had your chance and it didn't work. It's time to change."[266]

Perot also performed well. Challenged on his lack of governmental experience, he shot back:

> I don't have any experience in running up a $4 trillion debt. I don't have any experience in gridlock government where nobody takes responsibility for anything and everybody blames everybody else. I don't have any experience in creating the worst public-school system in the industrialized world, the most violent crime-ridden society in the industrialized world. But I do have a lot of experience in getting things done.[267]

The polls ranked Clinton and Perot as winners, the President as the night's looser. Carville knew that meant they had to do even better. It wasn't enough to beat Bush, they had to outperform Perot as well. Clinton needed a television moment, something that would lift him above both Bush and Perot and portray him as the real deal; empathic, presidential, and serious about bringing change to the country.

The second debate four days later was the perfect setting for such a moment. It would be framed as a townhall meeting, where the large audience of voters would ask their own questions of the candidates. Clinton loved people, he was a master of empathy, using his eyes, his tone of voice and his body language to make instant connections with strangers in a way few others could. He had always had this gift. His friends guessed it was a mix of a unique natural talent and a deep-seated interest in people's stories. If he could manage to show this side of himself to the tens of millions watching, it would give his image an instant boost. In other words, the town hall format was made for him. Carville had been astonished that the President had agreed to go mano a mano with Clinton in such a setting.

Even so, nothing was left to chance. The format called for the three adversaries to be sitting on high stools, facing the audience. So the campaign trained Clinton to sit on the same kind of stools in rehearsal. They wanted him sitting on the edge of his stool, leaning forward, ready to jump up and engage anyone from the audience, if the opportunity arose to make a real human connection. In fact, they went further; to make their candidate feel at ease and confident, they arrived at the venue hours before any of the others, and secretly replaced the stools set out by the organizers with their own – the exact same stools Clinton had used in his rehearsals.[268] This way, he felt at home from the very first second of sitting down, and every part of the ready-to-leap-up pose he had practiced could be copied perfectly.

About halfway through the debate, Clinton got his chance. A woman in the audience asked, "How has the national debt personally affected each of your lives? And if it hasn't, how can you honestly find a cure for the economic problems of the common people if you have no experience in what's ailing them?"

The first to answer was Bush. He struggled to understand the question. After a few sentences, he blurted out, "I'm not sure I get...help me with the question and I'll try to answer it." He seemed a little confused and out of energy.

Just like they had rehearsed, Clinton sprang up from his stool, and walked all the way over to the audience. He didn't jump into an answer, but instead he started a short conversation with the woman. "Tell me how it's affected you again," he asked, "do you know people who've lost their jobs and lost their homes?" She nodded and answered yes. "Well, I've been governor of a small state for 12 years," Clinton said. "I'll tell you how it's affected me. ...I have seen what's happened in this last 4 years when – in my state, when people lose their jobs there's a good chance I'll know them by their names. When a factory closes, I know the people who ran it. When the businesses go bankrupt, I know them."[269]

Standing as close to the audience as he could, Clinton got personal. As he spoke, the woman and the rest of the hall fell quiet, looking him in the eyes, resting on his every word, nodding their approval. "And I've been out here for 13 months meeting in meetings just like this, with people like you all over America, people that have lost their jobs, lost their livelihood, lost their health insurance," Clinton went on. "It is because America has not invested in its people. It is because we have not grown. ... Most people are working harder for less money than they were making ten years ago."[270]

More important than his words was the way he created a connection with the audience. They were listening intently now, nodding their approval. The image projected to millions watching at home was that this wasn't just some groomed politician, this was a real person, a real leader, who understood their troubles, who really cared.

Carville knew he had just witnessed a truly magical moment – perhaps the most important moment in Clinton's political life. Ever since he first met him, he had known his candidate was special.

"However smart and whatever ability to connect with people you think Bill Clinton has, you have no idea. He's so much better in person than you think he is," he had mused.[271]

And now the whole country had seen it, experienced it in a rare moment of real human connection and empathy through the television screen.

While Clinton had captured hearts and minds, Bush had clearly been uncomfortable. The camera captured the President glancing at his watch several times during the debate, like he couldn't wait for the ordeal to be over. It was a slam dunk in the Clinton-Bush contest. The only downside was that Perot also had done well. Clinton was still in the lead, but Perot was slicing new voters of his base every day. Carville wondered if their lead would hold long enough to reach election day, with enough votes to win the necessary majority in the electoral college.

As the final weeks melted away and judgement day grew closer, the Bush campaign saw Perot's surge as their only hope.

If their attacks could hurt the Arkansas governor enough for a sufficient number of voters to switch from the Democrats to Perot, the outcome could in fact be a narrow victory for Bush. By attacking Clinton, they hoped they could push more anti-Bush voters into Perot's camp, eroding Clinton's vote share. So, they intensified their attacks. The climax came when the Bush campaign launched a new television ad called "Vulture." It showed Arkansas as a wasteland with vultures in the scorched trees, while the narrator spoke of Clinton's alleged failures as governor.[272]

Under Carville's energetic leadership, the War Room worked day and night to beat back the attacks, and barely managed to stay on the offensive. Up until October, their hard work had succeeded in making the contest a referendum on the president. But now Bush's attacks and Perot's presence had switched the race back into a referendum on Clinton's record and character.

"How scared are you?" George Stephanopoulos asked Carville in the midst of the republican onslaught.

"How scared?" the Ragin' Cajun strategist replied, "I'm *this* scared: if we lose, I won't commit suicide, but I'll *seriously* contemplate it."[273]

It didn't help Carville's nerves that his candidate strayed off message just as Election Day closed in. Clinton was getting mightily frustrated by the Republican barrage of attacks on his character, and at last he snapped.

"The very idea that the word 'trust' could ever come out of Bush's mouth, after what he has done to this country and the way he has trampled the truth, is a travesty," he blurted out on camera. It was a major gaffe. Instead of sticking to their strategy of change and their mantra of "it's the economy, stupid," Clinton had in a single stroke cemented the issue of character and trust as the agenda of the last days of the campaign.

At Bush's campaign HQ there were high fives all around.

"We loved it," Matalin remembered. "There is nothing cooler than getting the other guy on your turf... Now we had Clinton where we wanted him."

Over at the War Room the mood was low.

"I was jumpy. I was damn jumpy," said Carville. "I had sat on a lead the last two weeks of the Dick Davis race in 1982 and lost; I didn't want to do that again."[274]

Not everyone on Carville's team were quite so pessimistic. While the Ragin' Cajun's nerves were on edge, the top number cruncher told them not to panic. Pollster Stan Greenberg's state-by-state polling showed that while the national numbers were crumbling, they were holding up where it really mattered. They were mainly losing ground in Bush's strongest states (where they couldn't win anyway) and in Clinton's strongest states (where he still had a huge margin to go on), not in the states were Clinton's leads were narrow. When he was fed the numbers, Carville's pulse slowed noticeably. Clinton was up by 18 in Illinois, 14 in Delaware, 21 in Massachusetts, seven in Georgia...and on it went. Consuming the numbers like a starving man finally getting his hands on some chow, Carville cracked a broad smile.

"Whoop!" he exclaimed happily. "They're breaking for us boys, they're breaking for us!"[275]

They were indeed. In the last two weeks, Perot's momentum evaporated. As it became evident that he had no way of winning, the press lost interest and focused instead fully on the duel between Clinton and Bush. The Clinton campaign also got two gifts thrown right into their lap. These gifts were wrapped in what was at first sight might look like bad news. But they were in fact blessings in disguise.

The first came with only six days to go until Election Day. Gallup published a survey showing Bush closing in, now only a few points behind Clinton.[276] It was like giant billboards had lit up across the nation, bearing the message, "If you want change, you have to get up from the couch and go vote for Clinton!" It mobilized and solidified Clinton's support and brought scores of voters back from the Perot camp.

The second unexpected gift was the release of a report showing a strong uptick of 2.7 percent in GDP. This in itself didn't help Clinton, but the President's reaction did. In his desperation, Bush seized on the news and tried to spin it as evidence that the economy was in fact in a better state than his opponents and the press pretended. The backlash from frustrated and disgruntled voters was swift. They couldn't believe Bush still hadn't grasped their precarious situation.

Like Carville had predicted, the election had come down to the state of the economy. That didn't mean they were guaranteed victory, of course. As he reminded everyone, several presidential incumbents had struggled with the economy and still won reelection. It was the Bush campaign's failure to grasp the reality of the situation on the ground, the hardship experienced every day by ordinary Americans, that did them in.[277]

Clinton wasn't the only candidate slipping up in the heat of the last days of the race. In pure desperation, the President lashed out at the Democratic ticket.

"My dog Millie knows more about foreign policy than these two bozos. It's crazy," Bush told the crowd at one of his last rallies.

Nicknaming Gore "the Ozone Man," the President declaimed; "This guy's crazy. He's way out. Far out, man."

This time it was Carville's turn to share high fives with his team.

"Calling Clinton and Gore Bozos was a huge error. A mistake of the first order," he concluded. "It's the Thursday night before the election and...Bush is not talking about stature or experience, the natural concerns that people had about Bill Clinton. All he's on the news talking about is 'crazy' and 'bozo' and 'Ozone Man'. I was delighted."[278]

On the eve of the day before Election Day, confident smiles could finally be seen in the War Room. They knew they had it in the bag. They had been through so much. They had taken so many body blows, survived so many press-driven scandals. And they were still standing – in a way it felt almost unreal. As they took it all in, feelings that had been bottled up for a long time under extreme pressure, broke through to the surface.

They gathered the senior staff for a short speech by George Stephanopoulos, lavishing praise on Carville.

"He wrote what I call our haiku: 'Change versus more of the same. The economy stupid. Don't forget healthcare.' I was kidding James yesterday. I said he was about to pass from the role of a regular human being to the role of legend," Stephanopoulos told the staff. "And I think he really deserves it, because in the first time in a generation, tomorrow we're going to win."[279] Tears were running down the faces of the people packed closely together in the War Room. They were awestruck by the moment.

An emotional Carville rose to speak:

There's a simple quote, that outside of a person's love the most sacred thing they can give is their labor. And somehow along the way we tend to forget that. And labor is a very precious thing that you have. ... I'm a political professional. That's what I do for a living. And I'm proud of it.

Tearing up he thanked his staff:

We've changed the way campaigns work... And people are going go tell you that you're lucky. You're not. [The professional golf player] Ben Hogan said that 'Golf is a game of luck – the more I practice, the luckier I get.' Well, the harder you work the 'luckier' you are. I was 33 years old before I ever went to Washington. I was 42 before I won my first campaign. You've been part of something special in my life, and I'll never forget what you did.[280]

Carville started crying.

The candidate himself was on a marathon run of rallies, winging around the country in 30 hours of ceaseless campaigning, in a last dash to persuade voters. It was in many ways a repeat of the frantic, high-energy, last-minute effort he had shown fighting for every last vote during the primary in New Hampshire. It was a 4,106-mile trip, with no sleep.[281]

He touched down for brief appearances in nine states, ending at home in Arkansas on Tuesday morning. The crowds, large and enthusiastic, smiled and waved and jumped up and down, as the campaigns rock anthem "Don't Stop Thinking About Tomorrow" blared from the speakers. Clinton's voice a rough-edged ruin after the relentless schedule of speeches, he limited himself to the bare essential of his pitch, the message of change that he and Carville had carved out in what now seemed a lifetime ago.

Starting Tomorrow, You're Going to be Famous

Election night was a triumph. In the three-way race, up against an incumbent Republican President and a billionaire populist, Clinton got 43 percent, to Bush's 37, and Perot's 19. Clinton captured 370 electoral votes, Bush a scant 168 proving that their state-targeting strategy had been on the button, and very well executed. The middle class, black voters, and the suburbs favored Clinton. As did veterans, showing the futility of Bush's last-minute hammering of the draft issue.

The election didn't just propel Clinton into the White House, it also changed Carville's life, making him a huge international celebrity. As the dust settled, he took Mary Matalin to Venice.

"We both needed a vacation after such a long, grueling campaign, and we'd planned to take that trip no matter who won. But when we got to Italy, there were paparazzi camped out there waiting for me. It was insane," he remembers. "It wasn't like anybody sat me down and said, 'Starting tomorrow, you're going to be famous.' Nobody prepares you for that transition."[282]

He decided not to follow Clinton into the White House. He wanted to do television, books, speeches, and international consulting.

"That surprised some people," he observed, "but it felt right. I was almost fifty years old by the time Clinton got to the White House. I didn't have a hell of a lot of money in the bank." Even so, he remained one of the new President's closest confidants. He spoke often with both the President and the First Lady. Describing the Clinton era in American politics, Carville writes:

You were constantly up and then down. Something good would happen; something awful would happen. ...Along the way, Mary and I got hitched in late 1993. Matty was born in 1995. Emerson came along in 1998. It was all a blur. Most days, I was just trying to keep my head above water.[283]

James Carville had started out a fighter. He had lost so many races. He had sat on the sidewalk, in the pouring rain, sobbing, feeling alone and desperate. He had stared down into the abyss. But he had survived. He had built a new career. And now he had won the big one. He was a superstar. And he had at last, as he married and had kids, found profound happiness.

Obviously, the Clinton victory wasn't Carville's alone. No presidential campaign ever comes down to just one person. The candidate too was a true Master of Politics. So was his wife. Moreover, Carville's partner Paul Begala and a handful of other central players also wielded a high degree of influence over the campaign. The Ragin' Cajun himself pointed to the political genius of Bill Clinton, saying, "I'm the tail. The candidate's the dog."[284]

But there is no doubt Carville was absolutely crucial to the Clinton campaign in at least three ways: First by sharpening the campaign's strategy of immediate response to any charges; second by formulating the campaign's message and making sure it stayed focused on that message; third by mastering the crucial tactical decisions of the primary. He brought invaluable energy and focus to the campaign, and a message he had honed for years. As it's general, the Ragin' Cajun ran the iconic War Room in a way that changed and professionalized presidential campaigns profoundly.

James Carville has, through strategic genius, hard work and sheer persistence, earned his place among the high echelons of the political Master Strategists.

CHAPTER 5

THE ARCHITECT

Karl Rove

"Politics is often considered a contact sport. And it is."

- Karl Rove

The Joke About the Norwegian Farmer

In the midst of the historic 1960 showdown between Richard Nixon and John F. Kennedy, the allegiance of nine-year-old Karl Rove was never in doubt. He rooted for Nixon. Young Karl got his hands on a Nixon bumper sticker which he attached to his bike before riding around the neighborhood to promote his candidate. But he was not the only kid on the block with a favorite. A girl who was a couple of years older and who was enthusiastically for Kennedy, pulled him from his bike and – in Roves own words – "beat the heck out of me, leaving me with a bloody nose and a tattered ego."[285] It was Rove's first experience with politics as a contact sport. It would not be his last.

Growing up in Colorado and Nevada, Karl seems to have always been a political creature. He was once asked when his obsession with being on the inside of presidential power and history began, and simply answered: "December 25, 1950."[286] The day he was born.

As a teenager, Karl's biggest hero was the conservative icon Barry Goldwater. While other teens collected baseball cards and posters of movie stars, he collected buttons, stickers and posters of Goldwater. His idol's book *The Conscience of a Con-*

servative – attacking liberalism and describing new right-wing ideals – was an especially treasured item. Karl wasn't very good at sports and would rather dive into his books, like Milton Friedman's *Capitalism and Freedom* and Adam Smith's *Wealth of Nations*. And as he absorbed their ideas, his conservatism naturally grew stronger.

Roves younger years were no walk in the park. His mother, Reba Wood, while appearing strong and in control to the outside world, was fragile and unstable. Her problems haunted both her and her family. While Karl's mother struggled to get control over her emotions, his father was another story. In his autobiography Rove writes "Have you heard the joke about the Norwegian farmer who loved his wife so much he almost told her? My father – Louis C. Rove, Jr – was a Norwegian, one of those taciturn Midwesterners who held back a lot."[287]

His father always holding back his feelings, his mother displaying them erratically. This was not the most stable of emotional environments for a young boy to grow up in. His parents loved Karl and his siblings. They showed their affection in their own way. But Karl's unusually strong need for success and recognition in later life might well stem from this time. Certainly, it is obvious that the adult version of Karl Rove became someone who not only craved success but needed it. Needed it badly. And he was willing to go to great lengths to achieve it.

His family was not among the most affluent, and as a teenager Karl often took the odd job to get his hands on a little extra money. He waited tables and washed dishes. He worked as a clerk and in a hospital kitchen. Between junior high and high school, he got a summer internship in the Washoe County clerk's office

– his first real meeting with government – and he was thrilled by the experience.

At the Salt Lake County High School, Rove joined the debate team and immediately felt at home. He developed an obsession for thorough preparation. Even at that age, he craved better research than his opponents, a trait that would become part of his modus operandi. His diligence paid off. Soon, he was elected vice president of the student body.

In 1968, he became his high school's chairman of Students for Bennet, the senior United States Senator from Utah, in that year's election. He managed a small campaign, feeling he had contributed a tiny part to the Senator's victory. Living in the midst of that year's historic presidential campaign – with candidates like Richard Nixon, Hubert Humphrey, George Wallace, Robert Kennedy, Nelson Rockefeller, and Ronald Reagan all fighting for their ideas in the same arena – could have shaped and sharpened any political mind. Especially someone as intelligent and driven as Karl Rove. He was irrevocably smitten with politics. Just as important, he was starting to shape his basic operational principles as a political operative.

In the fall of 1969, he enrolled in his studies at the University of Utah and joined the College Republicans. But while he was mapping out his path in life, his family was falling apart. That Christmas, his parents split up. They moved away to different parts of the country, basically leaving Rove to fend for himself. He especially had a hard time financially. Years later it would emerge that the child support sent regularly by his father had been withheld by his mother, who lied about never receiving it. Karl was broke.

He found a place to live, asked for more hours at the job he had, and found other jobs, among those an internship at the Utah Republican Party that came with a small stipend. He found his footing, even if his family dissolved. His mother could never achieve the lasting happiness she so desperately craved. Twelve years later, she killed herself. Naturally, this left a lasting mark on Karl. To this day, in spite of all their faults, he expresses a deep love for both his parents. The emotional and economic hurdles he had to face in these early years clearly helped shape the man he eventually became.

Free Beer, Free Food, Girls and a Good Time for Nothing

Rove loved working for the College Republicans (CR). In the spring of 1970, he got a job offer from the College Republican National Committee and jumped at the opportunity, leaving school to travel to Illinois. The National Committee wanted him to organize college students for the campaign of Republican Senator Ralph Smith. Then CR president at the University of Illinois, Bob Kjellander, remembers Rove arriving:

> He was incredibly energetic and full of ideas. He was a ball of fire. He could get kids motivated, and you have to remember that this was at the height of the Vietnam War. Being a Republican on a college campus in 1970 was not popular, but Karl motivated people and got them working.

At the Smith campaign's headquarters, the 19-year-old Rove met an attractive young woman working as a receptionist. He wanted to impress her and came up with a plan. The Democrat Alan J. Dixon, who was running for state treasurer, was hosting an opening of his new campaign headquarter, and Rove got his hands on an invitation. Using it, he and some other college Republicans made their own false invitation to the event, promising "Free Beer, Free Food, Girls and A Good Time for Nothing." They printed hundreds of copies and distributed them to vagrants, homeless people, and drifters. Loads of hungry and thirsty people from the street arrived at Dixon's event, almost causing a riot. The press was thrilled; the thirsty vagrants not so much. But Dixon turned it around, declaring that the crowd showed that "the Democratic Party is the people's party...the Party of everyone." [288]

According to Rove, "all heck broke loose" back at the Smith headquarters when the flyer became public. He was told to get out of town and lay low. He spent the rest of the campaign in far-flung corners of the state. Kjellander later told *The Harrisburg Register*, "It wasn't a big deal. It's just one of those funny little stories in life."[289] But still it was a lesson of sorts, and Rove later regretted the prank: "It was not only foolish and childish, it was unhelpful. Dixon won his race and the prank didn't even raise me in the eyes of the attractive receptionist at Smith headquarters."[290] Smith lost the Senate race.

After the 1970 elections, the CR national chairman stepped down. The vice chairman, Joe Abate, automatically moved up. Abate needed administrative help, and Rove was offered the job of executive director. The CR were housed in the Republican National Committee headquarters, where he got to meet some of the most powerful figures in the Party. The job also meant he was traveling all over the country, meeting local Republican leaders and candidates, and leading 150 local CR training schools. At 20, he was fast becoming a behind the scenes guy in the Republican landscape with an ever-growing list of friends and contacts.

In 1972, Chairman Abate's term was up, and Rove desperately wanted the job. His main opponent was Bob Edgeworth. Rove knew winning would take a lot of effort. Before long, he was expanding his supporter group and trading favors. To get the support and loyalty of the powerful South Carolina CR Chairman Lee Atwater, he made a deal: If he was elected chairman, Atwater would get Rove's old job of executive director. The two soon became close.

The CR's national convention was held in June, at the mountain resort Lake of the Ozarks, Missouri. At the state and regional conventions leading up to June, both sides staged credential challenges. The net result of all the challenges was that a number of states sent two competing delegations to the Lake of the Ozarks, one pledged to Edgeworth and the other to Rove, each claiming to be legitimate. Rove and Atwater's strategy was simply to win by dominating the credentials committee and getting most of their delegates approved. As a result, the committee's meeting turned into a chaotic rumble.

To anyone not familiar with the ferocity of young Republican politics, the fierceness of the fight would be both surprising and troubling.

"It was so raw," one of the attendees later told *The New Yorker*.[291] The Republican operator Roger Stone, another key player at the convention, later mused, "There's nothing more vicious than a young Republican fight, nothing, nothing."[292]

The convention ended in complete chaos, with both Rove and Edgeworth declaring victory. Now it was up to the chairman of the Republican National Committee, George H. W. Bush, to decide. During the summer of 1973, while Bush's staff was conducting an inquiry into the Lake of Ozarks election chaos, one of Edgeworth's supporters leaked a tape to *The Washington Post*. It was a clear attempt to smear Rove. In the tape, Rove and another College Republican can be heard recounting amusing stories about minor campaign espionage they had engaged in during various campaigns, to a group of College Republicans at a training weekend. The GOP started an investigation into the affair. This might have been of little interest to a national paper like the *Post* under normal circumstances. But the Watergate scandal was at a highpoint, so any scandalous revelation from inside the College Republicans was worth printing. The *Post* ran the story under the headline, "GOP probes Official as Teacher of 'Tricks.'"[293] The teacher of dirty tricks, of course, being Karl Rove.

Chairman Bush was furious with the leak and the extra media attention it produced. It was the last thing he needed in the midst of dealing with the Watergate debacle. It was obvious to all that the tip to the *Post* had come from Edgeworth. And Bush hated disloyalty more than anything. Edgeworth had miscalculated the situation. An enraged Bush named Rove as the winner of the convention vote.

The beaten Edgeworth wrote the GOP chairman asking for a layout of the basis of the ruling. Not long after, Bush answered him in "the angriest letter I have ever received in my life," according to Edgeworth. "I had leaked to *The Washington Post*, and now I was out of the Party forever."[294] Even so, Edgeworth's reminiscences of Rove is not entirely without praise. To *The New*

Yorker, he described him as a smart, funny, super competent young man with an obsession with political campaigning and a strong need to win.

Rove was now the new chairman of the CR National Committee. His first act was to deliver on his earlier promise, handing Lee Atwater his first Washington job. But the incident with the investigation into Rove's conduct also left its mark. It had been an extremely unpleasant experience. His sister Reba believed it permanently spoiled her brother's appetite for being the candidate himself.[295] From now on, Rove would only seek power through others. He would be the man behind the curtains, pulling the strings, not the candidate in front of the cameras.

Rove + Company

A few days after moving into his position as CR chairman in October '73, Karl got summoned to George H. W. Bush's office. He was struck by the gentility, calm and evident integrity of the lanky Texan. The feeling must have been mutual because a couple of weeks later he was offered a job as Bush's special assistant. It wasn't a glamorous job, but it brought Rove into the upper echelons of the Republican Party. It was a smart move by Bush, too, because Rove had a rolodex of valuable contacts throughout the country.

A few months later, he met one of the chairman's sons for the first time. It was a meeting that left a profound impression on the young operative. George W. Bush, or just "W," "was exuding more charisma than any one individual should be allowed to have," Rove later recounted. Neither of them understood the significance of their meeting at the time, but decades later, Rove would make W president of the United States.

In August 1974, the Watergate scandal left president Nixon little choice but to resign. Less than one month later, President Ford appointed George H. W. Bush as the new US envoy to China. Bush's successor as chairman let Rove stay on as an assistant, and before long, he was sent out to help build the campaign of Congresswoman Virginia Smith in Nebraska's 3rd District.

The campaign let Rove try out some of his theories in practice and honed his skills. Most importantly, he left Nebraska with a deep understanding of the importance for a campaign to be run by someone other than the candidate. The person put in charge of any campaign needed to have full operating authority. The candidate should not run the day-to-day campaign but instead focus on executing the strategy, on delivering the message. In a year that saw the devastation of the GOP at the polls, and with only six weeks to go, Rove saved Smith's campaign, and managed to irk through a victory with a slim margin.

His achievement was noticed and rewarded. In 1976, he got headhunted to become finance director of the Republican Party in Virginia. That same year, he also married his first wife, Val Wainright. In the Old Dominion, he helped mastermind the campaign of President Ford. Again, Rove contributed to a victory in the face of a national anti-GOP atmosphere, as Virginia became the only southern state where Ford won.

In what by now seemed almost a pattern of his life, as Karl's career was flourishing, his personal life was not. His wife missed her family terribly. The couple decided they would move back to

Texas to be closer to them. He did not know it at the time, but the move into Texas would set the course for the rest of his political career. His marriage was not to last, but Rove's fascination for Texas politics would never fade.

At the time, the Lone Star State didn't seem a particularly good place for an up-and-coming Republican. Democrats occupied every statewide office, and there were just 13 Republicans in the 150-member state house. But two important factors meant the Democratic hegemony of the state was about to change: The first was a shift in the demographic composition of the electorate, with the number of Republican's slowly growing thanks to immigration. The second, and probably just as important, was the political genius and war-time attitude of Karl Rove.

During the 1980s, the Democratic Party was becoming more liberal, thus moving away from many of the more traditional moderate Democratic voters in in the state. Rove saw an opening for changing this political landscape. Dramatically. But before he could enact his plan, he had to build a platform of influence. He soon got the opportunity he needed. His former boss, Texan George H. W. Bush, now based in Houston, had big plans for 1980 election cycle.

"I'm considering running for President, Karl," he told Rove, "and I'd like your help. Would you like to run my Political Action Committee?"

It was a perfect job for the 26-year-old, from where he could continue building his national network. Bush had brought in another old friend, James Baker, to chair the PAC, which he named the Fund for Limited Government. Flying around the country, Rove and Bush became close. The young man looked up to his boss.

"He displayed his essential decency to everyone he came in contact with. There was no elevator operator or busboy or complete stranger undeserving of his respect, nor any party leader or fat cat who merited slavish attention," Rove remembered.[296]

In 1978, the young George W. Bush was also running for the state senate. Just how involved Rove was in that campaign is not known. Bush's opponent in the Republican Primary distributed a letter warning that W was too liberal, and that he had "Rockefeller Republicans such as Karl Rove" working on his campaign. W denied it, telling one reporter that Rove was "a young twenty-seven-year-old guy who works in my Dad's office in Houston. He has nothing to do with my campaign. I doubt if he even supports Rockefeller." Many years later, W admitted Rove did, in fact, have a minor role in this early campaign.[297] W won the Republican Primary but lost in November.

That year's election was important to the Bushes for another reason, too. James Baker had made a run for the post of state attorney general, but he too had lost. That meant he was free to come handle Bush's presidential bid full time. As Baker started building his team, Rove left. He had other plans. He wanted to work for Bill Clements.

In 1978, Bill Clements had become the first Republican governor of Texas in more than a hundred years. Clements was a self-made millionaire, a Dallas oil man. He had built his personal political brand as unapologetically unrefined, outrageous, and outspoken. Clements launched his gubernatorial campaign by flinging a toy chicken across a banquet table at his opponent. The no-filter oil man was described by Rove as "tough as an old boot." More importantly, Clements was willing to give Rove a large part in his political operation, starting with fundraising.

The campaign was in deep in debt, owing $7.2 million. Rove was tasked with raising $200,000 in two years through direct mail. It is no exaggeration to say that he exceeded his boss's expectations. By the end of the first year, he had raised $1 million, and by 18 months the entire $7.2 million debt was retired. Rove's genius emerged full scale. It turned out, he was a master of building large donor bases, finding just the right message for just the right recipient and getting those greenbacks flowing in. In record time, Rove built and ran an impressive money-machine.

Rove was also in charge of coordinating Clements' activities, developing and building the Republican political machine across the state. For the 1980 presidential election, Clements, as chairman of Ronald Reagan's Victory Committee in the Lone Star State, appointed Rove as its executive director. Reagan picked Bush as his running mate, and Rove went all out for the Gipper and his old boss. He built a robust statewide grassroot organization in every single county. Copying the micro-targeting of his fundraising, he built micro campaigns for all the important voter groups. Rove would later joke that he had a plan and an organization to reach "every conceivable voter group…from farmers and ranchers to Hispanics to women to students to small business owners to doctors to African-Americans to left-handed orthodontists who played golf on alternate Thursdays."[298] This kind of operation cost a lot of money, of course. However, that wasn't a problem. Under Rove's leadership, the Texas Victory Committee raised more than all the other Victory Committees in the country – combined. The state went overwhelmingly for the Reagan-Bush ticket.

After the election, Rove decided the time had come to start his own business. He got Clements as his first client, giving him cash flow from day one and a solid base to build on. In October 1981, Rove + Company opened its doors in Austin. During the next 18 years, Rove + Company would handle over 75 different campaigns for governor, senator, or congress. Rove even worked for the Conservative Party in Sweden, Moderaterna. He was a highly sought-after operator, and his vast, and ever-expanding network of donors gave him buck loads of power and influence.

As Rove became a major player in the Republican political landscape, the roles in his business dealings got reversed. Potential candidates started seeking out Rove, not the other way around. This meant he could pick and choose, and actively position the candidates he preferred. *The New Yorker* observed:

> *By the mid-nineties, Rove had got himself into a highly unusual position for a political consultant - functioning more in the manner of an old-fashioned political boss... Rather than his pitching candidates for their business, candidates pitched him for his commitment.*[299]

Rove carefully picked his candidates, then financed their campaigns through his company's fundraising. He wrote their overall strategy and made sure it was effectively executed.

At Rove + Company he also found love again. A freelance graphics designer named Darby Hickson became his new obsession. The feeling was mutual. They would later marry and Darby would give Rove a son, Andrew. Talking about their relationship with Melinda Henneberger of *The New York Times* in 2000, Darby described Karl as a creative genius and a committed father, but she also said he can be fierce and quite intimidating.

"I told Karl the other day," she said, "'You see things in black and white. I see lots of gray."

They would divorce in 2009, and in June 2012, Rove would marry lobbyist Karen Johnson. With three marriages, Rove's love life might have been in periodic change. But he never wavered from his political path.

Building a powerbase in Texas in the 1980s wasn't done overnight. In '82, the Democrats saw what would turn out to be their last great election season in Texas, unseating Governor Clements and winning a score of other elective offices. But Rove stuck to his plan.

In '84, he orchestrated the election of the former Democrat-turned-Republican Phil Gramm as US Senator. In 1990, Rove convinced then-Democrat Rick Perry, who had planned to retire from the Texas legislature, into switching parties. Rove then helped him become agricultural commissioner. Perry would later go on to become governor of Texas in 2000, when W left for the White House. Rove also worked with out-of-state Republicans, such as John Ashcroft in Missouri and Orrin Hatch in Utah.

There are a number of interesting stories about Rove's creative maneuverings in Texas. One stems from 1986, when Bill Clements decided to try to recapture the governorship after his ouster four years earlier. Rove was his chief strategist and operator. With a month left, the race was a dead heat. Most thought the scheduled televised debate between Clements and the incumbent governor would tip the scale for one of the candidates, and the incumbent was expected to outperform old Clements. But on the morning of the big debate, Rove held a press conference where he announced that a secret electronic listening device had been found in his office, hidden behind a red, white, and blue needlepoint of the GOP elephant.[300] Predictably, this kicked of a frenzy of media coverage, totally overshadowing the debate. Rove never pointed his finger directly at their opponent, but he did say, "There is no doubt...that the only ones who would benefit from this detailed, sensitive information [that was picked up from the listening device] would be the political opposition."

The opposition hit back, suggesting it was all a trick to overshadow the debate, gain sympathy for Clements and drive up the negatives for the Democrats. No one ever figured out who was behind the affair, but the story became part of the Rove myth. In the words of one Austin political consultant, "You have to put this in the context of Karl Rove. Rove equates politics with war, you do whatever you have to do in order to win. ...That doesn't mean he did it. But in war you do what you have to do to destroy your enemy."[301] Rove's maneuverings helped Clements win back the Governorship.

Making Texas Red

At the Democratic Convention before the 1988 election, the Democrats needed a keynote speaker that could go after the Republican presidential nominee, George H. W. Bush. What they needed was someone who could get the job done in an effective and entertaining way, someone that could make a real impression on the tens-of-millions of voters tuning in. They found Texas' state treasurer Ann Richards.

Richards, an outspoken woman in her mid-'50s with a mane of silver hair, gave a speech that went down in history. In her folksy Texan drawl, she talked of being a grandmother and an American. She invoked women's rights, civil rights, and went after the Republican record. With her easy smile, she attacked Bush as a privileged out-of-touch politician, with the memorable catchphrase, "Poor George. He can't help it. He was born with a silver foot in his mouth." The crowd roared its approval. In an instant, Ann Richards became a national sensation and a rising star in Texas.

Richards ran for governor in 1990 and won, beating the Republican candidate Clayton Williams. Her campaign had especially targeted moderate suburban women, who came out in droves to vote for her. Williams, an even cruder old cowboy than old Clements, had gone through the campaign bragging that he hadn't always paid his taxes. He refused to shake Richards hand at a debate. And in a telling episode, when a thunderstorm descended on his farm, he entertained reporters by comparing the bad weather to rape: "You can't do anything about it, so you might as well lay back and enjoy it," he laughed.

Williams' insensitivity and crudeness seemed a stark contrast to Ann Richards' optimistic, cheerful tone as she described her dreams for the Lone Star State, always with her charismatic smile. When the campaign was over, she had become simply "Ann" to a large part of the Lone Star State constituency.

As the Republicans licked their wounds and got used to the new governor, Rove was already making plans to oust her in 1994. And he had found his candidate. The son of the former President Bush; George W. Bush. Eighteen years earlier, he had met W for the first time, a meeting which had left him with a strong impression of a captivating and charismatic man. Now he wanted to make the most out of these traits, as he molded Bush's image to best compete with the popular Ann Richards.

Rove essentially built the image of the folksy Bush. Asked years later whether the Republican takeover of Texas would have been possible without W, Rove thought about it for a minute, then said, "If George W. Bush didn't exist, we'd have to find a way to create somebody like him."[302] Luckily for the Rove, he didn't have to. He had found his candidate.

With Richards polling a job approval rating at 67 percent, Rove was keenly aware that they needed to beat Richards by marketing W's own charisma, rather than by personal attacks on the governor. When a Republican women's group in Dallas asked W to participate in a comedy skit, Rob Allyn – the consultant helping the women with the event – got a stern call from Rove: "He said Bush would make fun of himself, his mother or whatever, but he would not under any circumstances make fun of Ann Richards and would appear only on that condition."

Allyn was floored, "It's a year out! Bush hasn't even said he's running. This is a skit for the faithful. But Karl has decided that they're not going to run against Ann's personality, because she has a great personality, so he's on the phone, all serious."[303]

To many observers, W wasn't the obvious choice to run against Richards. Sure, he had buck loads of charm, his family name, his dad's contacts, and access to big donors. All that was obviously important. But he had only run for office once before, for a seat in the state senate, and lost. To step out from under his father's shadow and become a credible candidate in his own right, he needed both an issue and an opening.

Luckily for Rove, Richards provided both when the voters rejected her proposal to redistribute property tax revenues from wealthier school districts to poorer districts. In one poll, 63 percent of the electorate were against the proposition. Her strong personal appeal simply wasn't enough to convince voters to support the policy. Richards' most important educational proposal went down in flames and left an opening for George W. Bush.

Rove couldn't have been more pleased with the issue that had landed right in his lap. W was passionate about education. His wife, Laura Bush, was a teacher. Education – one of the most important issues in any election – was also the kind of issue Rove needed to lure women voters away from Ann Richards. W wanted to free local school districts from state mandates, so they could design their own curriculum, decide student-teacher ratios, and set teacher certification rules. These were positions that the Democrats were sure to object to, but that could be sold successfully to a majority of the voters. This gave Rove a huge advantage.

Bush also wanted to make new initiatives to fight poverty an important part of his platform. He wanted to empower churches, neighborhoods, and community groups to take a larger part in that work. And he wanted to focus on the problem of juvenile justice, seeking new ways to help young offenders find a better path in life. Education, poverty, and juvenile justice were hardly typical Republican issues, but Rove figured they could help pull voters away from Richards, framing his message in a conservative yet broad and inclusive way, while at the same time firing up traditionally conservative voters through W's focus on personal responsibility, choice and religion. It was a preamble of what would become his main theme as a presidential candidate: Compassionate conservatism.

But Rove also suggested adding one more issue to the platform: Tort reform. He argued that Texas was "awash in junk lawsuits filed by personal injury trial lawyers." The argument was that "jackpot justice" was costing Texans jobs and economic growth as businesses picked up and moved to other states.[304] But there was another reason why Rove wanted to make it a big issue: Trial lawyers were a very important donor-group for the Democrats. Attacking their business would over time make it harder for his opponents to raise money.

If Rove could use the governorship, the legislature or the Texas Supreme Court to push tort reform, he would weaken the Democrats substantially. As a master fundraiser, he knew the huge importance of money in politics all too well. Though he never admitted as much publicly, it was obvious that tort reform was an important part of his strategy to wrestle Texas away from the Democrats grip. To Rove, it was killing two birds with one stone – he could sell it as a populist issue in the campaign, raise cash from grateful business leaders, and at the same time help achieve his long-term goal of Republican dominance in the Lone Star State.

He coached W until his candidate was ready to enter the spotlight. On November 8, 1993, Bush finally announced he was running for governor. Rove had prepared an impressive speaking tour to get the campaign rolling, and W made speeches in 27 cities in just five days.

"If you're happy with the status quo, I'm not your candidate," Bush told the crowds. He also took a gentle swipe at Richards without mentioning her name, saying, "Our leaders should be judged by results, not by entertaining personalities or clever soundbites."

As the campaign progressed, obvious glitches became apparent in the campaign. These were always addressed and corrected.

As chief strategist and moneyman, Rove wasn't shy about firing people if things didn't go as planned. Neither was W.

"Out went the campaign manager, the press secretary, and half a dozen other people. The rest of the staff buckled down and redoubled its efforts," Rove later recalled.

The campaign was strengthened with Karen Hughes as communications chief. Rove and Hughes were a formidable team from day one, and they would stick together for a long time. Hughes, a former Dallas TV journalist, kept up a steady barrage of attacks against Richards. Most of the time, they succeeded in pushing the Democratic governor into full defensive mode. In the fall, they launched their television ads. Again, Rove was insisting they not make the election a referendum of the two candidates' personalities, but rather keep their focus on the issues that separated W from Richards.

Bush's ads featured the candidate looking straight into the camera, speaking about education, juvenile justice, and tort reform, highlighting the differences between Richards and himself. As in any campaign, the trick was to trigger the voter's sentiments and feelings. Rove knew exactly how to do that Texas-style. In one of the spots, Bush promised to take away both the driving licenses and "to show you how serious I am" even the hunting licenses of Texas men who failed to make child support payments.

While his campaign was hitting Richards on the issues, the candidate himself was as nice to her as he could possibly be. When Richards lost her temper and called W "some jerk" in one of her speeches, Bush laughed it off, saying, "The last time I was called a jerk was at Sam Houston Elementary School in Midlands, Texas. I'm not going to call the Governor names."

Then Richards unleashed an attack spot alleging that the companies on whose boards Bush had sat had lost hundreds of millions of dollars. Rove answered the attack with a spot where W, again talking straight into the camera, said Richards's "personal attacks" removed the focus from the real problems facing the people of Texas.

As the two contenders faced off in the only televised debate between them, Richards started off by complementing rescue efforts following a flood in Houston that week. Bush responded with a simple, "Well said, Governor." Throughout the campaign Bush came off as a statesman and a gentleman, while Richards seemed aggressive, not at all displaying the same charm that had gotten her elected the first time around. She seemed almost unrecognizable.

Rove's strategy worked just as he had planned. At election night, Bush beat the popular incumbent governor by 53.5 to 45.9 percent, the widest margin of any candidate in 20 years. Most importantly, suburban women voted for Bush, as did 37 percent of the Hispanic vote. They captured both the suburbs and rural Texas. Richards made her concession speech early. It had been an impressive campaign with an even more impressive result, and it got noticed across the nation. Bush knew whom he had to thank for his success. On his wall, Rove still has a picture from that night, inscribed by Bush to, "The Man with The Plan."

The victory over Ann Richards changed Rove's relationship with George W. Bush.

"I went from being a longtime friend to being a political partner," he remembers.[305] From this moment on, that's what they were. Partners. Texas law required a governor's political activity to be run through a private committee, and the newly elected governor asked Rove to lead his.

This new position gave him immense power over the Bush organization. He would coordinate W's teams in all 254 counties, handle the fund-raising, vet potential appointees, recruit and back candidates for state and local office, muster support for the Governor's legislative agenda and start to plan for his 1998 reelection campaign. At the same time, he kept control of Rove + Company.

They made sure they hit the ground running, using the first term to secure a tax cut, rewrite the juvenile justice code, delivering what W had promised on education, and clamping down on "lawsuit abuse." The Governor proved adept at forging political alliances to guide his proposals through, and with Roves help all the measures they initiated passed the legislature.

To the outside world, Bush and Rove were in full control of the Texas GOP. However, there was one faction inside the Party that Rove had underestimated: The evangelical Christians. At the '94 Republican state convention, this group displayed their strength, dominating the convention floor. The new evangelical majority gave Bush's chairmanship candidate Fred Meyer thumbs down. Hurriedly, Rove recruited a candidate he thought could win over some of the evangelicals; Congressman "Pro-Life Joe" Barton. But the evangelicals wouldn't budge. They pushed forward with their own candidate to the chairmanship, Tom Pauken.

Only after it became clear that Pauken had secured commitments from an overwhelming majority at the convention did Rove back down. The evangelicals under Pauken's leadership went on to embrace a platform that supported constitutional rights for the unborn, the repeal of the Clean Air Act and the Endangered Species Act, a repeal of the minimum wage and a return to the gold standard. Rove made sure Bush was seen to immediately distanced himself from the platform.

The relationship between Pauken and Rove was kept cordial. At least until Bush and Rove decided it was time to capture the White House. While they quietly started building what was to become Bush's presidential campaign, Pauken suddenly entered the race to become new national chairman of the Republican Party. Rove understood that it was absolutely necessary to forge an alliance with the emerging Christian right. Still, he knew that Pauken was totally out of his control. According to Pauken, former Governor Clements suddenly offered him a job if he would withdraw from the race for the national chairmanship. But he declared he wouldn't be bought off.[306] Luckily for Rove, Pauken lost the chairmanship race.

Still, the feud continued. Pauken made sure Rove + Company lost the Republican Party's direct mail contract. Then he went after W in the state legislature, accusing him – even in newspaper ads – of wanting to raise taxes. Pauken got Republican legislators to vote against Bush's tax bill. So, the Governor's bill died in the Republican controlled state senate, killed off by the state Republican chairman. Rove was furious.

When Pauken announced he was entering the Republican Primary for attorney general, the strategist decided enough was enough. According to Pauken, Rove talked John Cornyn, a Texas Supreme Court judge, into standing against him in the primary. He also wielded his fundraising magic, so that Cornyn could outspend Pauken. Even then, Pauken still had his strong core of evangelicals, and for a while, it looked as if he could win. Rove needed to make another move. Out of the blue, Karl's former client Barry Williamson joined the race and started launching fierce attacks on Pauken.

Now, two well-connected and well-funded candidates were running against Pauken. The impression many observers were left with was that Williamson was there to attack Pauken and pull his numbers down, while Cornyn was presented as the candidate most likely to win against the Democrats in the fall election. With $1.5 million provided by a tort-reform PAC and hundreds of thousands of dollars in contributions from tobacco-companies with connections to Rove + Company, Cornyn beat the under-funded Pauken.

Finally, Rove and Bush had more or less complete control in Texas. Looking at the list of Rove's clients, there is no question who was the mastermind behind the Republican take-over of the second largest state in America. The list includes several governors, railroad commissioners, state treasurer, a large number of state senators and congressmen, and by the late '90s, every Republican member of the Texas Supreme Court. Rove was *the* kingmaker.

Creating the Dream Candidate

"I can't remember the day when the idea of Bush's running for president first came up – though I was the one brash enough to bring it up," Rove modestly wrote in his autobiography.

This was something of an understatement. Even before Bob Dole lost to Clinton in the '96 presidential election, Rove had his eye on the biggest trophy of them all – the White House. In the younger Bush, he had found a disciplined candidate with unmatched name recognition. They had built a solid political image through the governorship. They now commanded both the skills and the donor base they would need to get a presidential campaign off the ground.

But to have a chance nationally, they would need to bag a decisive reelection victory in the '98 governor race to prove to the world that they were more than a Texan one-hit-wonder. To get everybody's attention, Rove made sure he raised more money than their Democratic opponent Garry Mauro. A whole lot more. When all was said and done, the Bush campaign had raised and spent a staggering $25 million on the campaign, compared to Mauro's $3 million.

It also helped that a small chunk of that money came from the most unlikely of sources. At a Bush fundraiser in June 1997, then Lieutenant Governor of Texas, Democrat Bob Bullock, suddenly showed up with a $2,500 contribution to the Bush campaign. Later in the race, Bullock even issued a statement saying, "I respect and admire Governor George Bush and feel he deserves reelection to a second term. During my public career, I've served under seven governors, and Governor Bush is the best I've served under." It was a hard blow to Mauro, who had campaigned for his fellow Democrat Bullock, and who had even made Bullock the godfather to one of his children. To Rove, this was like manna from heaven. It made it easier to convince the national press corps that Bush's appeal reached far into the ranks of both independents and Democrats alike.

One part of Rove's master plan was to use the gubernatorial campaign to impress on a national audience that Bush had strong support among Hispanics. The heavily Democratic and Latino El Paso would be the biggest challenge, and for that exact reason, the campaign built a strong organization there and made sure the Republican state convention was held in the city. They even secured the endorsement of El Paso's Democratic Mayor. Rove also saw to it that the campaign spent more on Spanish language radio ads than their opponent spent on his entire campaign combined.

On election night, Bush won with 68.2 percent of the vote to Mauro's 31.2 percent. He carried every region and 240 of 254 counties, and received 49 percent of the Hispanic vote, 65 percent of women, and 70 percent of independents. Rove and Bush had done exactly what they had set out to do: Proven Bush's broad appeal and electability to the rest of the country. It was a tremendous feat.

"The rule in Texas is: Never underestimate Karl," said Bill Miller, a consultant in Austin who has worked for both Republicans and Democrats.[307]

As the dust settled on the gubernatorial campaign, Bush sat down for a difficult conversation with his chief strategist. He told Rove that he had to sell his life's work of 18 years, Rove + Company, and devote his full attention to his 2000 presidential campaign. He needed Rove's full commitment, day and night. It was a blow to Karl; it was not something he had expected. His sister Reba said her family was surprised that W made such a demand. But Rove said he understood. He sold his company. Now he was in it with both feet. The presidential campaign would be all or nothing.[308]

In March 1999, Bush created his exploratory committee, consisting among others of Condoleezza Rice, Haley Barbour, and

George Shultz. Of course, Rove had a hand on the wheel in the selection of the impressive group. In June, they officially announced that Bush was running.

Rove's grand strategy was based on winning some "invisible primaries" before facing the real one. One was "the Money Primary"; Bush needed to raise more money than any of his Republican contenders. Rove, the country's most adept fundraiser, made sure this part went according to plan. By the end of June, his team had raised $36.4 million[309] – more than the aggregated total raised by all of Bush's primary opponents, and twice as much as the Democrats' probable nominee, Vice President All Gore.

The next move was winning what Rove called "the Establishment Primary." Bush needed to show he had the support from the establishment and key players in the GOP. Typically, this meant traveling the country, doing the many face to face meetings that were needed. But that would prove a problem. Bush was governor of a large state and had an ambitious agenda he needed to push through to show he was a strong leader that could deliver on his promises. This meant he couldn't travel nearly as much as was needed to succeed in "the Establishment Primary."

Seeking a solution to this conundrum, Rove drew inspiration from the 1896 presidential campaign of William McKinley. McKinley had faced the Democratic populist William Jennings Bryan. Bryan set out on an unprecedented speaking tour across the country, visiting some 27 states. At the end of the campaign, approximately five million Americans had heard the Democrat speak. This was a staggering amount considering only 13.6 million would cast their vote in that year's election. What's more,

Bryan was a spectacular speaker, completely captivating his audiences with his colorful oratory. When McKinley was pressed by his staff to set out on a similar speaking-tour of his own, he waved the suggestion aside; "I might just as well put up a trapeze on my front lawn and compete with some professional athlete as go out speaking against Bryan."

So the McKinley campaign developed an alternative strategy. Instead of their presidential candidate touring the country, the country would come to him. In a carefully orchestrated front porch campaign, delegations from all over the county came to see the candidate at his home in Canton, Ohio. McKinley would politely listen to their pre-edited remarks, and then give some remarks of his own. Each group was hand-picked to leave the right impression, and the press was given full access and copies of the remarks made by McKinley. The Republican candidate saw some 750,000 people cross his front lawn, and the historic "front porch campaign" captivated the press and the country, letting McKinley frame the agenda through the press.[310]

Karl was fascinated by the McKinley campaign and would later go on to write a book about it. In the summer of 1998, he stole a page from McKinley's playbook, as Bush and Rove began their own version of the "front porch campaign." Bringing selected groups of important Republican players to the Governor's Mansion in Austin, W would greet them and make sure the press was aware of the visit, before the visitors got a private audience. Senators and congressmen, party chairmen and people from all the important states, and of course contributors, all soon started flowing into Texas for a visit with Bush. Just like in the McKinley campaign, the media were fed stories connected to the visits, all intended to show Bush's massive support and build his political image. It was an effective way of showing off W's strong position in the GOP, without having to travel extensively.

Besides demonstrating Bush's commitment to the campaign (which had not yet formally begun) the meetings also managed to enlist most of the Republican Party's top fund-raisers very early in the campaign cycle. The move took their rivals by surprise. Said a prominent Republican fund-raiser:

> It was very stealthy, and people did not realize it was happening. It was an amazing thing to watch. While he was doing his legislative work, he has sat down and had lunch with people from around the country - basically letting the money people come to him. And he pulled some of the top fund-raisers off the table, and the other Republican candidates did not know what hit them.[311]

All this meant Bush entered the real primary contest as the clear front runner. He had the backing of the establishment, he had the money and the fundraising ability, and he had his faith. In Rove's eyes, Bush's faith was an important attribute. His Texas struggle with the evangelicals meant he had learned the hard way never to underestimate the Christian vote. When the moderator of a primary debate asked the candidates which political philosopher or thinker they most identified with, the other candidates mentioned people like Jefferson, Lincoln, and Reagan. Bush just said, "Christ, because he changed my heart." When the moderator asked him to expound on his answer, Bush explained, "When you turn your heart and your life over to Christ, when you accept Christ as the savior, it changes your heart. It changes your life. And that's what happened to me." The response drew loud applause from the audience and got media attention across the country. Rove had made this a central part of Bush's message to draw the evangelicals into their coalition.[312]

Beating the Maverick

Rove's many years of preparation and hard work had made Bush the instant Republican favorite. The start of primary season almost looked more like a Bush coronation than a real primary fight. In the Iowa caucus, Bush beat his closest competitor, Steve Forbes, by a 10-point margin. With such a showing in the first primary contest, Rove was jubilant.

But he had underestimated Senator John McCain. McCain skipped the Iowa caucus because he was concentrating on the New Hampshire primary. Nicknamed "the Maverick," the Senator was famous for his straight talk, often criticizing his own party and voting against the GOP line. Now the Maverick built his whole campaign around his special brand of independence. Riding with the press on his campaign bus, "The Straight Talk Express," he gave them almost unlimited access, answering all kinds of questions with humor and frankness. The press was awed. The result was a lot of free media.

John McCain had a captivating life history. He had been a Navy pilot during the Vietnam War, where he was shot down over enemy territory, captured, and severely tortured. Being the son of an admiral, the communists believed releasing him would produce a propaganda victory. But when he was offered early release, he cited the military Code of Conduct, which specified that prisoners must be released in the order they were captured. For his refusals, he was subjected to so much torture that for the rest of his life he would walk with a limp and be incapable of lifting his arms higher than his shoulders. After five long years in captivity, he finally got released, returning to America a celebrated hero.

In the winter of 2000, Senator McCain crisscrossed New Hampshire, doing over 100 town hall meetings. Everywhere he went, he pledged to always be honest with the American people and to enact extensive campaign reform that would "clean up politics." His numbers rose rapidly, taking Rove by surprise. McCain won the New Hampshire primary with 49 percent of the vote to Bush's 30 percent. In politics, most people are inclined to appreciate a true David and Goliath story, and the media loved the fact that McCain had beaten Bush – the perceived too-strong-to-beat frontrunner – in the face of overwhelming odds. Rove knew this meant that the race was now wide open.

Bush's national numbers cratered, going from 50 points to 22 points in just four days. As they entered the crucial South Carolina primary, the primary race was now an open contest between Bush and McCain. Under the headline "McCain's Moment," CNN's Nancy Gibbs asked the question that was on everyone's mind; "The GOP party crasher upset the plans for a Bush coronation. Can he sustain his amazing surge once the Empire strikes back?"[313]

Landing in the Palmetto State, Rove understood that if McCain won there, the Bush campaign would most probably be over. If his instinct for full out political war hadn't kicked in earlier, it most certainly did now. Rove's only focus was that McCain had to be stopped. He had to be stopped *now*. The campaign suited up for total war.

Several stories have circulated about the dirty tricks that were used to attack McCain in the South Carolina primary. Under the headline "Dirty Tricks, South Carolina and John McCain," Ann Banks of *The Nation* claimed that Rove invented "a uniquely injurious fiction for his operatives to circulate via a phony poll," where voters were asked: "Would you be more or less likely to vote for John McCain…if you knew he had fathered an illegitimate black child?" Added Banks, "This was no random slur. McCain was at the time campaigning with his dark-skinned daughter, Bridget, adopted from Bangladesh."[314]

Bestselling author and former *Wall Street Journal* writer Ron Suskind stated that Rove is the prime suspect behind the stunt. The suspect himself vehemently denied being behind any such push poll, dismissing the story as a myth, calling Banks a left-wing journalist, and writing that Suskind "…has a dusty Pulitzer in his closet somewhere and that gave him license to sling mud." No actual proof has so far been put forward to support Bank's claim. Either way, the story is a telling example of the strong emotions and toxic mood during the Republican Primary contest in South Carolina in the summer of 2000.

What is indisputable is that Rove set out for the kill. In the beginning of the primary contest, Bush had positioned himself as a statesman that didn't get down in the mud to wrestle his opponents. But that was then. Now he sharpened his rhetoric considerably, blasting McCain's "Washington double-talk"; McCain was casting himself as a reformer while flying on corporate jets and planning Washington fundraisers where he schmoozed with the lobbyists he was vilifying on the trail, he lambasted.[315]

Rove also launched a new slogan "Bush – A Reformer with Results." By shamelessly stealing McCain's central message of "reformer," the Bush campaign enticed the media to start focusing more on the last part of the slogan – "with Results." Rove argued that Governor Bush had reformed Texas in several ways, among them education, juvenile justice, and tort reform. McCain, on the other hand, who had faced massive opposition to his reform ideas in the Senate, had less of an actual record to show. As expected, the tactic drove McCain mad. He even made an amateurish mistake, publicly accusing the Bush campaign of stealing his message. This way, he turned more public attention toward Bush's reform record.

There lay opportunities in McCain's temper, Rove knew. If he could get McCain angry enough, the Senator might start making more mistakes. And nothing could arouse the veteran's anger as much as getting unfairly attacked on issues concerning prisoners of war. They had Thomas Burch, the chairman of the National Vietnam and Gulf War Veterans, introduce Bush at a rally. Burch attacked McCain vehemently, accusing him of having abandoned veterans.

"He came home from Vietnam and forgot us," Burch shouted.

It was dirty and untrue, and McCain's reaction was highly predictable. He flew in a rage, calling Burch "some whacko." Rove reveled in the way they had gotten under the Maverick's skin. Hitting back, McCain launched a television add that asked, "Do we really want another politician in the White House America can't trust?" – referring back to President Clinton lying to the American people about his affair with Monica Lewinsky.

Then McCain put out another add, claiming that Bush's ads "twist the truth like Clinton."

Rove wrote the script for the response add. It featured Bush looking into the camera, saying, "Politics is tough. But when John McCain compared me to Bill Clinton and said I was untrustworthy, that's over the line. Disagree with me, fine. But don't challenge my integrity." McCain had played directly into Rove's hands.

Rove had through a series of chess moves portrayed the Maverick as something of a hothead.

"This was the worst insult one Republican could hurl at another. Those seven words cost McCain the South Carolina primary... Not one in a hundred Republicans thought George W. Bush was the moral equivalent of Bill Clinton," Rove later wrote of McCain's allegation. "South Carolinians liked both Bush and McCain, but McCain had crossed a bright red line. The reaction was negative and powerful." Check mate.[316]

McCain had been up by 8 points just before the controversy erupted. After it, McCain plummeted in the polls. Less than a week later, Bush had moved into a five-point lead, and his lead would continue to strengthen. When the South Carolina primary votes were finally counted, Bush received 53.4 percent to McCain's 41.9 percent. It destroyed McCain's momentum and resurrected Bush as the chosen one. And with that, victory in the Republican Primary was more or less in the bag. Rove could soon turn his attention to beating the Democratic nominee, Vice President Al Gore.

A Supreme Strategy and a Dangerous Secret

Every Republican knew that the 2000 election was theirs to lose. The economy was in a good shape, an achievement the majority of voters attributed to Clinton and Gore. On top of that, the Republicans in Congress had overplayed their attacks on President Clinton for his affair with Monica Lewinsky, with impeachment proceedings that went nowhere. Clinton had a higher Gallup poll approval rating than any other departing president, which was bound to bolster Gore. For years, voters had been moving away from Newt Gingrich's right-wing "Contract with America," towards a more moderate direction, helping the Democrats both in the 1996 and 1998 elections.

Knowing they had to capture as many votes as possible from independents, moderates and minorities in 2000, Rove packaged Bush as a "Compassionate Conservative." The idea was to attract centrist voters by having Bush champion issues like education and advocating initiatives for communities and churches fighting poverty. Rove's advice even led Bush to denounce the House GOP's proposals to eviscerate tax credit payments for low-income people.

"I don't think they ought to balance their budget on the backs of the poor," W said, "I'm concerned for someone who is moving from near-poverty to middle class."[317]

Bush was loudly pushing for centrist policies, trying to build a winning majority between conservatives and moderates. At the same time, in the more conservative media outlets, Rove pushed Bush's conservative credentials, especially faith-based policies. The Compassionate Conservatism-brand helped Rove balance these two conflicting images. After all, what was a Compassionate Conservative? To conservatives, it sounded like a traditional faith-based conservatism. To independents and moderates it sounded like a whole new brand, a more moderate centrist approach.

Rove saw to it that the Republican convention was customized to underpin the impression of a modern, inclusive and more compassionate conservatism than that of old. The lineup consisted of, among others, Colin Powell and Condoleezza Rice, Bush's young Hispanic nephew George P. Bush, and Abel Malonado, who was raised in an immigrant family and who addressed the convention in Spanish.

On the opening day of the convention, the popular Powel told the tens of millions of Americans watching at home, "In pursuing educational reform as well as in all other parts of his agenda for Texas, Governor Bush has reached out to all Texans – white, black, Latino, Asian, Native American." Likewise, the most memorable political initiative coming out of the convention was not on an issue people would traditionally expect from a Republican convention, such as military strength, moral absolutism or fiscal responsibility. Rather, it was an extensive new educational initiative under the slogan "Leave No Child Behind." Someone wandering in off the street could almost have mistaken it for the Democratic convention.

On important strategical issues, Bush nearly always followed Rove's advice. But on one crucial question, he refused to listen to Rove: The question of his choice of running mate. Rove had pushed for former Senator John Danforth of Missouri as their Vice-Presidential candidate. Compassionate Conservatism fit Danforth's image like a glove. He was from a battleground State, and while a moderate Republican on many issues and well liked among Democrats, he was also pro-life and a person of deep faith that could appeal to the Christian Right. From Rove's strategic point of view, Danforth was as good as they come. But in spite of all this, Bush turned his deaf ear to Rove's advice. He chose Dick Cheney instead.

Cheney had been a Wyoming congressman and Bush senior's defense secretary, before becoming Chairman of the Board and Chief Executive Officer of Halliburton, a Fortune 500 company. He was not particularly popular among neither Democrats or independents, and he had a strongly conservative voting record from his years in Congress. This didn't fit the Compassionate Conservative image at all. Besides, Rove pointed out, Wyoming wasn't a swing state; its electoral votes were already secure in the Republican column.

But Bush resisted Rove's arguments regarding campaign tactics and viewed the choice as too important to let short-term considerations trump his main concern. He wanted to choose a candidate that would be ready to lead the nation from day one, if the worst was to happen. Even so, Bush didn't simply brush Rove aside. What happened next shows how much emphasis W put on Rove's opinion and support. He sat down with Rove and Cheney, just the three of them, and let Rove present his arguments against Cheney straight to his face. It's hard to imagine any other presidential candidate lending such weight to his campaign manager or even to one of his closest friends. But for Rove, Bush went the extra mile.

The Cheney-choice might have been what Bush viewed as the responsible choice, but it didn't translate into any uplift in the polls. The choice of Cheney also looked bleak and boring compared to Gore's choice of running mate: Senator Joseph Lieberman. The Senator significantly expanded the Gore-ticket's appeal. Lieberman was as moderate as a Democrat could get. He had often stood against his own party on a range of issues, like supporting school choice and privatization of Social Security. The fact that he was the first Jewish candidate to be nominated on the national top ticket also lent a feeling of historic occasion to the Gore-Lieberman ticket. Rove felt Bush had thrown away an important opportunity to gain a few crucial points by not listening to his advice when choosing his running mate. But for once, Rove had to accept defeat and move on.

Rove is a perfectionist on most matters, and this is especially the case when it comes to opposition research. As the campaign progressed, Rove gathered a team of about 30 people – lawyers, budget analysts, accountants and other staffers – and set them to work digging up everything they could find on Gore. Analyzing the enormous amount of material, Rove decided to go after Gore as a flip-flopper (on the issues) and as an exaggerator (on everything else).

The strategist ordered the campaign to look for any and every opportunity to attack Gore as an incurable exaggerator, because "…it was Gore's exaggerations that most damaged him." They would attack Gore for – among other things – having claimed to invent the Internet, discovered the Love Canal chemical disaster, sent people to jail as a reporter, and faced enemy fire in Vietnam. Rove decided they would to a lesser extent focus on Gore's policies because "…if [Gore] lost voters because of these weaknesses, it wouldn't matter where he was on the issues."[318] If anyone inside the campaign thought Rove's strategy was tantamount to choosing a mudslinging campaign rather than discussing the issues, they didn't voice their opposition.

As always, Rove was a stickler for details. He developed a model for each of the battleground states, and shamelessly named his plan "The Ideal Campaign." It set specific targets for everything from voter registration, doors to be knocked and number of local headquarters, down to yard signs and stickers. Rove adopted an innovative state strategy that carried a lot of risk: He wanted to compete seriously not only in the traditional battleground states, but also a range of other states – including the home states of Clinton and Gore, Arkansas and Tennessee. Spreading the Bush campaign resources to cover states most observers considered securely in Gore's column was a high-risk gamble. But as it turned out, Rove's plan would prove a stroke of pure genius. Bush would go on to win in both Tennessee and Arkansas. Had he not done so, he would have lost the election and never become president.

In many of the states that Rove wanted to capture, he identified the Latino vote as especially important. Copying his targeting of this group from the earlier Texas campaigns, he made sure this consideration penetrated all parts of the Bush campaign. During the convention week in Philadelphia, for example, there were a lot of speeches and music in Spanish, and signs of "Viva Bush" and "Un Nuevo Dia." Bush himself even addressed the convention in a few Spanish phrases. In selected areas, Rove had Spanish language newspaper ads printed, under headlines like, "Cuando Hay Education, Hay Opertunidad" ("When there is education, there is opportunity"). This is just one example of how he subdivided the campaign's voter-group targeting effort.

Rove also made sure every part of the micro-initiatives strengthened the main theme, Bush as a Compassionate Conservative. All the hard work paid off. In the polls, Bush's lead continued to grow steadily. Coming into the last weeks of the campaign, a Bush victory seemed like a very good bet. Only something totally unforeseen could derail their train to victory.

And then that's exactly what happened.

Rove had known about the hidden Bush secret for years. On Labor Day weekend back in 1976, W had gotten drunk with some friends before getting in his car to drive home. When he passed a police officer, driving at a very slow pace, slipping on and off the curb, the officer pulled him over. Bush was arrested and fined. Even though Rove had known about the incident for a long time, he had not pressed Bush to go public with it before entering the campaign. It was one of the worst tactical mistakes of his career.

On November 2, Fox News called asking for a confirmation that Bush had indeed been arrested for driving under the influence of alcohol. Obviously, Rove should have made Bush go public much earlier, in a controlled environment. Then they could have presented the story in an air of honesty and put it into context – perhaps even using the occasion to underpin why Bush later chose to let his faith play a larger part in his life. But now they had no control over the story, and to most voters, it seemed Bush had tried to hide his arrest from the public. Instead of a story about how Bush had made a mistake and then turned his life around, it had become an exposed scandal.

With only five days to go until Election Day, this was a worst-case scenario. Once it broke, Rove considered it crucial that Bush respond immediately. Only W himself could explain why he had kept his arrest hidden, and the whole election now hinged on whether people would believe his explanation. At a hastily called press conference, Bush owned up to his mistake. He told the press corps what had happened, and said of the Fox News story, "It's an accurate story. I'm not proud of that. I've often times said that years ago I made some mistakes; I occasionally drank too much. I did on that night. I was pulled over. I admitted to the policeman that I had been drinking. I paid the fine. I regretted that it happened. I learned my lesson."

It was handled well, considering the circumstances. But why hadn't Rove made sure the story of the arrest was made public early and under controlled circumstances? Of course, there were personal considerations. Bush had wanted to keep the arrest hidden from his children. Even so, the strategist knew the reality of a presidential campaign: Everything gets out. No matter what. Everything. Always. But Rove had stuck his head in the sand, hoping it wouldn't come up. In his biography, Rove admits his mistake, writing, "I helped George W. Bush keep a secret that almost cost him the White House." From a master of the game like Rove, it was a stupid, rookie mistake.

Going into the last stretch of the race, the story became a huge problem. First, Rove and his people had spent months attacking Gore's character, but now it was Bush that seemed deeply flawed. It looked like he had tried to hide a DUI arrest from the American people. Second, it stole all the headlines, knocking the Bush campaign off message in the last crucial days of the campaign. It also consumed most of Rove's attention and energy, which should have been used better.

With the story of the DUI dominating press coverage the last week of the election, Gore rose in the polls every day until Election Day. As Rove himself acknowledged:

> *If Bush did drop 2 percent nationally in the vote because of the DUI revelation, then it probably cost him four additional states that he lost by less than 1 percent - New Mexico, Iowa, Wisconsin, and Oregon. Had he won them, this would have added a total of thirty electoral votes to Bush's column, which would have allowed him to win the White House without Florida.[319]*

But because of the DUI scandal, everything *did* come down to Florida. It became one of the closest and most thrilling US presidential elections in modern history. As election night progressed, the television networks first called Florida for Gore, then backtracked – stating that the Sunshine State was too close to call. Vice President Gore even called Governor Bush to concede, but then he too put out a statement saying the election was too close to call.

In the days after the election, it became clear that the final outcome would be decided by the courts. Gore kept pushing for more recounts in Florida, but Bush – who held a very narrow lead – protested. This left Rove on the sidelines, as the legal battles over which votes to recount were raging in the courts. He hated the uncertainty. He hated not being in control. It was a period he describes as "thirty-six days in Hell."[320] When the US Supreme Court eventually decided in a 5-4 vote that the counting was over, the five nerve-racking weeks finally came to an end. Rove could relax. George W. Bush would be the 43rd president of the United States.

Karl Is the Sun and Everyone Else Is the Moon

The President-elect announced that he wanted the man who had orchestrated his campaign to serve as his senior White House adviser. Bush gave Rove an unusually broad portfolio. According to *The New York Times*, many of Rove's political associates had assumed he would want to be chairman of the Republican National Committee, which was the route Lee Atwater had chosen. But Rove wanted to be closer to the President and to the policy crafting of the White House.

He was already planning for Bush's reelection in 2004. Who could blame him? The fact that it had taken weeks of fighting in the courts to secure the presidency didn't exactly produce the sweet taste of victory that Rove had craved for so long. He wasn't feeling like the kingmaker he had wanted to be. He knew, among other things, that he had helped Bush keep the DUI story a secret until it broke at the worst possible time. It was the one mistake that had almost cost Bush his presidency, and it had robbed Rove of an uncontested win. That January when people told him, "Hey, great job," he simply answered, "If it was such a great job, why did it take 36 days?"[321] Rove made himself a solemn promise that the next round would produce an unassailable victory, an absolute victory. And this time, he was willing to go to even greater lengths to get there.

In his new White House office, Karl hung symbols to let everyone know who he was and where he came from. Pictures and memorabilia from William McKinley, Abraham Lincoln, Teddy Roosevelt, and three framed passport documents from his Norwegian great-grandfather, Olaf Rove, adorned the walls. Rove's special role in the White House gave him great power. While all the other key staff had their specific areas of influence, Rove could move among all three areas of policy, politics and publicity.[322]

Of course, like any loyal top staffer, Rove followed the President's instructions when a final decision was made. But more than anyone else, he had Bush's ear and confidence, and his influence in domestic policy was far reaching, farther than most understood. "There's never been another like him on a president's staff," wrote conservative columnist Fred Barnes of *The Weekly Standard*, quoting a Bush aide saying of Rove, "On the big policies, Karl is the sun and everyone else is the moon."[323]

Rove set about to secure and expand the electoral base that had sent Bush to the White House. He wanted to build a lasting national Republican majority, based on their new brand of Compassionate Conservatism. To achieve this, they would first have to deliver on the education initiative they had presented during the campaign. That would prove to the voters that the GOP had changed and was more attuned to the hopes and dreams of the middle class than it had been during the 1990s.

Only three days after the inauguration, Bush sent Congress the No Child Left Behind bill. The bill required states to develop assessments in basic skills. To receive federal school funding, states had to give these assessments to all students at select grade levels. Rove made sure they got the bill passed. One could argue about whether No Child Left Behind was a success. What is undeniable is that the political benefits of Bush's strong focus on education were significant. Four years earlier, only 16 percent of voters for whom education was the top issue voted for the Republican presidential candidate. In 2000, after the Bush campaign had talked endlessly about No Child Left Behind, Bush received 44 percent of the voters for whom education was the top issue.

It is one of the achievements of which Rove was most proud.

"In March 2001, Gallup reported that for the first time in its sixty-six years of polling, Americans trusted Republicans more on education than Democrats," he boasted in his autobiography. It was more than just an issue – it was a political tool Rove used to reshape voter patterns. He had changed Texas from a blue state to a red state. Now he was well on his way to changing the country.

Rove made sure the President was seen selling his passion for education on every possible occasion. One of those many occasions was the President visiting the Emma E. Booker Elementary School, where Bush was reading to the children on the morning of September 11, 2001. As he read, the first of two passenger planes crashed into the World Trade Center in New York. It was Rove who told the President of the attack that was to change America and the world. After the second plane crashed into the two towers, Bush said, "We're at war." Then the terrorists crashed a plane into the very symbol of Americas military strength, the Pentagon. America had never before experienced such an attack on its mainland. In a few hours, everything in Rove's world changed dramatically.

King Karl

As soon as Bush, Rove, and the rest of the presidential entourage boarded Airforce One to get the president to safety, Rove called his wife and told her what had happened. Like everyone else, he was shaken. Still uncertain of how the rest of the day and the days to come would unfold, he was sure of only one thing: The political landscape had changed dramatically. His old plan of building a centrist base for the GOP had become obsolete in an instance. Now, everything would be about strength and leadership. And in his mind a new long-term plan was already forming.

Three days after the brutal attacks that killed almost 3,000 innocent civilians, Bush entered the pulpit of the National Cathedral. There, before four presidents, the leaders of Congress, and hundreds of mourners, he spoke to the nation and the world. Rove had worked on the speech with the President. Their goal was to rally the country behind a forceful reaction – answering the attacks with military might and strength.

"War has been waged against us by stealth and deceit and murder," the President told the world from the pulpit. "This nation is peaceful, but fierce when stirred to anger. This conflict was begun on the timing and terms of others; it will end in a way and at an hour of our choosing." The ceremony ended with "The Battle Hymn of the Republic." Singing of a "terrible swift sword," Rove felt a deep and burning anger.

A few days later, in a speech to Congress, the President stated, "Our enemy is a radical network of terrorists and every government that supports them." They had defined their enemy and staked their course. Rove knew this was what the large majority of the country wanted. And he also knew this was a path that would rally voters behind the GOP. The strategy of capturing the hearts of the voters in the suburbs and the middle class by focusing on education, diversity, and compassion would no longer be the hymn of the Bush administration. Their new message was war, strength, and leadership. It was a new plan, for a new world. Even in the midst of the sudden chaos in those September days in 2001, Rove's eyes never strayed of the 2004 election.

On September 20, 2001, President Bush delivered an ultimatum to the Taliban, the government of Afghanistan. They had to turn over Osama bin Laden and other al-Qaeda leaders operating in the country, or face attack. When the Taliban demurred, US forces, together with coalition allies, invaded Afghanistan. One and a half years later, in March 2003, the Iraq War began. The Bush administration argued the war was a necessary consequence of the war on terror and claimed that Saddam Hussein had weapons of mass destruction. (The latter was later to prove untrue.) Rove's role in the discussions leading up to the Iraq invasion is no open book, but he certainly was on board with the decision.

With the country engaged in the war on terror and American soldiers dying on foreign battlefields, the national mood was set for the 2004 presidential election. This was an environment Rove felt at home in. For him, politics had always been like war. He knew what it meant to be all in, to fight to crush your enemy, being willing to go to great lengths to win, totally dedicated to victory. Now the American people shared many of the same emotions.

Rove planned to make the 2004 campaign a mirror of the one in 1864, when Abraham Lincoln won reelection in the middle of the civil war.

"Voters then asked themselves if they should, in the words of Lincoln, 'swap horses when crossing streams,'" Rove pointed out. "I thought that if we showed Bush to be a strong, decisive war-time leader, voters wouldn't want to swap horses."[324]

In a January 2002 address to a Republican luncheon in Austin, he explained, "We can go to the country on this issue because they trust the Republican Party to do a better job protecting and strengthening America's military might and thereby protecting America. Americans trust the Republicans to do a better job of keeping our communities and our families safe."[325] Rove would use the war on terror as an effective tool to mobilize voters for Bush in 2004. A prelude to this was seen in the 2002 midterm elections, when Rove masterminded a stunning Republican victory in the post 9/11 political landscape.

Usually, the incumbent president's party loses seats in both chambers of Congress in a midterm election. But in 2002, the Republicans picked up net gains of two Senate seats and eight House seats. It was only the third time since the Civil War that the president's party gained seats in a midterm election, and the first time that this happened under a Republican president. Now the GOP controlled both the White House and both houses of Congress. The stunning midterm ascendancy of the Republicans boosted Rove into a new category. One-party rule had returned to Washington.

"It's an amazing moment," said one senior White House official. "Karl just went from prime minister to king. ...Pure power."[326]

Presidential reelection campaigns have a tendency to sabotage themselves from inside, as the "policy achievements trump all" staff at the White House and the "victory is all that matters" campaign staff start clashing over policy and the use of the Presidents time. To make sure this would not happen, Rove structured the campaign in such a way that all information between the White House and the campaign had to go through just one person. Himself. This gave him a tremendous power over all the important day to day decisions as well as being in full control of the strategy.

Rove's first decision was to hire Ken Mehlman as the campaign manager. Together they developed a geographical strategy divided into four tiers, from the states W had a solid grip on that the campaign didn't need to worry about, down to states that would most probably vote Democratic. In between were the states W could win, and the states W needed to win to capture a majority in the electoral college. With his scientific approach, Rove was careful not to jump to premature conclusions. He called in a selected group of Republican political scientists who tested all his assumptions and helped him decide which tier the different states really belonged in. Only after this expansive exercise was done, the organization, money and resources were allocated – not only to each of the states but down to each local region.

Constructing such a campaign was as complex as building a supertanker. You had to plan for everything from the design of the hull, the number of main tanks, the bridge, the gas system and a thousand other factors needed to give it the necessary speed and accuracy. The structure had to be strong enough, and this one had to be able to withstand the heavy storms and massive waves you encounter in a presidential election. Rove grasped this complex architecture and mastered it like few others.

For 30 years Rove had used micro targeting in his fundraising and campaigns, and now the same approach was put to use in the 2004 reelection campaign.

"This complex analytical effort drew upon as many as 225 pieces of information we could collect on an individual household to help identify which members were likely to support Bush and turn out to vote for him," Rove explained, continuing:

> Among the pieces of information we sought were whether they own a gun, whether their children attended private schools, what kind of magazines they subscribed to, what kind of car they owned, even what kind of liquor they preferred. No one piece of information was a reliable indicator by itself. The complicated algorithms that made sense of the relationship among these data points were prized secrets.[327]

Rove's team spent three years and millions of dollars perfecting this microtargeting tool.

He executed the campaign with the goal of expanding the Republican base in the suburbs and rural areas. He used a "72-Hour Task Force" to mobilize that base the last three days up to Election Day. He used discrete spending programs and microtargeting to pick off vulnerable Democratic constituencies among Hispanics, African Americans, and Catholics. These tactical maneuvers should guarantee a Republican majority.[328] And Rove knew these swing voters were absolutely necessary to create a winning majority because the percentage of true independents – people who split their ballot – had shrunk to just seven percent of the electorate.

There was also the issue of the 4 million evangelicals that had failed to turn out in 2000. The lessons from Texas, where Rove at one point had lost control of this group, and thereby his party, were not forgotten. He needed them and he knew how to mobilize them. Rove made sure the Republican Party in some states took steps to make it worthwhile for evangelicals to vote, by raising specific issues that would get them to the polls. For example, the question of allowing or banning gay marriage was put on the ballot in some states, ensuring these voters would turn up on Election Day. Rove knew that once they were standing in the voting booth to cast their vote against gay marriage, most of them would also pull the lever for Bush.

Politicians have a tendency to run for re-election by ticking of long lists of past achievements. The most famous example might be Winston Churchill, the Prime Minister who against all odds led Britain to victory against Nazi-Germany and then got kicked out of Number 10 by the voters in 1945.

"Incumbents who run on past achievements often get defeated," Rove explained. "Bush's campaign [in 2004] needed to be about big, important things for the future – 'something new plus more of what he's doing,' as one planning document put it."[329]

How unique was Rove's approach? Some of the data driven work he oversaw could perhaps have been executed by other savvy political operators. But he wasn't just the data hungry, systematic workaholic. He was also an unmatched long-term strategical thinker. Part of his political genius came from his gut. And it was his gut that told him they needed to take down the Democratic nominee, Senator John Kerry, by going after his most prominent strength; his service record. This was especially crucial in an election so colored by the wars that the US was fighting in Afghanistan and Iraq.

During the Vietnam War, Bush had stayed home, serving as a pilot in the Texas Air National Guard. Kerry on the other hand served on the battlefield on the other side of the world, getting awarded several combat medals for his heroic achievements – including the Silver Star Medal, the Bronze Star Medal, and three Purple Heart Medals. As captain of a Swift Boat, Kerry had saved comrades under fire, showing exceptional bravery and leadership in the field.

The contrasts between Kerry's and Bush's service records were evident for all to see. And it was especially damaging to Bush in '04 when the country was involved in two wars. Rove knew they had to destroy Kerry's strength on the issue. First, he would go after Kerry's leadership image by portraying him as a flip-flopper. Second, he would make sure the personal story of Kerry the War Hero was discredited and brought into doubt.

For the first task, they got a little help from the Senator himself. Kerry used many of his campaign appearances to criticize Bush for his handling of the Iraq War. The Democratic nominee had initially voted in support of authorizing Bush to use force in dealing with Saddam Hussein, but then he had voted against an $87 billion supplemental appropriations bill to pay for the subsequent war. Rove decided to use these two seemingly contrasting votes to portray the Democratic candidate as a flip-flopper. The Bush campaign put out an ad that said, "Few votes in Congress are as important as funding our troops at war. Though John Kerry voted in 2002 for military action in Iraq, he later voted against funding our soldiers."

Trying to answer the attack and explain his vote at a meeting in West Virginia, Kerry stumbled, saying, "I actually did vote for the $87 billion before I voted against it."

Rove had hit jackpot. This was an invaluable soundbite. In ad after ad, and speech after speech, the Bush campaign used it to portray Kerry as a flip-flopper, a man lacking the leadership abilities needed to lead the nation securely through its time of crisis.

For the second task, Rove thought Kerry's war record could actually be turned on its head.

"I knew we could prevail when I saw Kerry mount the convention stage and open his speech by saying, 'I'm John Kerry and I'm reporting for duty,'" Rove remembered, "He bet that his Vietnam service would convince Americans he was the strong leader they wanted…" It was a bet Rove would make sure Kerry lost.

Only weeks after Kerry had "reported for duty" in front of the Democratic Convention and millions of television viewers, a brand-new political guerrilla group appeared on the political stage. Swift Boat Veterans for Truth was a group formed with the sole purpose of opposing Kerry's candidacy. These veterans of the Vietnam War claimed that Kerry was "unfit to serve" as president, based upon his alleged "willful distortion of the conduct" of American servicemen during that war. They stated that "Kerry's phony war crimes charges, his exaggerated claims about his own service in Vietnam, and his deliberate misrepresentation of the nature and effectiveness of Swift boat operations compel us to step forward." The group put forward their claims in television ads that ran in several swing states, as well as in the vast media coverage they received.

One of the group's adds had several decorated veterans speaking into the camera; "John Kerry has not been honest about what happened in Vietnam"; "He's lying about his record"; "John Kerry is lying about his first Purple Heart, because I treated him for that injury"; "John Kerry lied about his Bronze Star – I know, I was there, I saw what happened"; "His account of what happened, and what actually happened, are like night and day"; "John Kerry has not been honest"; "He lacks the capacity to lead"; "When the chips were down, you could not count on John Kerry"; "John Kerry is no war hero"; "I served with John Kerry. John Kerry cannot be trusted." It was a devastating charge of attacks from a large group of veterans, effectively creating doubt about Kerry's character and service record.

Most of the claims were later proven untrue and misleading. And it would emerge that most of the organization's members had not been in a position to actually assess Kerry at all. In fact, most of the Vietnam veterans who actually had served with him supported Kerry's version of events. But in spite of the facts, the attacks had done what the group had set out to do: Destroy Kerry's biggest advantage in his fight with Bush. Swift Boat Veterans for Truth was nothing more, nothing less than a dirty but successful political smear campaign.

Karl Rove have repeatedly stated that he had nothing to do with the group's attacks on Kerry. However, producing and running the ads cost a small fortune, and the group had – somehow miraculously – gotten hold of more than $11 million in donations in a very short time.[330] Most of the money was provided by prominent individuals who had close ties to the Republican Party. According to information released by the IRS, more than half of the group's reported contributions came from just three sources, all prominent Republican donors from Rove's home base of Texas.[331] Whoever was the de facto architect behind the Swift Boat Veterans for Truth and steered money their way, their campaign was so damaging to Kerry that it inspired the widely used political pejorative "swift-boating" to describe an unfair or untrue political attack.

Many commentators thought that Rove's grand strategy for the 2004 election was solely a "base strategy," an appeal only to conservatives and Republicans. But the numbers showed a different story. Yes, Rove counted on expanding Bush's support among traditional Republican voters. But the strategy was "far deeper and wider," said Bush campaign adviser Peter Wehner. It was tailored to increase his vote among Catholics, Jews, Hispanics, and blacks, and it succeeded in doing so.[332]

John Kerry never fully recovered from the "swift-boating" and the "flip-flopper" attacks. On Election Day, Bush won the popular vote with a comfortable margin. He won 31 states to Kerry's 19, and captured 286 in the Electoral College to Kerry's 251. They had won a second term for Bush. And this time it was a more solid win. There were no courtroom fights, just the sweet taste of victory. Rove had achieved his goal. In fact, he was probably even happier than the President. He had finally gotten what he had longed for so long – an unassailable victory in a presidential election.

Having received Kerry's concession call, Bush walked on to the podium to give his victory speech. With millions watching, the President pointed to Rove and told everyone who didn't already know that his strategist was "the Architect" of his victory.[333] The Architect himself smiled from ear to ear. The 2004 Bush campaign would forever be attributed to Karl Rove, in all its genius and hard work and dirty tricks.

It's Time to Get Serious

"Bush wants a policy legacy and a political legacy," a senior strategist explained, "and he counts on Karl for both."[334]

Rove certainly wanted to deliver. But in the last term of Bush's presidency, he would embroil the White House in controversy. One controversial issue was the Valerie Plame affair. Plame was a covert CIA operations officer whose identity was leaked to and subsequently published by Robert Novak of *The Washington Post*, causing her to lose her job at the CIA. According to the *Post*, Rove was identified as a source of the leak.[335] She later filed a civil lawsuit against Rove and other senior White House officials, but the lawsuit was dismissed on jurisdictional grounds. Still, the controversy hurt Rove.

Another scandal involving the chief strategist was the unwarranted firing of nine US attorneys because they would not investigate certain Democrats that the White House wanted investigated. Even though he denied involvement, both Congressional and Justice Department investigations found that he played a central role in the politically motivated firings. The investigators concluded that Rove, in tandem with other White House officials, "had pushed to fire the federal prosecutors because they were not aggressively pursuing investigations against Democrats".[336]

Rove was also accused of pressing for the conviction of Alabama's former democratic Governor Don Siegelman for federal bribery and conspiracy charges, as part of an effort to prevent him from winning a second term. Again, Rove denied any involvement.

No one could pin any crime on him; it was mostly just circumstantial. But the press didn't really bother whether there was any proof, as long as they could earn a buck on a good story. Bush did what any good leader would do in such a situation; he supported the guy that had gotten him elected. Still, the high number of controversies made it increasingly difficult for Rove to focus fully on his work. It was a position he didn't appreciate. He also found it unfair that his many huge achievements, of which he was so proud, seemed to fade away while his controversial image got center focus. He needed to move on. So, in August 2007, Rove resigned from his White House job.

As he walked out of the gate and strolled down Pennsylvania Avenue, he was still a relatively young man. But in spite of his age, he had reached goals most other operatives could only dream of in a lifetime. He had helped turn Texas from an overwhelmingly blue to an overwhelmingly red state. He had help orchestrate the campaign strategies in a range of successful campaigns. And he had built the image of George W. Bush, getting him elected first governor, then president for two consecutive terms.

How could one man achieve all this? Obviously, he has extraordinary strategic abilities and a relentless need to win. When combined with hard work, this made him a political force of nature. One of Rove's traits is that he is always multitasking. He might be talking on the phone while simultaneously reading a memo, conducting a meeting, or fielding queries from his staff. He also has an uncanny ability to remember data. Discussing Bush's focus on education with one reporter in mid-2000, for example, Rove said without any notes in front of him, "Remember, in 1996, if education's your No.1 issue, you vote for Clinton-

Gore over Dole-Kemp by 76-16. By 2000 you vote for Bush-Cheney by 52-44."[337] His head is full of data and he knows how to analyze it and distil from the vast amount of numbers a clear strategy for victory.

Rove's brain was almost a kind of supercomputer that was utilized on a day-to-day basis to dissect and solve political challenges. But even while maintaining such a high degree of detailed knowledge, what he was best at was creating long-term strategy. He always did more long-term strategic planning than most other political consultants. He produced written plans far in advance for his campaigns, outlining not only strategy, messaging and fundraising, but also analyzing and mapping out the campaign as it would progress. He had an amazing knack for understanding how to break through to each individual voter, and how to trigger that person's feelings and sympathies. These complex qualities are part of the reason President George W. Bush, in addition to naming him "the Architect," also gave him the nickname "Boy Genius."

Rove is still working on pushing America towards conservatism. He is doing it in the way he knows best – raising money and distributing it according to his long-term strategy. Rove had learned more from the 1896-campaign of William McKinley than just the front porch campaign he had copied in Texas in the '90s. McKinley's chief strategist had been the Republican Senator Mark Hanna, who famously said, "There are only two things that are important in politics. The first is money, and I can't remember what the second is." Hanna is one of Rove's heroes.

His close ties to large republican donors is built on a vision of shaping the future of Republican politics for a long time to come. At a meeting with wealthy donors, he declared, "People call us a vast right-wing conspiracy, but we're really a half-assed right-wing conspiracy. Now, it's time to get serious!"[338]

The last ten years he has been instrumental in the launching of several super PACs, like American Crossroads in 2010, and Crossroads GPS, a politically active nonprofit. Both organizations raised and spent enormous sums to support conservative candidates and issues. He has ties to at least one other dark money organization as well, One Nation. In the 2016 election cycle, One Nation spent $40 million, according to the Center for Responsive Politics.[339] Through organizations like these, Rove still has a substantial impact on American politics, albeit more hidden than before.

To the deep dismay of his foes and to the delight of those who share his political ambitions, the Architect is still out there, hard at work.

CHAPTER 6
THE AXE

David Axelrod

"When I was a kid, my father and I would occasionally watch chess masters in the park, who silently moved from board to board as they took on multiple opponents at the same time. Such too, is the life of a political consultant."

- David Axelrod

Hooked for Life

Senator Robert Kennedy had just scored a major victory in the Democratic nomination, having won the California primary. Every American remembered where they had been the day his brother, JFK, had been shot five years earlier. Now Bobby seemed destined to pick up the mantle of his older brother. But destiny works in mysterious ways. After addressing his supporters in the Ambassador Hotel in Los Angeles, Bobby was also shot and mortally wounded, when leaving the ballroom through the hotel kitchen. Lying bleeding on the floor, he asked, "Is everybody OK?"[340]

The year was 1968, and Bobby's sudden death left a 13-year-old named David Axelrod totally crushed. The boy had been transfixed by the two Kennedy brothers, and their crusades. To this day, David still remembers the day he first saw JFK, even though he was only five years old at the time.

"Not everybody can point to a moment, the exact time and place, when a lifelong passion began. I can," he wrote of that day in 1960 when he saw JFK campaigning just two blocks away from his New York childhood home. "The scene was pure magic, electric and important. From that moment on, I was hooked. I wanted to be part of the action."[341]

The young boy had watched the murder of JFK on television, in horror and morbid fascination. When Bobby Kennedy moved to New York to run for the US Senate in 1964, David went to his local Democratic club to volunteer. And when Kennedy four years later ran for President, as a torchbearer against the war in Vietnam, David volunteered again. Though he mostly did menial tasks like distributing campaign literature, he felt part of something larger, something important. His admiration for Bobby Kennedy would come to guide the way he crafted his strategies in his later campaigns.

"Nearly forty years later, when Barack Obama was considering his candidacy for president, I talked with him about Bobby and the campaign of '68," Axelrod recalled in his autobiography. He even compared Obama to the slain Kennedy:

> Bobby inspired and spoke for a whole generation that believed we could do better, I told Obama, another young senator poised to challenge an unpopular war and the established world order. If you run, we need to be as bold, and rekindle that kind of hope.[342]

This observation was not merely about idealism. Where others saw a long-gone torch for change, David Axelrod saw a still powerful political message, a clear strategy to victory. He realized that the political hopes and aspirations of the majority of the American people really hadn't changed. He felt that the energy of young people still was an energy that could be harnessed, this time to help propel the first African American into the White House. And David Axelrod would guide him there.

David was born on February 22, 1955. His father, Joseph Axelrod, ran a small psychotherapy practice. He was warm, caring, and funny, but had little drive. His mother was the exact opposite. A journalist and researcher, she craved acknowledgement and focused mostly on her career. She was always striving for perfection, both in herself and in her kids. She was, in Axelrod's own words, "subtle as a sledgehammer." His mother simply didn't have the time or emotional bandwidth for him. It left Axe with deep scares.

As much as he struggled with his relationship with his mother, he also admired her in some ways. He attributes some of his own relentless need to win to his mother.

"On one hand, I credit much of my professional success to the drive and skills I drew from her," he says, adding:

> On the other, I have spent my life fighting off the same debilitating self-doubt, too often fretting over the very same questions that obsessed her; "What did they say? What did they think?" It's painful to acknowledge that my own children also paid a price, often losing out to my career in the battle for my attention.[343]

The huge differences in his parents' temperaments lead them to divorce when David was 13. After their split, his mother remarried, and he soon found himself in a frosty relationship with his stepfather. The result was that he kept spending as little time as possible at home. As soon as he graduated from high school, he left New York and his strained home environment, and headed for the University of Chicago.

There was another reason for the move as well; Chicago had the most interesting political landscape of any major American city. Mayor Richard J. Daley, who ran the last of the big-city machines as a political boss, had been instrumental in electing JFK president. Chicago was divided into 50 wards with strong, ethnic identities. Daley's genius was forging local leaders into one powerful political whole, using patronage and demands of absolute loyalty to keep this powerful Democratic juggernaut vital and strong. But as years went by, many voters grew disillusioned with the corrupt system. Inside the Democratic Party, challengers started emerging. This was the world Axelrod entered when he came to Chicago. He found it both fascinating and alluring.

The early '70s was a time for exceptional political journalism. It was a time when journalism was still driven by a relentless focus on the truth, rather than just scandal. Because of this, it was a time when journalists were widely respected and admired. By uncovering the coverup behind the Watergate break-in, journalists Bernstein and Woodward emerged as the unlikely assassins of Nixon's presidency. And Mike Royko of *The Chicago Daily News* had just published his book *Boss*, shedding light on Daley and his machine. Axelrod saw journalism as a great way to quench his thirst for politics. It was certainly the easiest way into the political world for a young man without any experience or contacts.

Starting out in internships in the weekly community newspapers *The Villager* and *The Hyde Park Herald*, Axelrod grew his network of contacts as well as his credentials. On graduating from college he landed a job at the prestigious Chicago Tribune. At the *Tribune* he flourished. Before long, he was covering local, state and national politics, eventually advancing to City Hall bureau chief.

Perhaps because of his strained relationship to his mother, Axelrod developed a deeper connection to his father. They talked often on the phone. Mostly Axe called him for advice or solace, or to ask for a few bucks to tide him over. His father at times hinted that he was struggling economically, but as most young people, David paid little attention. One day in the spring of '74 he got an unusual call from his dad, who told Axe that he was proud of him and sure he was going to do well in life.

"His message had a strange, parting tone," Axe remembered. "A few days later, there was a knock on the door of the shabby off-campus apartment…" It was a police officer, telling him that his father had committed suicide. He had financial difficulties, he had gotten fired from his job, and had gone into some sort of dark depression. David was angry with himself for missing the clues, and angry with his dad for not seeking help. He felt helpless; "My father was dead. My mother, distant. I was completely on my own."[344]

A few years later, Axe started dating a local girl, Susan Landau. She was a perfect match for him. Since the death of his father, Axe had felt alone in the world. In Susan, who had lost two brothers to illness, he found a partner that shared with him a common understanding of life's deep setbacks. They understood each other in a way few others could. They had long talks. They took care of each other. Axe didn't feel so alone anymore. Before long, they married.

Three years later, Susan gave birth to their first child, Lauren. But before the little girl had reached her first birthday, she was hit hard by epileptic seizures. Having already been through so much grief in their lives, this hardly seemed fair. Axe and Susan were still young newlyweds, trying to build their life together. Now they would also struggle to take care of Lauren, who required constant care. For Susan, her daughter's illness would become a life mission, trying somehow to balance Lauren's needs while raising their other two children and embarking on a political crusade for epilepsy research. It tied them all together. In hardship and joy, his family became Axe's anchor in life.

The One Guy I Never Want to See Lobbing Grenades at Me Again

Axelrod's years as a journalist gave him a lot of insight into the complex machine that was Chicago politics. His network of sources, friends and allies continued to grow. But even as his career blossomed, he knew deep down that he wasn't meant for a career in journalism. It was his fascination for politics that had gotten him into journalism in the first place, and it was that same fascination that made him leave.

With the 1984 election cycle approaching, Congressman Paul Simon asked Axe to come work for him as his communication director. Simon had set his eyes on a US Senate seat. At first Axe hesitated, but when Simon won the heavily contested Democratic Primary, he decided to take the plunge. He admired Simon, a liberal who had dropped out of college and bought a little newspaper in Troy, Illinois. He had used the paper to crusade against a local gambling syndicate. Not being able to persuade anyone to challenge local officials beholden to the mob, Simon had run himself and won a seat in the state legislature.

The 29-year-old Axelrod understood that Simon wanted him as much for the vast network he had built as a journalist, as his political abilities.

"We had a good relationship, and he apparently felt my contacts and cachet as a political writer for the state's largest paper would redound to his benefit." The shrewdness of the move didn't dampen Axe's admiration for the candidate. "Even as the amiable Simon maintained friendships with machine Democrats, he was a steadfast voice for reform in a legislature dominated by politicians who profited handsomely from the corrupt status quo," he remembered.[345]

Axe had been hired as the communication director, but after an internal shake up, Simon promoted him to be his campaign manager. It was his first campaign as a political operative – and now he was running it. Axe befriended another young operative working on the campaign, the energetic, merciless, hard-driving 24-year-old Rahm Emanuel. (Emanuel would go on to become Clinton's chief of fundraising, engineer the Democrat's takeover of the House of Representatives, serve as President Obama's Chief of Staff, and get elected Mayor of Chicago.) He was also impressed by the 26-year-old Forrest Claypool, whom he made his lieutenant.

The election battle was fought between Simon and Republican incumbent Charles Percy. Axe put his researcher to work collecting all the information on Percy they could get their hands on. Watching Illinois races closely from the outside for years, he had learnt how the naive campaigns most often faltered. A campaign was war, you had to be willing to do what was necessary to win. The relentless drive and ambition he had inherited from his mother was an inescapable part of him. Behind his soft demeanor and idealistic world view, Axe was every bit as shrewd and brutal as he needed to be to succeed.

In his autobiography, he admits that he went after all parts of Percy's record, "however obscure," mentioning one telling example:

> *An abstruse technical vote he had cast in committee...allowed us to say that Percy had cast the deciding vote in favor of President Carter's grain embargo against the Russians that Congressman Simon had opposed. This would become fodder for press hits, direct mail, and TV ads in normally Republican downstate Illinois, where grain farmers abounded.*

If he could pin something damaging on Percy, he would.

Opponents came to learn that a fight with Axe was no walk in the park. One who was left bloodied on the battlefield was famed Republican strategist Ed Rollins. He concluded that of all the Democratic operatives he had come up against, Axe was on the very top of his list of "guys I never want to see lobbing grenades at me again."[346] Axelrod was becoming known for his take-no-prisoners approach, always going after the jugular. The fight against Percy was no exception. His hardball politics paid off. Even as President Reagan swept Illinois in a landslide, Simon won the Senate seat. Axe had delivered his first win.

During the election season of '84, there was another valuable lesson to be learnt as well. At that year's Democratic Convention, Mario Cuomo, who had been elected Mayor of New York just two years earlier, gave a memorable keynote speech. With clarity and vigor, Cuomo rallied millions behind his powerful vision of a warmer and more inclusive America. The speech made him an instant celebrity and lifted his status on national stage.

"I learned from his star turn how, overnight, a single, soaring convention speech, viewed by tens of millions, could instantly transform a relatively unknown politician into a potential presidential candidate," Axe later wrote. He made a mental note of the immense impact of a perfectly delivered convention speech.[347]

After guiding Simon to victory, Axelrod and Claypool formed Axelrod and Associates. Trying to build their venture into a successful business, they begged their way into long-shot races for small, local offices. One was for Chuck Bernardini, a candidate for the Cook County Board of Commissioners. To help his candidate break through the media noise and get noticed in the myriad of races and candidates, Axe wrote a series of playful radio ads. He got a local improv actor named Dan Castellano to do the voice. Castellano would become famous a few years later as the voice of Homer Simpson from the popular TV show. Bernardini won his race.

Axe's reputation as an effective, smart, and hard-hitting operative continued to grow. Time and time again he proved that he would go to great lengths to achieve victory. When *Chicago Magazine* wrote the first major profile on him, they titled it, "Hatchet Man: The Rise of David Axelrod."[348] So, when Democratic Chicago Mayor Harold Washington against huge odds decided to run for reelection in 1987, he knew whom to turn to. He hired the Hatchet Man.

City politics in Chicago had always been a blood sport. The Democratic mayoral primary looked especially daunting, with several fractions inside the party ganging up to oust Washington, who was the first black mayor of the city.

"This is going to be a brawl," the mayor told Axelrod. "These guys will do anything to beat me."[349] What really pissed off some of Washington's opponents was his fight to end the old corrupt patronage system.

But Washington had a strategist who knew how to maneuver through this particular battlefield. Axe developed a strategy that entailed building a winning coalition based on the nearly unanimous support from the black community, a solid Hispanic majority, and enough white votes to carry the mayor over the finishing line. Everything from the grassroot organization to the campaign's carefully crafted message was aimed at convincing these selected voter-groups. This voter coalition proved strong enough to brush aside all of Washington's challengers in the primary and gave him 54 percent in the general election.

"I would say that Barack Obama stood on Harold Washington's shoulders," Axe reminisced. "Had Washington not been elected Mayor in 1983, I don't know that the political conditions would have been there for Barack Obama to rise in Illinois politics the way he did."[350]

Washington's '87 campaign was important in another way, too. It was here that Axe first constructed a strategy of building a winning coalition between the black community, Hispanic voters, and a necessary share of the white vote – the same strategy he years later used to carry Obama to victory in the contest for the White House. It is a well-known fact that most good strategists that make it on the national stage, have developed and honed their approach in local and state races for years before succeeding. Axe was no exception.

That same year, he also ran message and strategy for his old friend, Paul Simon, who had now entered the race for president. The jug-eared, bow-tied, liberal Senator stood little chance in the age of Reagan, of course. But by the time he lost the first primary contest in Iowa and bowed out of the race, Axe had developed a strong message for Simon focusing on hope and change under the slogan, "Isn't it time to believe again?"

It was a message he would develop further in the years to come, seeing how many voters – even when dismissing Simon as a future president – got fired up by the vision of real change and thrilled by a candidate who had the audacity to believe in it. Not surprisingly, Simon's candidacy burst into flames and crashed almost before leaving the ground. Axe had gotten his first taste of how different and demanding a presidential campaign could be. It appealed to him. And now he had some ideas of how to build one around a message of real change.

What made Axelrod and Associates famous was their work on a range of successful mayoral campaigns. One was the campaign of Chicago's Richard M. Daley, the son of late Mayor Daley, who under Axelrod's guidance followed in his father's footsteps. Another was Cleveland mayoral candidate Michael White. Once again, Axelrod built his campaign on the basis of a message of change and of hope for a less divided community coming together.

White was a long-shot come-from-nothing candidate who surprised the pundits by winning the democratic primary. Wanting to get ahead of what looked to be a ferocious general election contest, Axe wrote a brilliant script for a television ad that could foreshadow the anticipated attacks. In the spot, White told Clevelanders:

> *The experts said that our campaign was a dream that would end in the primary, but thanks to you the dream is alive. A dream of a Cleveland that rises above racial politics and name-*

calling. A dream of One City, working together to fight drugs, crime, poor schools and neighborhood decline. In these final weeks, the forces of division will launch their last stand. They will say or do anything to keep us from working together. But, you know, it's hard to stop a dream whose time has come!

By defining the attacks before they had even been launched, he had in effect framed them as proof of White's authentic struggle for change. In one clever stroke, he had given his candidate armor against the expected onslaught. White won in a landslide.

There were a myriad of lessons that could be picked up from running campaigns in the big cities. But Axelrod couldn't shake off his craving for larger prey. His reputation as the ultimate "change"-strategist made him a hot commodity in the Democratic Party. When Bill Clinton started his run for the '92 presidential nomination, he reached out to Axelrod for a meeting. Axe was immediately taken with Clinton.

"He was palpably brilliant, but as a southerner with a great personal story, he spoke in a colloquial way folks could grasp," he wrote, adding:

Moreover, Clinton shared my view that to win, the Democratic party had to update its vision and speak to (as well as for) an increasingly embattled middle class. ... If his purpose was to corral me, Clinton succeeded halfway through that first meeting.[351]

In the weeks leading up to Clinton's campaign launch, Axe traveled to Little Rock, for one-on-one meetings with Clinton. They kept in touch, and after Clinton won the Democratic Primary, he was offered a job as the campaign's communication director. He pondered the opportunity. This could be the chance of a lifetime. But the thought of leaving his wife and kids was too much. His family needed him around.

His daughter Lauren still suffered severe epileptic seizures. More than once, David and his wife Susan would rush into her room at night. They would sit by their little girl as she had repeated seizures, again and again, coming around just long enough to grab her mother's hand and cry out, "Mommy, make them stop!" Sitting like that, feeling totally powerless in the darkness by their daughter's bed, he and his wife would cry together.[352] Axe knew this was not the time to leave his family for a 24/7, yearlong campaign. He told Clinton no.

Trying to spend as much time as possible with his family while also maintaining his business, he spent most of the '90s working for candidates like Congressman Patrick Kennedy, Congressman Dan Rostenkowski, Congressman Rod Blagojevich, and Governor Tom Vilsack. It was an impressive slate of candidates and victories that kept him in the top tier on the list of the most sought-after political Democratic consultants.

As the upcoming 2000 presidential election campaign approached, Vice President Al Gore called Axelrod, inviting him to Washington to talk about joining his campaign. This time, Susan urged him to go see Gore.

"The kids are older now," she said. "We can manage. If you miss another chance, you don't know when, or if, the next one will come along."[353]

He decided to go for it. But just as he was about to accept Gore's offer, doctors found out Susan had breast cancer. They had gone through so much misery in their life, it sometimes seemed there would be no end to it. Even though the prognosis was good, the illness was a wake-up call. Again, Axe turned down the offer of a presidential campaign.

In hindsight, it seems faith had other plans for him.

When He Speaks, It's Like - It's Like Magic

He liked Gore. Still, it wasn't just that the timing had been bad. For a future run, another candidate was simmering in Axe's mind. Someone he felt really good about. Someone he knew could go a long way. A young man with both great potential and great ambitions. A person that shared Axe's relentless drive to win. A man who would not only hire him to play a central role in his campaign, but *the* central role.

Axelrod had first met Barack Obama only as a favor to a friend. The meeting took place in '92, after Obama had graduated from Harvard Law School. At Harvard, Barack had become the first African American to lead the prestigious Harvard Law Review. After returning to Chicago, he was organizing a voter registration drive focused on minority voters. It was democratic activist Bettylu Saltzman who had called Axe to set up the meeting. Saltzman told him she thought Obama could even become the first black President.

Saltzman was a liberal stalwart and an important player in Democratic politics in Chicago. She had inherited a fortune from her father, a Chicago-area builder, and had a vast array of contacts and friends, yielding her significant influence. She also ran the Chicago-based office of Senator Paul Simon for several years, forging a close relation to Axelrod in the process. Completely smitten with Obama, she wanted Axe to help the young man succeed.

"When he speaks, it's like – it's like magic," she fawned.

A nod from Saltzman was no small feat, and Axe went to the meeting with Obama intrigued. Even if he wasn't as thunderstruck as Saltzman, he left their first encounter duly impressed, sensing that Obama had an innate talent for politics. Then, Obama went after a state senate seat in '96 and Axe got to see his savvier side. It became obvious that the young man was made of the kind of material needed to play successfully in the hardball world of politics.

An opportunity arose for Obama when Illinois State Senator Alice Palmer, who came from Obama's South Side district was seeking a US Congress seat. She announced that she would not be seeking reelection to the state senate. With her help, Obama launched his own campaign to succeed her. Palmer lent Obama her endorsement and help, but when she lost her bid for the national stage in a special election, she rescinded her pledge to leave the state senate and asked Barack to pull out of the race.

But Obama – who by now had been gearing up for the campaign – refused, even though he knew he was in for a hell of a nomination fight. Palmer would be a formidable adversary, being an established political figure in the district with a lot of contacts and a solid list of donors. So, the savvy Obama took another route, trying to avoid a primary fight with Palmer by instead challenging her hastily prepared candidacy petitions. He won the legal fight, and Palmer was thrown off the ballot for lack of sufficient signatures.

By challenging his popular former ally and going after her in such a controversial fashion, basically killing her political career on a technically, Obama had shown his shrewd competitive inner core and his formidable strength. Axelrod saw in Obama a candidate who just had to win and who would go to unusual lengths to beat his competition, even when it was a former ally.

"In ending her career to launch his own, Barack had engaged in the bare-knuckle politics that they didn't teach at Harvard," Axe remembered. "Clearly he could be though, unsentimental, and even bruising when the situation demanded."[354] This time, Axe was *really* impressed.

When Obama ended up winning both the primary and the election, Axe decided this was a horse he could bet on – and bet big. The two started working more closely together, developing a friendship as well as a tight professional relationship. They sparred over strategy and message. And through their new alliance, a real friendship sprouted.

Time and time again, Obama proved to be every bit the political warrior Axelrod had seen in him. One example came when Illinois Democrats, after toiling in the minority in the Illinois Senate, gerrymandered the state to produce a Democratic majority. While drafting the new political map, Obama helped redraw his own district northward to include some of Chicago's wealthiest citizens, making the district a powerful financial and political base that he could use in later campaigns.[355] It was just one example of how Obama and Axe were always thinking ahead.

As the 2004 election cycle approached, Axelrod had been honing his great strategic abilities for more than two decades. His mastery of message and strategy would give any candidate that hired him an edge over his competitors. All the big players in Illinois knew what an asset Axel was. Wrote Obama biographer David Mendel:

> *Each serious candidate in the 2004 Senate contest ranked Axelrod the overwhelming first choice among media advisors to hire. ...In being the most sought-after advisor, Axelrod was dealing from a position of extreme power when selecting an employer. No one grasped the demographic and political dynamics of the entire state and urban Chicago as astutely as Axelrod. ...The candidate who won his services would have the sharpest, most ruthless political mind in the state at his disposal, immediately providing that person with a huge advantage amid a competitive field.*[356]

When Obama decided to launch his bid for a US Senate seat in 2004, Axe at first cautioned him. He suggested they should make him mayor of Chicago instead, which would be a more solid platform for a future national career. But Obama didn't waver. He craved the national stage more than Axelrod. He wanted the US Senate seat. And he wanted it now. Obama was intelligent enough, competitive enough, more than hungry enough, and willing to gamble his political career in one bold move.

Obama had a compelling life story that had not yet been conveyed to the large mass of voters. This meant Axe was free to shape his overall message in a way he couldn't with someone who was already defined in the public eye. Obama shared his strategist's deep conviction that what voters wanted more than anything was a message of real change. Axe had honed this message for more than a decade, shaping it into a political tool used to build new coalitions of voters. Now he had identified his one-man army, the force that could put all of Axe's knowledge and strategic mastery to use: Barack Obama.

Their first big decision was how to handle the upcoming US Senate vote on the authorization of military action in Iraq. It had been just a year since the devastating attacks on 9/11. Betty Saltzman had invited Obama to speak at an antiwar rally in Chicago. He was clearly against the war, but he needed Axelrod's guidance. He didn't know whether he should attend the rally. In the short-term tactical view, he should clearly stay away and not openly oppose a war in Iraq. The majority of the voters were supporting the war, rallying behind their president in a time of crisis. So were most prominent Democrats.

But such short-term goals didn't fit in with Axe's and Obama's long-term strategy: Building Obama as the torchbearer for real change. Building such an image included saying unpopular things that could cost them support in the short run, if they thought it would help in the long run. Trusting his instincts, Axelrod told Obama to go to the rally and speak his mind. He did.

Obama told the crowd he wasn't against all wars;

> *What I am opposed to is the cynical attempt by...armchair, weekend warriors in [the Bush] administration to shove their own ideological agendas down our throats, irrespective of the cost in lives lost and in hardships borne. What I am opposed to is political hacks like Karl Rove to distract us from a rice in the uninsured, a rise in the poverty rate, a drop in the median income... That's what I'm opposed to. A dumb war. A rash war.*[357]

There and then, the speech didn't seem all that important. But as time passed by and Democratic voters changed their views on the Iraq invasion, the speech elevated Obama's reputation. This was a guy who would stand by his convictions even at a time when most other Democratic leaders didn't dare. This was a guy that embodied change.

Obama Delivers

On January 2003, Axelrod called the press conference where Obama announced his candidacy for the US Senate. To make sure everyone understood this was a strong and credible candidate, they worked hard at local endorsements and fundraising. This time, too, as with Simon years before, it was clear to Axe that he was not the only one capitalizing on their relationship; "[Obama] knew that I had credibility with the state's political players and press corps. If I were willing to bet on him, Obama bluntly acknowledged, others would give him a longer look."[358] Axe knew he brought the heavyweight image to Obama's candidacy, as well as his strategic savvy.

Axelrod's unique talent for producing television commercials that highlighted the best sale points of a candidate is perhaps unsurpassed. For the primary campaign, he decided to keep a lock on their money, spending on TV only in the last three weeks of the campaign. This way, he could define his candidate in the public conciseness in those last weeks when the voters really began paying attention. Axe's goal was to make the voters see Obama as the only real change candidate.

One of the most memorable ads had the candidate telling the viewers:

They said an African-American had never led the Harvard Law Review. Until I changed that. In the state senate, they said we couldn't force insurance companies to cover routine mammograms. But we did. They said we couldn't find the money to cover uninsured children, or give tax relief to the working poor, or pass new laws to stop wrongful executions. But I have. Now they say we can't change Washington. I'm Barack Obama, I'm running for the United States Senate, and I approved this message to say: Yes We Can!

All the ads Axe made for Obama in the 2004 cycle ended with the "Yes We Can" slogan, which became an Obama-Axelrod trademark and would capture the worlds imagination four years later. It was a message of change that the Democratic voters were hungry for. Obama ended up winning an amazing 53 percent of the vote in the seven-candidate primary race. He did well in most voter segments. The breadth of Obama's support impressed even his chief strategist.

"The most surprising and gratifying thing was when those numbers rolled in on primary night," Axe wrote. "What those numbers meant was that we had passed a Rubicon in the politics of [Illinois], where a guy could come along who was an African American candidate, but who had universal appeal and people were willing to look beyond race."

In the general election, Obama faced off with Jack Ryan, a formidable rising star in the Republican Party. Ryan had formerly worked both at Casa Juan Diego, a refugee camp for Latinos fleeing the Central American civil wars, as well as climbing to be a partner at Goldman Sachs. In addition to embodying both compassion and ambition, he had tons of charisma.

But Ryan had an Achilles heel – his divorce five years earlier from famed actress Jeri Ryan. The former couple had agreed to not make the custody records public, because they felt these contained details that could be harmful to their son if released. During the GOP primary, Ryan's opponents began pushing for the release of the records. So did *The Chicago Tribune* and WLS-TV, the local ABC affiliate, who took the case to court. There were whispers that Axe was spurring them on.

In late March of 2004, a Los Angeles judge ruled that several of the custody records should be opened to the press and the public. The files contained statements that Ryan took his then wife to sex clubs in New York, New Orleans, and Paris in the late 1990s, where he allegedly insisted that the two have public sex, which his wife had angrily refused. The documents also contained juicy detailed descriptions of the sex clubs in mention.

Obama publicly called on fellow Democrats to refrain from trying to inject the divorce files into the campaign, telling *The Chicago Sun-Times*, "I don't think it's an appropriate topic for debate."[359]

But prominent figures from Ryan's own party kept hammering him. Representative Ray LaHood said that Ryan "needs to immediately withdraw from the race," and Ryan's former primary opponent Jim Oberweis said, "If the allegations made were true, it would end the candidacy."

Many of his fellow Republicans in Washington left him for dead. An advisor to President Bush said that the revelation made it more likely the Bush-Cheney campaign would steer clear of Illinois.[360] Even talk-show-host Jay Leno got in a shot, joking, "Jack Ryan, I've heard of going after the 'swing vote' but this is ridiculous."[361]

Dismissing all ethical standards, the media gorged in the personal details of the former couple – even though they both had fought together in court to keep it a personal matter, insisting publication would hurt their son.

It was a media storm that was impossible to fight. Ryan's ex-wife released a statement calling him a good man and a loving father, saying she had "no doubt that he will make an excellent senator."[362] But it was too late. One week after the custody records were opened, Ryan was forced to pull out of the race. It had been a successful ambush by the press, but also a brutal and undignified one. Said Senator Fitzgerald, "I think the public stoning of Jack Ryan is one of the most grotesque things I've seen in politics."[363]

Ryan's departure left the Illinois GOP in complete disarray. As the Republicans argued over how to tackle the crisis, Obama got a telephone call that would change his life. Axelrod had never forgotten the elevation of New York Mayor Mario Cuomo to national prominence after his successful Democratic Convention speech 20 years earlier. For some time, he been maneuvering to get Obama up on that stage, lobbying high party officials to win his candidate a key speaking slot at the Democratic National Convention in Boston in 2004.[364] He was sure such an opportunity could elevate Obama into national prominence much like it had Cuomo.

John Kerry, the Democratic presidential nominee, had campaigned with Obama in Illinois. He had been impressed by Obama's style and the enthusiastic crowds. Now, the phone rang. Obama got the opportunity of his lifetime. Axe and his candidate threw themselves into writing what they hoped would be a memorable speech.

It turned out to be far better than memorable. It proved perhaps the best convention speeches since William Jennings Bryan captured the Democratic nomination on the basis of his speech alone, 108 years earlier. Obama bewitched the convention hall in Boston and millions of Americans watching at home. He told his life story, crafted in simple language. He spoke of hope and change:

> Tonight is a particular honor for me because, let's face it, my presence on this stage is pretty unlikely. My father was a foreign student, born and raised in a small village in Kenya. ... [My mother] was born in a town on the other side of the world, in Kansas. ...My parents shared not only an improbable love; they shared an abiding faith in the possibilities of this nation. They would give me an African name, Barack, or 'blessed', believing that in a tolerant America your name is no barrier to success. They imagined me going to the best schools in the land, even though they weren't rich, because in a generous America you don't have to be rich to achieve your potential...

Obama went on to speak of people he had met campaigning throughout Illinois, describing the challenges they faced, their dreams and hopes. He told the enthusiastic crowd:

> Yet even as we speak, there are those who are preparing to divide us, the spin masters and negative ad peddlers who embrace the politics of anything goes. Well, I say to them tonight, there's not a liberal America and a conservative America - there's the United States of America. There's not a black America and white America and Latino America and Asian America; there's the United States of America. ...There are patriots who

opposed the war in Iraq and patriots who supported it. We are one people, all of us pledging allegiance to the stars and stripes, all of us defending the United States of America.

Underscoring the very essence of the Obama-Axelrod mantra, Obama went on:

In the end, that's what this election is about. Do we participate in a politics of cynicism or a politics of hope? ... I'm not talking about blind optimism here ... I'm talking about something more substantial. It's the hope of slaves sitting around a fire singing freedom songs; the hope of immigrants setting out for distant shores; the hope of a young naval lieutenant bravely patrolling the Mekong Delta; ...the hope of a skinny kid with a funny name who believes that America has a place for him, too.[365]

The delegates on the convention floor erupted in pandemonium. Axe knew that the speech had captured the hearts of millions of Americans – many of whom would be voting in the presidential primary four years later.

Back in Illinois, *The Chicago Sun-Times* declared, "Obama delivers!" *The Chicago Tribune* nicknamed Obama, "The Phenom." The magical performance also helped the fundraising efforts significantly, giving Axelrod a large war chest to get his message out.

Disillusioned and in disarray, the Illinois GOP still needed a candidate to run against Obama in the US Senate race after Ryan's sudden departure. But the post-speech Obama tidal wave was enough to scare away all credible Republican contenders. In desperation, they finally settled on Alan Keys, a big-mouthed African American radio talk show host. Keys was the opposite of the normally moderate, soft-spoken Republicans that Illinois voters were used to. And he used what was left of the campaign to voice his views vehemently. As Keys grabbed the headlines with his inflaming political ramblings, many moderate Republican voters fled in disgust.

On election night, Axe felt happier than he had for a long time. Obama captured a staggering 70 percent of the vote. Wrote Obama biographer David Mendel, "In Chicago, political insiders marveled at how artfully Axelrod and Obama's brain trust had managed his campaign amid the truly bizarre circumstances of the race..." Most were equally impressed.

"It was a thing of beauty to watch from the outside, like watching a play that David Axelrod had written, with all the acts progressing into each one another perfectly," another Chicago operative said in admiration.[366]

John Street and John Edwards

Amid the Obama US Senate campaign of 2004, Axelrod had also handled several other candidates. He helped advise his friend Rahm Emanuel's race for the US Congress, and he got Governor Tom Vilsack reelected in Iowa. One particularly clever move came in the reelection campaign of Mayor John F. Street of Philadelphia.

As the race entered its last month, Axe got an unusual call from Street's deputy, saying they had found a listening device in the mayor's office. The bug obviously belonged to the United

States government. A candidate under investigation by the Justice Department would have been any other every political consultant's worst nightmare. But where others saw the makings of defeat, Axelrod saw a huge opportunity.

By now, the Iraq War wasn't turning out like the Bush administration had promised. Instead of a clear and solid victory, it was evident that the American military was becoming mired in sectarian warfare with no clear end in sight. More and more, people felt betrayed or let down by the Bush administration. The president's poll numbers plummeted. Axe knew that "in an overwhelmingly Democratic town, a probe launched by the Republican Justice Department in Washington would surely be greeted by skepticism, perhaps even outrage." Especially so when it was targeted at a Democratic Mayor in the midst of an election.

Axe told Street to hastily call a news conference on the steps of City Hall, to accuse the Republican's in Washington of trying to steal the local election through dirty tricks. He wrote a memorable line for the Mayor: "I'm happy to speak into a microphone I can see."

Axe's maneuvering worked like a charm and carried Street to victory. Or as the headline in *The Philadelphia Daily News* put it; "We Interrupt This Probe for a Landslide!"[367]

Later that year *PoliticsPA* named Mayor Street "Politician of the Year," stating, "It takes an extremely shrewd and effective politician to turn an FBI bugging of the mayor's office into a positive…"[368] But that was exactly what Axe had done.

That same year, he also had a brief stint with John Edwards primary campaign for the presidential nomination. He clashed with both the candidate and the candidate's wife, none of whom understood how they could capitalize on his ability to shape a candidate's image. Axe resolved to never again work on a presidential race unless he had a close, trusting relationship with the candidate that could yield a high degree of influence. And he knew he didn't need to compromise. He had his candidate: With a compelling life story, Barack Obama had adopted Axe's message of hope and change, essentially making it his own. Obama was smart, determined and competitive, and had shown how far he was willing to go and how hard he was willing to work.

By now, Obama was also a political celebrity, having captured the hearts and minds of the nation with his once-in-a-lifetime convention speech. He had captured his Senate seat in a breathtaking landslide – especially impressive in a year when Democrats lost both the presidency and seats in both houses of Congress. Most importantly, Obama always listened to Axe, valuing and mostly following his strategist's advice. It was all the materials Axe needed to build a new platform for a presidential run.

Change, Change, Change

Throughout the 2006 midterm election season, Axe continued working for other clients, but his eyes never strayed from Obama. In the late fall of that year, he wrote a 12-page strategic memo focusing on how they could win the 2008 presidential race.

"The most influential politician in 2008 won't be on the ballot," Axe concluded, continuing:

His name is George W Bush. ...Now we are entering a campaign that will be defined by vivid perceptions of Bush, his record and his style of leadership. And that's our opportunity. Where Bush is hyper-partisan, ideological and unyielding, voters will be looking for the next leader to rally and unify the country around our common interests and mutual obligations as Americans.

In the memo, Axelrod went on to tell Obama that the time had come for their brand of politics.

The bottom line is this: Voters are primed to turn the page and choose a candidate who offers an inspiring, inclusive, confident and HOPEFUL vision for America ... They want to believe again in themselves, their country and their future.[369]

Running through Obama's most likely opponents, Axe wrote:

Hillary Clinton is a formidable candidate, who should be considered the frontrunner for the nomination because of her strength, intellect, discipline, and of course, access to an array of assets far in excess of any other candidate. ...But for all her advantages, she is not a healing figure...making herself the candidate of the future will be a challenge.

At the time, this conclusion was running against the conventional wisdom. Most pundits believed that voters in times of war always seek towards tested and proven leaders, like Hillary. Not Axelrod. His conclusion showed some of his remarkable strategic insights. In 2008, voters would be more focused on change than experience. And he would make sure that real change would be personified by Obama.

Of the Democratic nominees' Republican opponents, he wrote:

The GOP hierarchy...seems resigned to McCain. But his nomination won't come without a fight or a cost. ...And at the age of 73, he also will have a problem presenting himself as the candidate of the future. McCain is formidable, to be sure. But he is not unbeatable.

Finally, Axe ended the memo by strongly rejecting the counsel of those advising Obama to get more experience in national politics before running for president. He told Obama:

You will never be hotter than you are right now. And with the longevity favored by the Washington establishment comes all the baggage. You could wind up calcified in the Senate, with a voting record that hangs from your neck like the anchor from Lusitania.

Axe didn't sugarcoat the challenges of a presidential campaign, but his advice was unequivocal. After working through the ups and downs with his wife, Obama finally heeded his strategist's advice. He was all in.[370]

Their first move was to set up the top team of a presidential Obama campaign. Drawing a parallel between himself and the character Danny Ocean from the movie *Ocean's Eleven*, who also gather a team of highly skilled specialists to achieve his goals, Axe set out to create what he dubbed a "dream team" of consultants, recruiting among others Larry Grisolano, Joel Benenson, David

Binder, and Jim Margolis. These four became the core of his force. They would develop and execute the overall strategy, under Axe's leadership. Robert Gibbs and Dan Pfeiffer were also an important part of the media handling team, while the enormous task of getting the campaign operations to run smoothly had already been handed over to Axe's long-time partner, the operational genius David Plouffe. With his dream team all fired up and ready to go, Axe went to work.

On February 10, 2007, Obama announced his candidacy. He stood outside the Old State Capitol building in Springfield, Illinois, where Abraham Lincoln had delivered his House Divided speech.

"Look, I recognize that there is a certain presumptuousness in this, a certain audacity, to this announcement," he told the large crowd that had gathered on that chilly winter day:

> I know that I haven't spent a lot of time learning the ways of Washington. But I've been there long enough to know that the ways of Washington must change. ...Each and every time, a new generation has risen up and done what's needed to be done. Today we are called once more, and it is time for our generation to answer that call. For that is our unyielding faith - that in the face of impossible odds, people who love their country can change it.[371]

The theme was pure Axelrod. He had even written the defining line, which answered the criticism of Obama's lack of tenure in Washington; "I know that I haven't spent a lot of time learning the ways of Washington. But I've been there long enough to know that the ways of Washington must change."[372] You could sum up Axelrod's strategy and overriding message in this one word: Change. Axe had used this theme as the strategic basis for campaigns many times before, and he knew exactly how to build a successful strategy and campaign around it, crafting it into so much more than a mere slogan.

The results of the 2006 midterm elections, in which the Democrats had retaken majorities in both houses of Congress, was also a good indication that 2008 would be a "change election," much like the 1992 election that had swept Bill Clinton into the White House. The pollster Peter Hart found that three-quarters of the country wanted the next president's approach to be different from Bush. In other words, a change of party wasn't enough for many voters. They wanted a change of *approach*. Hart sensed that this would be a year where authenticity was particularly salient.

Hart's conclusions fitted perfectly with the image Obama had been cultivating for years. Axe perfected three different tactics to persuade voters that his candidate was a credible champion for change. First, present new policies. Second, talk about fighting special interest. Third, say things people didn't want to hear.[373] These were intended to boost Obamas credibility. They also put the Clintons, who had been around for so long and taken so much special interest money, on the spot.

Early on, the Clinton campaign made two major strategic mistakes. Their first was executing what Clinton's campaign manager Patti Solis Doyle called a "shock and awe" strategy, aimed at scaring off opponents early, by delivering big endorsements, early primary victories, and a huge lead in fundraising. When this strategy fell apart – after Obama won in Iowa and surged in endorsements and fundraising – the Clinton campaign had no real backup plan, and essentially had to wing it for the rest of the race. That was almost like flying blind.

The second major mistake was when Hillary made the unprecedented move of giving her chief strategist Mark Penn the dual roles of both chief strategist and chief pollster. Penn was a brilliant strategist, but even brilliant strategist gets it wrong sometimes and needs correction. By giving him control over the interpretations of every poll, a crucial corrective was lost. By contrast, Axe had made sure to recruit some of the best pollsters around, all of whom continually challenged his assumptions and tactical moves.

There was also a fundamental difference between Axelrod's and Penn's strategic approaches. Axe believed strongly that a campaign needs one single, clear overreaching theme. This should work with several different groups of voters and would be the foundation of all other strategic and tactical decisions. For him, this was "change." If something didn't fit under that overreaching theme, it wouldn't be part of their agenda.

Penn on the other hand, was shaped by his experience from working under Dick Morris during the 1996 campaign to reelect President Clinton. This meant his approach was completely opposite to Axe's. Penn dismissed overall themes aimed at creating or feeding off of a specific mood in the electorate, as mere slogans. Instead, he was constantly searching for programs and policies that could appeal to small micro-slices of voters without much regard to the overall picture.

From the 2004 and 2006 campaigns he had worked on, Axe's most essential takeaway was that the Internet was turning political communications into a two-way exchange. A new form of dialogue had arisen between the candidate (i.e. the campaign leadership) and the voters. Even more important, this could be used to communicate with the thousands of activists working on the ground. He and Plouffe saw to it that the 2008 campaign took full advantage of this technology, using peer-to-peer communication for persuasion, get out the vote efforts, and fundraising.

Axe knew that between 2001 and 2004, Karl Rove had been developing improved methods for getting out the vote. Rove's research had proved that getting contacted by someone who knew the targeted voter or was affiliated with the same church or social group as her or him, were vastly more effective than calls from someone without these common ties. Using this insight, the Obama campaign – as the first campaign to ever do so – developed a bottom-up approach that combined grassroots organizing and social media. By May 2007, the campaign was already running a three-day school called Camp Obama, where unpaid volunteers learned how to use personal contacts, stories, and examples to engage and convince voters effectively.[374]

Their first challenge was Iowa. The Obama campaign understood that if they were to have any chance against the establishment candidates, they needed to make a real show of force in the Hawkeye state. Axe's strategy was as hard to execute as it was simple to understand. While Clinton argued she was the Democrats' best bet to *win* the partisan war against the Republicans, Obama would argue he was *above* the partisan war fare. Axe's bet was simply that the country was tired of the partisan warfare in Washington. All the other contenders in the Democratic primary wanted to compete with Clinton on her terms, on who played the partisan game best. Obama would compete on completely different terms; advocating an end to partisan warfare. This was how he would stand out.

At first glance, such a strategy might seem to rise above dirty tactics. But that was only in the optics. Axelrod wasn't shy about going after Hillary. Even before surveying his opposition research, he knew her weak spots. Having worked on her Senate race in New York in 2000, he had seen her vulnerabilities in her own research. He especially remembered the apprehension among voters who thought of her as being calculating and slippery with the truth. The trick was to revive the voters' worst memories of her, the negatives that were bubbling just below the surface of her popularity, by inciting it subtly, using implication and inference. It was a cunning approach.[375]

While the battle between the candidates still raged in Iowa, he wrote Obama a memo where he advised him to attack Clinton. In the memo, Axe wrote that all campaign communications, even the new slogan they had created – Change We Can Believe In – had to emphasize distinctions with Clinton on character rather than on policy. Meaning you couldn't really trust Hillary as an agent of change. The slogan "was intended to frame the argument along the character fault line, and this is where we can and must win this fight," the memo said.

Axe wanted the campaign to paint Hillary as an untrustworthy liar, too calculating to be trusted with the mantle of leadership.

"Clinton can't be trusted or believed when it comes to change," because "she's driven by political calculation not conviction, regularly backing away and shifting positions," Axe wrote. "She embodies trench warfare vs. Republicans, and is consumed with beating them rather than unifying the country and building consensus to get things done."[376] By going after Clinton's character, he wanted to demobilize her support, whilst portraying Obama as the only real alternative to the partisan warfare of Washington.

This message was hammered into voters at every opportunity. One of the main battlegrounds of the Iowa contest was the Jefferson-Jackson Day dinner, where all the candidates would give their speeches to a large crowd of Democratic activists. The JJ dinner was seen as a testing ground for the different campaign's abilities to organize and mobilize its supporters, traits that would be essential on caucus day when Iowans selected their candidates. Nearly 10,000 people jammed into the gym for the event, and at the end of the night, Axe felt they had nailed it. To him, the highlight of the day was a raucous march from the campaign headquarters to the arena, several blocks away.

"It was led by a smiling, playful Barack and Michelle, who danced along to the beat of a local drum corps, followed by a sea of delirious supporters," Axe said.

Obama delivered a speech that went for Hillary's jugular, just as Axe had urged him to. The speech had been road tested it a week before in South Carolina. Without mentioning her name directly, Obama drew a stark contrast between himself and Hillary, in difference of leadership and – just as Axe's memo had stated – implying that Clinton couldn't be trusted or believed when it came to implementing change. Obama told the crowd:

This party...has always made the biggest difference in the lives of the American people when we led, not by polls, but by principle; not by calculation, but by conviction; when we summoned the entire nation to a common purpose - a higher purpose. And I run for the Presidency of the United States of America because that's the party America needs us to be right now... A party that doesn't just offer change as a slogan, but real, meaningful change - change that America can believe in.[377]

The call to rise above the fray to summon the entire nation around a common purpose was a stark contrast to the speech that Clinton gave. It was built around the theme "Turn up the heat!" – a slogan her supporters were chanting while she spoke. Nobody in Hillary's entourage had liked it, except Penn, who claimed it tested well in his polling.

"As Harry Truman said, 'if you can't stand the heat, get out of the kitchen'," Hillary told the crowd. "And I'll tell you what, I feel really comfortable in the kitchen. ...I believe we should be turning up the heat on the Republicans; they deserve all the heat we can give them."[378]

Portraying herself as the ultimate partisan warrior, she seemed less like a national leader than Obama.

"Standing against the bleachers as Hillary spoke, I thought she had done a fine job of executing her strategy, but she had also played right into ours," Axe remembered. A couple of days later, Penn had to report to Clinton that she was in trouble. Her negatives had risen sharply in the poll after the JJ dinner.

Throughout the last month of the Iowa primary race, the polls showed Clinton and Obama head-to-head. For Obama, this was a strong showing against Clinton, who for months had been seen as the almost unbeatable frontrunner. In fact, the situation on the ground was even better for Obama than the polls revealed.

With scores of engaged activists working around the clock to rally up voter support in the upcoming caucuses, the Obama campaign had created an impressive mobilizing machine.

Their message was especially appealing to younger generations and first-time voters, who were hungry for something new and different, and who would turn out in larger numbers than most polls had predicted. From the start Axelrod and Plouffe had believed that the only way they could win against the strong established Clinton-brand, was by attracting completely new voters. This, they believed, would be easier than to persuade people to switch away from Clinton.

On caucus night, even Axe was taken by surprise by just how effective their strategy had been. Obama captured Iowa with 37.6 percent to Clinton's 29.4 percent. Everywhere in the Hawkeye State, attendance soared. Twice as many attended in 2008 as four years earlier, a total of just over 250,000 people.

"You have done what the cynics said we couldn't do," Obama told his enthusiastic supporters in his victory speech that night. "You have done what the state of New Hampshire can do in five days. ...Our time for change has come!"

The Long Brawl

To the Clinton camp, Iowa was a brutal wake up call. But those who underestimated Hillary's fighting ability were about to get a surprise. She threw herself into the battle with dedication, ferocity, and discipline like never before. She also started showing a more human side, even crying at a campaign stop when pressed on how she could keep fighting under such heavy fire. Her tears provided a moment of emotion and empathy that many voters had been waiting to see in the battle-hardened Clinton, and it certainly made her a more attractive candidate.

New Hampshire had always been good to the Clintons when they showed their vulnerable side. The state had rescued Bill Clinton's candidacy from doom back in 1992 after he got embroiled in several media driven controversies. This time around, the Granite State would help Hillary survive. Five days after losing Iowa to Obama, she captured New Hampshire with a three-point margin. Like her husband 16 years earlier, the win made her the "comeback kid" of the race. Suddenly, she had new momentum.

Obama had hoped to clutch the primary by another win in New Hampshire, but it was not to be. After he got the news of Clinton's victory, he looked at Axelrod and said with a deep sigh, "This is going to go on for a while, isn't it?"[379] That, as it turned out, was something of an understatement. For the next six months, Obama and Clinton battled it out in a political war that would go down in history as one of the fiercest Democratic primary battles in modern history. The two campaigns were locked in a drawn-out, hard-fought contest right to the very end.

"That campaign generated so much heat, it increased global warming," Bill Clinton later joked dryly.[380]

During their long primary war, both of the two combatants had their ups and downs. The biggest crisis in the Obama camp came when the media took a closer look at Reverend Jeremiah Wright, the minister from Obama's church. Wright had been a guiding presence through parts of Obama's life. In his book

Dreams from my Father, he had told the story of how one of Wrights sermons had been the inspiration behind his much-used tagline "The Audacity of Hope," which was also the title of Obama's second book. He had also said that it was Wright that "brought me to Jesus."

Now ABC News used excerpts of videotapes of Wright's sermons, showing a picture of a minister unhinged. The excerpts were incendiary and anti-white. Wright called his country the "US of KKKA," After 9/11, he told his congregation, "We bombed Hiroshima, we bombed Nagasaki, and we nuked far more than the thousands in New York and the Pentagon, and we never batted an eye... America's chickens are coming home to roost." In another sermon he railed against the injustices African Americans had suffered at the hands of white Americans, shouting "God bless America? No, no, no, not God bless America. God *damn* America!" The media ran the story in a continues loop. The press was having a field day. *The New York Post* dubbed Wright the "Minister of Hate."

Axelrod was livid. Nervously, he told the campaign's inner circle, "Do you guys understand, this could be it? This could be the whole campaign!" [381] He urged Obama to get as much distance between himself and Wright as he possibly could – as fast as humanly possible.

Obama survived the media storm only by labeling Wright's statements "inflammatory and appalling" and giving a rousing speech on race. In the speech, Obama elaborated on Wright's comments, denouncing them as "expressing a profoundly distorted view of our country" and "divisive at a time when we need unity." But in a clever twist, Obama's speech was about much more than Wright's sermons. He spoke of the history of race in America, of the living resentment between whites and people of color, and of how the country needed go forward to build a more perfect union. After reading the first draft, Axe was blown away, telling Obama, "This is why you should be president."[382] The speech was widely viewed as a defining moment of the campaign.

Another controversy that arose, though far from as damaging as the Wright incident, concerned a real estate deal. Years before, the Clintons had also taken part in a real estate deal, Whitewater, which had grown to a controversy fueled by the media. It had ended only after it had become clear that no laws had been broken. Now, it surfaced that the Obamas had taken part in their own real estate transaction. Obama had struck a deal with Tony Rezko, a Chicago developer who was a personal friend. The media – in particularly the local Chicago papers – had a lot of questions. But like in the case of Whitewater, the controversy eventually faded away when it became clear that no laws had been broken, and Obama apologized for handling the matter unwisely. Only some local reporters kept harassing him over the issue, and that didn't bother Axelrod all that much.

The earliest clashes between the Obama and Clinton campaigns were mild. Axe had told Obama not to end up in a face-to-face fight with Clinton. He had positioned his candidate above the fray, as someone who spurned ugly tactics, a harbinger of real change. So, it was important that he didn't get embroiled in an ugly fight with Clinton face to face. At first, the candidate managed to keep cool under fire. In a vain effort to show that Obama was not quite as self-sacrificing and un-ambitious as he came off, the Clinton campaign published a press release that cited an essay written by the then five-year-old Barack titled "I want to be president." But he simply brushed it off, saying, "It's silly season."

The Clinton campaign also sent out direct mail assailing Obama for voting "present" on abortion legislation in the Illinois state senate. This, too, the candidate let slide, playing it cool. For a while it, seemed like Obama would be every bit as laidback under fire as Axe urged him to be. But then things got heated up to a point where Obama simply couldn't contain himself any longer.

In the Democratic debate in Myrtle Beach, South Carolina, Hillary attacked him for having praised Ronald Reagan and the Republican's ideas of the '80s.

"That's not true," Obama snapped, "...while I was working on those streets watching those folks see their jobs shift overseas, you were a corporate lawyer sitting on the board at Wal-Mart."

People had never heard him go for his opponent's throat like this. Hillary's face went red.

"[The Republicans] did have ideas, and they were bad ideas," she shot back. "Bad for America, and I was fighting those ideas when you were practicing law and representing your contributor, Rezko, in his slum landlord business in inner-city Chicago."

It was the most personal attacks of the primary, and the debate instantly became known as the Brawl on the Beach.

As the race heated up, Axe knew this new line of tough confrontation between the two frontrunners would hurt Obama's chances. His candidate's bitter tone came off as politics as usual, not change, and gave Hillary a boost. As the state primaries progressed, neither of the two candidates were able to capture the needed majority and clutch the nomination. Axe worked 24/7 to ensure that his "Change and Hope" theme was not weakened by the skirmishes between the two prizefighters who were slugging it out in the ring.

He also worked relentlessly to ensure every part of the campaign's communications ended up painting the complete picture he wanted to leave the voters with. Every press release, every ad, every rally was designed to fit as a piece of the complete puzzle he was constructing. One of those following the campaign closely was journalist Matt Bai, who captured the strategist's essence brilliantly:

> *Mr. Axelrod is an ad guy. A man who perfected the craft of encapsulating an entire life in 30 seconds, he has a gift for telling personal stories in ways that people can understand. ...Mr. Axelrod's essential insight - the idea that has made him successful where others might have failed - is that the modern campaign really isn't about the policy arcana or the candidate's record; it's about a more visceral, more personal narrative. This is probably a big reason why Mr. Obama has, from the start, focused almost exclusively on broad themes of "hope" and "change," drawing heavily on his own life story, rather than staking out any particularly new policy ground. In its tone and emphasis, Mr. Obama's campaign reflects all the attributes of a truly great political ad: the stirring words, the beautiful pictures, the simple and elegant storyline of a ruined political system and the man whose moment has arrived.*

Bai was struck by the remarkable consistency in Axelrod's approach. Even in the speeches Obama gave after losing some states, the message stayed the same. Rather than seek to reassure viewers about his gravitas, Axe's script never changed. Wrote Bai,

"Such is the unwavering, almost defiant faith that Mr. Axelrod and his candidate have in the transformative power of their story."[383] Still, it went even deeper than Bai recognized. Those who had studied Axe's long professional history, would see that his message and his strategy always were one and the same.

Eventually Obama's lead broadened. But Hillary seemed to have found her calling in the contest itself; Never giving up, fighting it out until the bitter end, taking every blow, and then getting back up. It was almost like seeing her husband 16 years earlier. After winning the large states of Texas and Ohio, she told millions of Americans watching at home:

> For everyone here in Ohio and across America who's ever been counted out but refused to be knocked out, and for everyone who has stumbled but stood right back up, and for everyone who works hard and never gives up - this one is for you!

Axelrod's old friend Rahm Emanuel, who had a history with the Clintons, warned that quitting simply wasn't in their bloodstream.[384] Hillary kept defending her ground, even as her odds became worse by the day. The battle raged on until early June 2008, when Obama finally captured the magical number of delegates needed for a majority on the convention floor: 2,025. Shortly thereafter, Clinton finally conceded. The nomination fight of a lifetime was over. Axe's candidate had prevailed, at last.

Hillary understood the need for her and her husband to show that – with the primary battle now over – they would join Barack's army in battling the Republicans. To make a show of common cause, Obama and Clinton traveled together on a joint campaign trip to a small town in New Hampshire, where both of them had gotten exactly 107 votes each during the primary. The town was aptly named Unity.

On the campaign bus carrying them there, Axe approached Clinton and asked to have a quick word. He told her it was never his plan to work against her and that he admired her for the kindness she had shown towards his wife and family in their work for epilepsy research. He felt they had a good conversation and hoped he had managed to ease some of the hard feelings created by the prolonged primary fight.[385]

Hillary listened politely to Axelrod's plea. But it was still much too early for her to make peace. After all, he had been the chief strategist behind many of the toughest attacks on her character. After their talk, when she was alone again with her closest aides, she compared her conversation with Axe to having a root canal. She said it had made her want to throw up.[386] But at least their struggle was now over. Axe could turn his full attention towards John McCain and the Republicans.

The Maverick, the Celebrity, and the Running Mate

John McCain was an opponent no one should underestimate. A decorated war hero, he had spent five long years in a Vietnamese refugee camp where he underwent extreme torture. After returning home, he had been elected to the House of Representatives in 1983. Four years later, he won his race for the US Senate from Arizona, a seat he would hold until his death 31 years later. McCain, nicknamed the Maverick for his independence, often stood up against his own party on a number of matters. In 2000, he had challenged Bush for the nomination, and in 2001, he had even been one of only two Senate Republicans to vote against the Bush tax cuts.

Bush's popularity had declined sharply during the last years of his presidency, and by 2008, McCain's independence from the now unpopular president was one of his greatest assets. To counter this, Axe labeled his opponent "Bush-McCain," tying McCain to the unpopular president. McCain was running to continue Bush's policies, Axe argued, and the McCain candidacy was nothing more than "four more years of Bush." This message was repeated over and over in paid media, speeches, flyers and phone calls.

Another challenge facing Axe was McCain's comprehensive experience on the national and international stage. This stood in sharp contrast to Obama's two meager years in the Senate. In domestic policy this was hardly a problem, as Obama ran "to change the ways of Washington." The problem was on foreign policy and national security, were most voters wanted experience. Compared to McCain, Obama was perceived as somewhat of a novice on these issues. This was obviously a huge problem, as foreign policy and national security lay at the core of a president's job. To shore up Obama's credentials, Axe and the campaign team decided to have him make a trip abroad.

The trip turned out to be a brilliant tactical move. Starting with Afghanistan and Iraq, the news cycles at home were filled with great footage of Obama meeting many of the key players in the region and touring Iraq in a helicopter with General David Petraeus, both in sunglasses, grinning. The Iraqi Prime Minister Nouri al-Maliki even embraced Obama's proposed timetable for the withdrawal of American troops – a huge scoop for any president, let alone a presidential candidate. In Israel, Obama met with the top leaders from both the Israeli and Palestinian side. He especially hit it off with Israeli President Shimon Peres, managing to dampen concerns in the American Jewish community about his commitment to Israel's security.

The trip ended with a visit to Berlin, where more than 200,000 people gathered in the Tiergarten to listen to Obama outlining his vision of a world with more international cooperation and less conflict. The image drew a natural parallel between Obama and the two other Americans who had attracted such huge crowds with their speeches in Berlin – John F. Kennedy and Ronald Reagan. It made Obama look presidential. Axelrod was genuinely moved as he listened to the speech which he had helped write, taking in the large crowd chanting, "Obama, Obama, Obama." He felt the immense historic importance of the moment.

Someone less pleased was John McCain. For a year, almost all media time had been focused on Obama and Hillary slugging it out in the Democratic primary, leaving McCain little room to grab the electorates attention. Now, with the Democratic Primary brawl finally over, Obama kept grabbing the headlines with his trip abroad. Frustration reached an all-time high in McCain's HQ. His generals didn't know what to do. They just couldn't seem to find a way to break through the noise. It was driving McCain's chief strategist crazy.

Steve Schmidt, nicknamed 'Bullet' by Karl Rove, was a shaven-headed operative that had worked on a score of Republican political campaigns, including those of President George W. Bush and California Governor Arnold Schwarzenegger. He had a relentless focus and zero tolerance for bullshit. Now he searched frantically for a countermove that would put his candidate front and center again. On the day that Obama returned stateside, Schmidt gathered a small group of advisors to sound out any suggestions.

"We're running against the biggest celebrity in the world," he complained.

"Well, let's turn that against him," McCain's lead adman Fred Davis suggested. "Big celebrity? So's Britney Spears! So's Paris Hilton!"

The idea was simple: By pointing out the obvious, they would try to get the voters to see through the imagery that Axe was creating.

Davis rushed off to produce a new ad, called "Celeb." The spot toggled images of Obama with those of Britney Spears and Paris Hilton, while a soft female voice asked, "He's the biggest celebrity in the world, but is he ready to lead?" The message wasn't lost on anyone; Obama was nothing more than an elitist with a big ego. That might be an image that was made for good television, but it wasn't the stuff that strong leadership is made of. Axe was caught off guard and knocked off balance by Celeb. The ad went viral and put a visible dent in the Obama myth. His negative ratings suddenly started inching upwards. By early August, the Gallup tracking poll projected the Obama-McCain race a dead heat.[387]

The thing McCain feared most was that Obama would choose Hillary as his running mate. If he did, he was sure that the two of them – and the ongoing storyline of how the visceral hate between them developed into a new political romance – would keep dominating the major news outlets. It would be a rerun of the previous six months; all Obama-Clinton, all the time.

But McCain needn't have worried. Axelrod and Plouffe had been working for months on the vice-presidential pick, continually checking in with Obama, and Hillary wasn't even on the final list of candidates. The battle scars of the nomination fight hadn't healed enough for that. In fact, no woman was on the list.

"In the political calculus, we concluded that we could pass on Hillary, but not for another woman," Axe admitted.[388] Their favorite was Senator Joe Biden of Delaware.

Biden was first elected a Senator in 1972, and as the chairman of the Senate Foreign Relations Committee, he would bring much needed political experience to the ticket. He also had a way of mobilizing the white middle class vote – a trait Axe and Obama knew they needed to build a majority. Biden was a formidable politician on his own and would bring competence and energy to the ticket. Still, Axe had misgivings about Biden's tendency to talk all the time. Obama had experienced it in the Senate. During the vetting process, Axe confronted Biden about his ability to control himself verbally.

"Forgive me for being so blunt, but how do we know you know how to shut up?" he asked Biden, who started to explain. "An hour later, he finished answering. So I asked him another question," Axe reminisced with a smile.[389]

But there was another side of Biden that really appealed to Axe; Biden's family. His family history was well known. Just a few weeks after the '72 election, Biden's wife Neilia and his daughter Naomi were killed in a car accident after doing some Christmas shopping. Biden's sons Beau and Hunter survived the accident, and to take care of them Biden started commuting back home from Washington on a daily basis. Later, he married his new wife

Jill, and they added their daughter Ashley to their midst. Biden's natural ease with his family – he was comfortable expressing affection to his wife and grown children publicly in a way that most politicians were not – was what made the strongest impression on Axe.[390]

"There's something special about this family," he told Obama after meeting the Bidens.[391] It was so different from his own upbringing. And to Axe, who often interpreted political candidates in terms of how he could make their personal history an important part of his sales pitch, this would be a welcome addition to the Obama ticket.

McCain knew Biden well. He knew his strengths. He knew he was a formidable politician. But when Obama announced his choice, McCain still felt a rush of relief. Biden wasn't Hillary! For all Biden's strengths, picking him wasn't a spectacular move that would lay siege to all media attention for the last months of the campaign. In fact, the Maverick had a plan of his own to steal attention away from Obama, and now he felt he had a fighting chance. But first he had to let the Democrats get through their convention.

Axelrod understood that the 2008 Democratic National Convention had to be spectacular to live up to the expectations the trip abroad had created. He couldn't risk having just a few thousand people attend Obama's acceptance speech in Colorado, after hundreds of thousands of Germans had chanted his name in Berlin. So, Axe and Plouffe came up with idea that the candidate should give his speech not in the convention hall, but rather in front of 75,000 supporters in the Denver Broncos stadium. Axelrod's idol, JFK, had given his acceptance speech in front of 50,000 people at a similar stadium event. The scene was massive, and it made Obama look even more the rock star, as the enormous crowd cheered him on. If nothing else, it was great television, and the enormous crowd proved that Obama was just as popular back home as abroad.

The other hurdle of the convention was how to make Hillary's delegates fall in line behind the man they felt had ended their dream of the first woman president. This was handled brilliantly by Hillary herself. After the rollcall had begun and the states had started casting their votes – some for Obama, some for Clinton – there was suddenly a dramatic stir on the convention floor. It was Hillary. The Senator made her way through the anticipating crowds to her state delegation of New York, from where she addressed the convention:

> *With eyes firmly fixed on the future in the spirit of unity, with the goal of victory, with faith in our party and country, let's declare together in one voice, right here and right now, that Barack Obama is our candidate and he will be our president!*[392]

Millions of Americans watched as the hall erupted in cheers. The convention was a formidable success. The polls showed a significant bump. It all looked good. What could possibly go wrong now?

Palinmania

Axe was elated when he called Obama to share the post-convention numbers.

"It was a home run," he said with gushing enthusiasm. But as soon as he got off the phone, his Blackberry started blowing up with reports that McCain was about to steal their thunder. The Maverick had decided to end the Obama momentum by announcing his own choice of running mate.

For a while, McCain had been seriously considering tapping his good friend, Democratic Senator Joe Lieberman, for the second spot on the ticket. The moderate Lieberman had been the vice presidential nominee on the Democratic ticket eight years earlier. Picking him would enforce McCain's maverick image, underscore his independence, and endear him to moderates. This would undermine Axelrod's attempts to portray the choice as one between Real Change vs. "McCain-Bush." How could anyone draw a parallel between McCain and Bush, if McCain had a running mate who had run against Bush? Picking Lieberman would be a real game changer.

Those who paid attention knew that the Democrat was a good friend of McCain and had already endorsed him. So, the possibility wasn't really that far-fetched. In fact, Axe was actually prepared for such an outcome and had even done opposition research on Lieberman. The Senator was as hawkish on matters of national security and foreign policy as McCain, but much more liberal on most domestic issues. Thus, a McCain-Lieberman ticket would be a truly bipartisan ticket, showing McCain's eagerness for national unity, putting country before party. Axe didn't like that at all. It would bury the very basis of his strategy, and force him to change it in the middle of the race.

On the other hand, Lieberman's liberal stands on domestic issues were also the biggest obstacles in getting him nominated at the Republican convention, without losing hardcore conservatives. This could only be accomplished if the pick was kept a complete surprise and sprung at the last minute, so the opposition didn't have time to organize and build momentum. But in early August, the possibility of a moderate pro-choice pick accidentally leaked, creating a frenzy on the right.

"If the McCain camp does that," bellowed conservative talk-show host Rush Limbaugh, "they will have effectively destroyed the Republican Party and put the conservative movement in the bleachers." Karl Rove privately told the McCain campaign that picking Lieberman would be a bad idea. It would, Rove pointed out, leave McCain with a split party and little time to repair the damage.

With the Republican convention just a week away, the Lieberman idea sank like a stone, never to resurface. Worst of all, time was running out, and McCain still needed a pick that would shake the political environment.

"We still need to have transformative, electrifying moment in this campaign," Schmidt told his candidate. McCain agreed wholeheartedly. But who could fit the bill? Schmidt had an novel idea. In all haste, the female governor of Alaska was contacted. Neither Schmidt nor his team had any opportunity to vet her properly. There simply wasn't time. But they desperately needed a game changer, and she was the best they could come up with.[393]

The first rumors of this unexpected development were what flooded Axelrod's Blackberry with messages the day after the Democratic convention, as he boarded the Obama campaign plane. It took him completely by surprise. Her name wasn't even on his opposition research list.

"Where the hell did this come from?" he shouted into the phone as one of his staffers called to share the news. He barely knew the Alaskan Governor and had never heard her speak. Racing up to the front cabin, Axe shared the breaking news with Obama and Biden. Biden's face went blank.

Looking at Axe he asked, "Who's Sarah Palin?" The same question would be asked by millions across America.

"Wow," Obama said. "Well, I guess she's change."[394]

Sarah Palin had been governor of Alaska for just 20 months and had an approval rating at 80 percent, which was impressive by any standard. A former small-town mayor of her hometown of Wasilla, she was conservative to the core; pro-life, pro-gun, anti-big government, and an avid defender of states' rights. As mayor, she had even approached the town librarian about the possibility of banning some books she found morally or socially objectionable. Palin, still in her early 40s, had won the governorship running as a reformer and relentlessly attacking the Republican Party's old guard in Alaska.

She had her special kind of charm. Living in Wasilla with her husband and her five children, she was a hunter, a former beauty queen, intensely competitive, and undeniably fascinating. And perhaps most important: She was a *she*! It was mere months since Hillary had conceded defeat in the Democratic primary, declaring, "Although we weren't able to shatter that highest, hardest glass ceiling this time, thanks to you, it's got about 18 million cracks in it." Now the McCain-Paling ticket gave women across America the chance to have another go, if they sent a woman to the White House as McCain's vice president.

"She is an aggressive reformer who isn't afraid to break glass, to bring change to Wasilla and later to the state of Alaska," said a spokesman for the McCain campaign. "Washington needs some of that."[395]

Beside the fact that they both could bring a new dynamic to the campaign, Palin and Lieberman had very little in common. Picking him would have attracted swing voters and moderates. Picking her attracted the right wing of the party. Picking him would have signaled that McCain put country over party. Picking her signaled that he was true to conservatives, putting his party first. It meant going in a completely other direction than he had originally planned.

Obviously, she was a big gamble. McCain and Schmidt knew almost as little about her as Axelrod did. They were in such a hurry, they had very little time for vetting, and she was untested with no national political experience. From the moment that her name was presented to the press, the phone lines in McCain's HQ were jammed with calls from reporters trying to figure out what she stood for and get details about her life. But McCain's press shop was as clueless as the callers.

The Republican establishment was as surprised as everyone else. Vice President Dick Cheney felt Palin was woefully unprepared and that McCain had made a reckless choice.[396] Everything about picking Palin was a gamble, but McCain's chief strategist still insisted it was the right move.

"I'd rather lose by 10 points trying to go for the win," Schmidt said, "than lose by 1 point and look back and say; Goddamn it, I should have gone for the win."

The Palin pick did indeed create the "transformative, electrifying moment" in the race that McCain was looking for. Overnight, Axe's candidate was no longer the hottest commodity in town. For months upon months, the news cycles had been all Obama, all the time. Now they were all Palin, all the time. She also managed what McCain and his centrist reformer image couldn't – she fired up the right wing of the GOP. Giving her speech to the Republican National Convention, she attacked Obama for being an elitist, an egotist, a taxer, a big spender, and an appeaser.

"I guess a small-town mayor is sort of like a community organizer, except that you have actual responsibilities," she quipped with a sarcastic smile. It sparked pandemonium among the Republican faithful. They loved her.

In the following days, Palin got the same reaction at every campaign stop where she spoke. Soon, it was clear that most of the crowds, which grew visibly by the day, hadn't come to hear McCain. They had come for her. But the Maverick didn't mind. For a long time, he had been overshadowed by Obamamania. Finally, he was back in the spotlight again.

"Change is coming, my friends," he kept shouting at the crowds at every stop. A week after the end of the GOP convention, McCain was pulling even with Obama in the polls again, some even had him a few points ahead.

Facing the new Palinmania, Obama told Axelrod, "This shit would be really interesting if we weren't in the middle of it." They knew they had to strike back. But at first they couldn't see many weaknesses in Palin's armor. They couldn't use personal attacks on her style or family or history, because that could easily be interpreted as unwarranted. After the prolonged fight between Obama and Hillary, many were wary of more attacks against a woman. Axe concluded that the only way they could go after Palin was to not go after her directly, but rather criticize McCain for having made a risky choice that could come back to hurt the country. If elected, Palin would serve as vice president under the oldest president ever elected to a first term, who also had serious health issues; McCain was 72 and had a history of recurring melanoma. So, the Democratic spin-meisters argued McCain should have chosen a running mate with real experience, someone who had been battle tested, since voting for the McCain-Palin ticket could mean voting for a Palin presidency.

A Bumpy Road to the Finish Line

While Axelrod struggled to come up with an effective strategy for dealing with Palin, storm clouds were gathering over the American economy. In mid-September, Axe called a meeting in his office to consider additional steps to blunt the McCain-Palin momentum. But Obama told his advisor and friend that there was something else they had to plan for as well. He had just been briefed by Treasury Secretary Henry Paulson that a major economic event was expected to occur in the near future. The next morning, the giant investment bank Lehman Brothers announced it was seeking Chapter 11 protection. It was the start of the biggest single bankruptcy in American history. Another investment bank, Bear Sterns, had crashed in March, and the government had recently taken control of the mortgage giants Fannie Mae and Freddie Mac.

The downfall of Lehman triggered a panic in the markets that would become known as the global financial crisis. Axelrod didn't know the scope of the crisis yet, but like Obama he understood that Lehman's demise was merely a symptom of the state of the economy. He also understood the political landscape was about to shift dramatically. The economy would overshadow all other issues for the last two months of the campaign.

Axe braced for the worst and started tuning his strategy, re-crafting the "hope and change" theme into a message with more emphasis on jobs and the economy. The Republican's failed economic policies had led to the crisis, he claimed, and that would change under Obama's leadership. Most importantly, Axe wanted to convey that Obama fully understood the seriousness of the situation, that he had a plan for how to deal with the mess, and that he was ready to act the moment he was given presidential power.

While he was working to paint a clear picture of how Obama would deal with the crisis, the McCain camp seemed to be in disarray. As the Dow plunged, McCain greeted the news with a vain effort to reassure the market and the public. "The fundamentals of our economy are strong…," he told the press. It was a blunder of historic proportions, and Axe jumped at it, using the statement to underscore his claim that McCain and the Republicans were completely out of touch with reality.

They got even more help from McCain when he, just hours later, declared that the financial situation was in a state of "total crisis," that America's financial markets had become a "casino" and that he would fire the head of the Securities and Exchange Commission if he became president. This backtracking of his earlier statement made it look like he had switched views under fire. It was made worse by the fact that the president doesn't actually have the power to fire head of the SEC, a fact McCain seemed to have missed. It provided Axe with all the ammunition he needed.

A few days later, Treasury Secretary Paulson presented to Congress his proposal to stop the crisis spiraling into an economic Armageddon: a $700 billion rescue plan. The Democrats in both houses gathered under Obama's banner and supported the plan, with some minor adjustments. As did the Senate Republicans. But in the House, the Republicans rebelled. Under normal circumstances, the Maverick himself would be opposed to any $700 billion bailout. But these were not normal circumstances. Both McCain and Schmidt knew the public would become more and more concerned as unemployment rose, loans grinded to a halt and more bankruptcies ensued. If the House Republicans shot down their own treasury secretary's rescue package in the Senate, they could end up with the blame for the crisis being allowed to spiral further out of control. That would be the end of McCain's presidential hopes.

The only option as Schmidt saw it was for McCain to fly to Washington and broker a deal that the House Republicans could swallow. If he managed that, he would be the hero of the day.

"I can do it," McCain thought, "I can cut this deal."[397]

He got President Bush to host a meeting with himself, Obama, and the congressional leaders from both parties. But at the meeting, it turned out he didn't have the political strength to reel in his own troops. The meeting ended without consensus being reached. House Republicans proceeded to vote against the rescue package, killing it. As a result, the stock market plunged and businesses went into deep anxiety. By injecting himself into the role of fixer, McCain was left with much of the blame for the chaos.

Five days later, when reality had finally dawned on the House Republicans, they caved and passed a $700 billion rescue package anyway. The victims of the delay were the American economy, the American people – and John McCain's presidential hopes.

Axelrod could hardly believe what was happening. A few weeks earlier, McCain had been head-to-head with his candidate in the polls. Sarah Palin had stolen Obama's spotlight, and fired up the whole conservative base. Things had looked bleak. Now, McCain was feeding Axe and his team every soundbite they needed to mount attack after attack, while Obama appeared more presidential by the day. Axe had dreamt of shepherding a worthy candidate into the highest office of the land for decades. Now that dream seemed on its way of becoming reality.

This was a time of high anxiety for the master strategist. He felt things could go either way. And then, out of the blue, the Palin comet that had shone so bright in the sky, that had seemed so untouchable, came hurdling into the atmosphere and crashed to Earth in an ear deafening explosion.

Inside the McCain campaign, it had become clear that McCain had actually picked a running mate who lacked basic knowledge about the world. Palin didn't know why North and South Korea were separate nations. She believed, wrongly, Saddam Hussein had been behind the 9/11 attacks. And she didn't know who or what the Federal Reserve was. The list went on and on. What's worse, she didn't seem to understand how little she actually knew. Many inside the campaign considered their VP candidate a ticking bomb. For a while, the senior staff managed to keep this disturbing knowledge from the outside world. But in a presidential campaign, few things stay hidden for long.

As journalists continued to dig around in her past and question her readiness for higher office, the depths of Palin's staggering ignorance became visible for all to see. In an interview with ABC's Charlie Gibson, she said Russia was so close to her home state, "you can actually see Russia from land here in Alaska." In two interviews with CBS's Katie Couric, Palin's answers about the financial crisis and the recovery package were totally incoherent. She couldn't name a single effort from McCain to regulate the economy. She couldn't name a single Supreme Court case beside Roe vs. Wade that she disagreed with. She couldn't name one national newspaper she read regularly. As her meltdowns filled the airwaves, the question most people were asking was why McCain had picked Palin as his running mate in the first place. What did this say about his judgement?

Inside his campaign, there were people who were ridden with guilt over elevating Palin to within a striking distance of the White House.[398] To be fair, many on the far right still loved her and felt she had been the subject of unfair coverage from the liberal media. But most moderates and swing voters – who's support McCain desperately needed to win – started having profound worries about the McCain-Palin ticket. Axe, of course, did everything possible to reinforce those concerns.

For the remainder of the campaign, Axe and his team kept pumping out the "hope and change" message. In a historic 30-minute infomercial shot by Davis Guggenheim, entitled "American Stories, American Solutions," one could detect the Axelrod recipe. The ad had the overall theme of hope and change bind together a string of stories about everyday Americans; a white married mother from Missouri, a black retired railroad worker from Ohio, a Hispanic widow, mother and teacher from New Mexico, and a white male Ford motor worker from Kentucky. Beginning with images of cornfields, railways and picket-fence homes over soaring strings, the infomercial cut to a shot of Obama standing before a wooden table and a large American flag: it wasn't the Oval Office, but the resemblance was no accident.

Obama spoke softly and personally – like FDR in his famous fireside chats – about the problems facing the country. The info-mercial was broadcasted simultaneously on NBC, CBS, Fox, Un-ivision, MSNBC, BET, and TV One, laying out Obama's policies and views on the major challenges America. It was a masterpiece of political communication, seen by nearly 34 million viewers.[399]

The final weeks of the campaign became a blur of strain and exhaustion. Axelrod knew the numbers indicated that they were on the path to victory. But so much could go wrong in the last inning, he didn't dare take anything for granted. On election night, he tried to relax with his wife, but that was easier said than done. Everything he had toiled for was at stake.

As the night progressed, state after state reported Obama vic-tories. Soon the major networks projected Obama the victor. He would end up with 52.9 percent of the vote to McCain's 45.7 per-cent, giving him a majority of 365 to 173 in the electoral college. Obama carried a majority of independent voters and captured nearly 10 percent of registered Republicans – many scared off by the Palin effect.

Axelrod had worked his whole life for this. The supreme strategist and his colleagues had guided their candidate into the highest office, the pinnacle of power. And not just any candidate. A few generations earlier, the only black men in the White House were servants. Now, Barack Hussein Obama was to be sworn in as the 44th President of the United States. Those who had followed his career for a decade knew that Obama most probably would not have succeeded, had it not been for Axelrod's unique expertise and strategic guidance – from the early times in Chicago all the way up to the presidential campaign.

Now it had all paid off. As the momentousness of the situation washed over him, Axelrod became overwhelmed. His lips quivered, and his eyes brimmed with tears. He had imagined this moment a thousand times. Yet now that it had finally arrived, it wasn't so much elation he felt, as a sense of awe. Just by winning, they had already made history. He had helped change the world in the most profound way. It was a moment he would never forget.

A Swooning Loyalist

Yet winning was only the start of a new chapter of his life. The President-elect wanted Axelrod to join him in the White House as his Senior Advisor. But the strategist had misgivings. He had thirsted for this victory his whole life. Taking a job at the White House was something different. He understood it meant a lot of time away from his family. Another consideration was the businesses he had built over a quarter century that he would have to sell off, if he accepted Obama's offer. He saw the magnitude of the economic problems facing the country, which would obviously swallow most of the administrations energy and focus for a long time to come. But Obama insisted; "You have a chance to work for a president who's your friend at a pretty important time for the country. You can make a difference. Isn't that what this is all about?"[400] So, Axe made a deal with the President-elect; he would come work for him at the White House for two years, then go back to Chicago to start working on the reelection campaign.

Obama also brought in several of Axe's old colleagues, among them his old friend Rahm Emanuel, who became Chief of Staff. One collegial challenge was the new Secretary of State. To everyone's surprise, the President picked Hillary Clinton. Right after the election, when Obama had told Axe that he was considering Hillary, the strategist was stunned. How could he make his former rival the top foreign policy appointee when she had run ads questioning his preparedness to be commander in chief? Axelrod vividly remembered their last meeting and their awkward conversation – the one Hillary privately had compared to having a root canal. But Obama didn't waver.

"She's very smart. She's tough, and I believe that if she's on the team, she'll be loyal," he said. Now Hillary and Axe had to find a way to work together. It took some getting used to – for the both of them.

But there were other, more pressing issues at hand. As he moved into his new White House office, situated right next door to the President, the deep crisis in the American economy seemed only to worsen. Thousands of jobs were vanishing each week. Businesses were going bankrupt. More and more people found themselves struggling, barely able to pay for food, electricity and housing.

The President's economic advisors argued about what was the right way forward, agreeing only on one point: Things were going to get worse before they got better. Axe couldn't help thinking about the political implications. Discussing the dire economic prospects that were facing tens of millions of Americans, he said to Obama, "I'll tell you one thing, we're going to have a one hell of a though midterm election."

The President just looked at him and walked away.[401]

Axe's role, besides being one of the President's closest advisors, was to monitor polling, guide the message from the administration, oversee the speechwriting process, and make sure the Obama campaign brand was maintained as best he could. Already a personified part of that brand, Axe would go on television to defend Obama's positions, answering hard questions or joking with hosts like Jay Leno, John Stewart, and David Letterman.

His iron grip on the White House message wasn't lost on anyone, even those placed high up on the totem pole. He kept close tabs on what all the members in the cabinet were saying and doing, intervening whenever he felt it necessary. This led to the occasional row with those he was "guiding." But most listened attentively when he reached out to them. They knew how close he was to the President, which gave him a tremendous amount of clout. Axe was someone you wanted as a friend, not an enemy.

Axelrod and Obama had been together for so many years, they were totally at ease with each other. Wrote one *New York Times* journalist that was interviewing Axe in 2010, "A few minutes later, Mr. Obama walked in unannounced, scattering two aides like startled pigeons. 'Hey,' Mr. Axelrod said by way of greeting (no 'sir' or 'Mr. President'.)" Axe was "the president's closest aide, longest-serving adviser and political alter ego." White House Chief of Staff Rahm Emanuel called him "an integrator of the three P's" – press, policy, and politics – "and how they make a whole." He would sit in on policy and national security meetings and was routinely the last person the president talked to before making important decisions.[402]

But the time at the White House took its toll on the 55-year-old Axelrod. His friends started worrying. His diet worsened, and his weight soared. He got little sleep.

"He is considerably older than many of the wunderkind workaholics of the West Wing," the *Times* noted. "He wakes at 6 in his rented condominium just blocks from the White House and typically returns around 11." It was a grueling pace. He often felt tired, and he missed his family back home in Chicago.[403]

During the campaign he had repeated the Obama message of bringing change to Washington so many times, he could recite it in his sleep. They had promised to bring a new start and seek bipartisan solutions, rather than fight purely partisan wars. Now Axe saw the hope of bipartisanism dwindle. The Obama victory had, if anything, hardened the fronts between the two parties. When they were finally able to pass the $787 billion American Recovery and Reinvestment Act in the House – to combat the financial crisis – it was without a single Republican vote. In the Senate, only three Republicans supported it.

As rhetoric on both sides got more and more extreme, the image of Obama as a reformative leader bringing a new tone to Washington, quickly faded. Axe knew the reelection campaign would depend on one thing – how well they could communicate their achievements to the voters. To make sure he and his team didn't fall out of touch with the mood in the American people, he gathered the key White House communication players and the campaign strategic team every Wednesday night at his apartment.

Together they would pore over polls and research, trying to translate the administration's plans into a coherent message that would resonate with the voters, while downing gallons of coffee and a few beers.

But no strategist could spin the administration out of the economic stranglehold that most people were experiencing during 2009 and 2010. The economy had started to improve slightly, but two years into their first term it still remained plagued by slow growth and an unemployment rate that hovered at 9.5 percent. Recovery might be on the way, but people didn't feel it yet. And that had serious political implications.

Just as Axe had predicted, the 2010 midterms turned out a disaster for the Democrats. They were stripped of 11 governorships, including those in the battleground states of Iowa, Michigan, Ohio, Pennsylvania, and Wisconsin. They lost six US Senate seats and 63 House seats, the worst midterm loss since 1938. It was a terrible way to start their reelection campaign of 2012. But like he had planned, in February 2011, Axe gathered his things, walked out of the West Wing and traveled back to Chicago to start working full time on the campaign.

He kept in close touch with the President. The two would hash it out when necessary. Axe would always speak his mind. But he was also a swooning loyalist.

"I've heard him be called a 'Moonie,'" his close friend, former Commerce Secretary William Daley told *The New York Times*. White House press secretary, Robert Gibbs, joked, "[Axe is] the guy who walks in front of the president with rose petals."[404] He admired his friend. But he also acknowledged the dangerous weak spots in Obama's psyche when it came to campaigning.

While Bill Clinton and Ronald Reagan had seen every speech and public appearance as another opportunity to sell their message to the electorate, Obama drew a stark line between governing and campaigning.

"I'm not a candidate now. I'm the president," he would reply whenever Axe complained about the length and construction of his answers.

That attitude didn't always make it easy to be the President's chief political strategist. Axe saw that he needed to get Obama into a "campaign frame of mind." Finally, after a five-hour strategy session in September 2011, he achieved his goal.

"We're in campaign mode now," Obama concluded as the meeting drew to a close. His closest advisor let out a sigh of relief.

To make the President fully understand what was expected of him, Axe at one meeting showed him a video presentation; a clip from the iconic keynote at the 2004 Democratic National Convention, compared to footage from the summer of 2011. The Obama pre-2008 was fiery, energetic, and hungry to connect. The Obama post-2008 appeared pallid and sluggish. Pointing to the earliest footage, Axe declared, "That's the guy they elected president, and that's the guy they want to be president. …You were seen as someone who would run through the wall for the middle class. We need to get back to that."[405]

One that could help them reconnect with the middle class was the 42nd President. In November, Axe and a handful of others traveled to New York to meet with Bill Clinton. They wanted to enlist him in the reelection effort, both as an advisor and as a public magnet for those middle-class voters who had lost faith in Obama. Clinton's name was a gold brand among Democratic and independent leaning voters, synonymous with a period of broad prosperity. Even during the battle with the Clintons in the down and dirty nomination contest four years earlier, Axe had really never lost his deep respect for the former president. Besides, the relationship between the Clintons and the Obama generals had gotten better after Hillary was brought into the administration as Secretary of State.

Bill Clinton had a tremendous capacity for raising money, and a long-standing relationship with white working-class voters in swing states, with Jewish swing voters in Florida, and with suburban voters across America – all of which were key to electoral success. In addition, Bill could be an even more efficient communicator than Barack. With the disastrous mid-terms, the gloomy horizon ahead and the 2012 election closing in, Axelrod needed Clinton's help.

The former President had been puzzled by Axe's failure to clearly define and disseminate the administration's agenda and accomplishments for the country.

"You've got to explain your accomplishments, boil them down to a card that fits in voters' pockets," Clinton thought. "Obama doesn't do it. I don't know why. It's not that hard!"[406]

Now Axe and the Obama team tried to quell Clinton's enormous appetite for data, going through their polling, electoral scenarios, tactical challenges, and strategy. Drilling down on low-income white voters, the ex-president argued that Obama could succeed in capturing a large chunk of their votes, especially if the Republicans selected Mitt Romney as their standard bearer. Romney's enormous personal wealth could be turned against him, particularly in this demographic, Clinton said. But to succeed, they would have to hammer that message until it broke through the media cacophony. Axe agreed wholeheartedly; Romney was beatable.

Fighting Mitt

Axe's counterpart in the Romney campaign was Stuart Stevens, an ad maker, TV writer, and film consultant turned political strategist. Originally from Mississippi, Stevens spoke in a lazy drawl and exuded a bundle of charm. His political clients tended to be moderate Republicans, such as former Senator Bob Dole and former Florida governor Charlie Crist. He had also helped Karl Rove elect George W. Bush.

Stevens had cautioned Romney from the start, pointing out that he would have a hard time energizing the more conservative elements of the GOP.

"The party will not drift to you," Stevens told Romney. "You're going to have to win it over." [407] That was easier said than done. Every time Romney seemed close to getting a lock on the nomination, another candidate captured the momentum and soared on the polls, before plummeting to the earth again.

First there were the lightweights, like Texas governor Rick Perry, CEO Herman Cain, and the liberal icon Ron Paul, who all had their 15 minutes of fame. Then there were the two heavyweights, who both came close to killing Romney's momentum; former Speaker of the House Newt Gingrich and former US Senator Rick Santorum. Gingrich won the early and important primary in South Carolina, with 40 percent of the votes to Romney's

28. But Romney beat him back, and Gingrich only managed to win one more state. After Gingrich's descent, Santorum rose as the peak challenger, winning 11 states.

As the Republican primary contest dragged out, the race got ugly. Watching the spectacle from the sidelines, Axelrod wanted to make sure Romney's wealth became an issue. What better way of doing that then inserting it into the GOP brawl? Since 2003, most of Romney's assets had been placed in blind trusts that he had set up for himself and his family. He had some $250 million wrapped up in a mazelike assemblage of holdings, notably Bain funds residing in Cayman Islands and foreign accounts in Switzerland, Luxemburg, and Bermuda. The public knew nothing of this, of course. At least not yet.

Romney had avoided releasing his tax returns for years. Now, a tweet intended to bait the press into going after those records appeared from Obama's official Twitter account: "Why won't Mitt Romney release his tax returns?" The tweet also linked to a DNC video that began, "Tax Havens. Offshore Accounts. Carried Interest. Mitt Romney has used every trick in the book." Referring to Romney's refusal to release his returns, it asked, "What is Mitt Romney Hiding?"[408]

Axe's decision to insert the tax issue into the GOP nomination contest worked even better than he had planned. Not only did the press immediately jump on the bandwagon, Romney's Republican rivals did, too. In the run-up to the Fox News debate, Santorum and Gingrich both raised the issue. And in the debate, Rick Perry even challenged Romney point blank.

"Mitt, we need for you to release your income tax so the people of this country can see how you made your money," he demanded. "We cannot fire our nominee in September. We need to know now."

Romney didn't have a good answer. The next day he tried to calm the issue by telling the press that he had paid maybe 15 percent in taxes on the income from his investments, adding that in addition, he had earned some "speaker fees from time to time, but not very much."

The press seized on Romney's definition of "not very much" as it turned out he had received more than $374,000 in speaker fees just the last year alone. Just as Axe had intended, it left the public with the impression that Romney had no idea what financial struggles ordinary people had to deal with. The pressure built to a tsunami, finally forcing Romney to release his returns.

Of course, they were nowhere near the tax returns most people are familiar with. Romney's went on for thousands and thousands of pages, and Axe's crew dove into every specific detail. They found a lot of ammunition. Putting out another video, they zeroed in on his Swiss bank account, laying out a litany of abuses connected with Swiss-banking secrecy, which left Romney looking like he had something to hide – even as he had just released his tax returns. It was a masterly piece of negative spin by Axelrod and his team.

Some of Romney's problems were of his own doing. Four years earlier, when Obama had come up with a rescue package to save the auto industry, Romney had written an Op-Ed in *The New York Times* arguing against the move. Romney wrote:

> *If General Motors, Ford and Chrysler get the bailout that their chief executives asked for yesterday, you can kiss the Ameri-*

can automotive industry goodbye. Without that bailout, De-
troit will need to drastically restructure itself. With it, the auto-
makers will stay the course - the suicidal course of declining
market shares, insurmountable labor and retiree burdens,
technology atrophy, product inferiority and never-ending job
losses. Detroit needs a turnaround, not a check.

The New York Times summarized Romney's arguments under the headline "Let Detroit Go Bankrupt." Instantly sensing how damaging the headline was, Romney protested that he had never actually written those words, but to no avail. The headline reflected his arguments, the paper argued.

Obama's rescue package to the car industry had worked, saving tens of thousands of jobs. Now, trying to neutralize the issue, Romney traveled to Ford Field in Detroit to speak at a large campaign event. Axe knew this was a red flag issue that could be used to undermine the Republican nominee in swing states where the auto industry employed a lot of people. The Democrats mobilized a spirited demonstration outside the stadium, with union workers marching and chanting slogans that referred to the Republican candidate's stance on the auto bailout. One read, "Let Romney Go Bankrupt."

But Romney didn't need any help hurting himself. Looking out at the assembled crowd, he said, "I like the fact that most of the cars I see are Detroit-made automobiles. I drive a Mustang and a Chevy pickup truck. [My wife] Ann drives a couple of Cadillacs, actually." Not many in attendance could imagine affording two such vehicles, much less four. Later, on a trip to Florida for the Daytona 500, he referred to his "great friends who are Nascar team owners."

Romney's problem obviously wasn't so much that he had a lot of money, it was more that he had lived secluded in a world of millionaires for too long. He didn't seem to get it. The Richie-Rich gaffes made it seem like he resided in another dimension – as far removed from the life of ordinary Americans as could be. It showed in the polls, too. Romney's ratings on the "he cares about me" question were abysmal. Axelrod was absolutely thrilled and kept pounding the issue.

With Romney clearly vulnerable, Axe thought it was time to hit him hard on substance. In April 2012, the Obama team decided to copy a script that Dick Morris and Bill Clinton had developed back in 1996 when they had linked then Republican nominee Bob Dole to Newt Gingrich. Then Speaker of the House Gingrich's "Contract with America," that included big governmental cuts in popular programs, was highly unpopular among the voters. The ads run by Morris and Clinton tied Dole to Gingrich in such an extent it left the impression that the unpopular Gingrich was Dole's running mate. The ads worked. Dole's negatives had spiked as he got dragged down, chained to Gingrich's dismal image among independents and moderate Republicans.

Axelrod recognized that the equivalent of the Dole-Gingrich relationship, was Romney's relationship with the chair of the House Budget Committee, Paul Ryan. Ryan was a well known Republican rising star and a self-proclaimed deficit hawk. A major proponent of Social Security privatization, Ryan advocated for the privatization of Medicare, huge tax cuts, and the repeal of Obama's signature achievement, the Affordable Care Act. His budget was well received by the conservative right, but it left most independents and moderate Republicans feeling squeamish.

Speaking at a lunch hosted by the Associated Press, Obama thundered against the newly released Ryan budget, describing it as "so far to the right it makes the Contract with America look like the New Deal." Linking Ryan's budget to Romney, Obama continued:

> *Governor Romney has said he hoped a similar version of this plan...would be introduced as a bill on day one of his presidency. He even called it 'marvelous' - which is a word you don't often hear when it comes to describing a budget.*

The cameras rolled as the crowd ate it up.[409]

But Axelrod was not the only one looking to steal a page from the Clinton playbook. Romney's strategist had his eyes on another campaign. Like Clinton in '92, Stevens's mantra was, "It's the economy stupid!" In fact, their whole game plan centered around the struggling economy. Everyone could see that this was Obama's Achilles Heel. People were still hurting, many still out of a job. Stevens decided to build Romney's image as a savior from the financial hardships, an experienced businessman who could clean up the economy and save the day.

Axelrod, on the other hand, saw something else. He thought that Stevens's one-sided focus left Romney vulnerable. Romney's "all in" on the economy meant that all the Obama campaign had to do to beat him was to undermine people's confidence in Romney's ability to steer the economy through the end of the recession. If Axe could achieve that, Romney didn't have any plan B to fall back on.

Furthermore, Axe saw the Romney campaign itself as flawed, lacking any overreaching long-term strategy. In his eyes, Romney and Stevens were just about short-term tactics, maneuvering farther and farther to the right to win the nomination, seemingly forgetting that they couldn't win the general election without capturing moderates, women and a significant chunk of the minorities vote. Axe wouldn't make such a mistake. He knew that Obama had to rely on high support and turnout among minorities, liberal white women and young voters, to build a majority on Election Day. It was the same type of coalition Axe had successfully built in so many of his races since the '90s. Their polls gave Obama a strong showing among these groups. According to one poll released by *The Washington Post* in April, Romney trailed Obama by 19 points among women. Obama also showed a big lead among the young, and he held huge leads among African Americans and Latinos.[410]

In spite of these strengths, Obama, Axe, and Plouffe still believed Romney could beat them in November. What they feared most was being outspent by the Republican super PACs – like the one that Karl Rove had built. They were bracing for the tidal wave of negative attacks that they expected from the PACs – ad campaigns that would be designed to lower the Latino turnout and keep young voters from voting, thus corroding Obamas fragile coalition.

Axe decided they needed to take a calculated political risk to prove to young voters that the President was wholeheartedly on their side. So, Obama promised to pursue immigration reform if reelected and took steps to ensure that hundreds of thousands of illegal immigrants who had come to the United States as children, would be allowed to remain in the country without fear of deportation and able to work under an executive action.[411] This catered to the Latino vote. He also began a very public all-out push to get Congress to stop a doubling of the interest rate on federal student loans, affecting nearly eight million students each year.[412] This had a broad appeal among the young.

In addition, Obama announced he was in favor of same sex marriages, a historic step for any president.[413] It was a calculated gamble. They knew it would assist Romney by mobilizing the conservative right. But Obama and his generals saw it as a necessary bold step to energize their base and try to rekindle the flame of change that had entranced so many young people four years earlier. The announcement also went over well with college educated women. (In the end Romney's advisors – many of them moderate on most social issues – mostly steered clear of the contentious debate on gay marriage.[414])

While Obama pushed his new agenda, Axe went on a preemptive strike. With the aim of preparing both the public and the media for the expected viciousness of the attacks from the Republican super PACs, he got on a conference call with reporters to label Karl Rove and the other PAC operatives "contract killers."[415] In fact, as all this was going on, a secret plan of attack had been hatched by a group of well-known Republican operatives – a 54-page war-plan document entitled "The Defeat of Barack Hussein Obama – the Ricketts Plan to End His Spending for Good."

The plans ostensible financial backer was the conservative billionaire Joe Ricketts, known for his intense distaste for Obama. The document's main thesis was that Obama could be defeated by an aggressive ad campaign featuring the inflammatory sermons of Reverend Jeremiah Wright – whom Obama had denounced four years earlier.

The document proclaimed:

Our plan is to...show the world how Barack Obama's opinions of America and the world were formed. And, why the influence of that misguided mentor and our president's formative years among left wing intellectuals has brought our country to its knees. The world is about to see Jeremiah Wright and understand his influence on Barack Obama for the first time in a big, attention-arresting way. The metrosexual black Abe Lincoln has emerged as a hyper-partisan, hyper-liberal, elitist politician with more than a bit of the trimmer in him.

The plan called for "incurring maximum attention in a limited amount of time" and recommended "hitting Barack right between the eyes" with a five-minute film about Wright.

The film was to be released at the opening of the 2012 Democratic National Convention. The plan laid out the details for a massive campaign to capture everybody's attention, using print space, newspaper ads, kiosks in the airport and around the convention site, as well as a barrage of one-minute mini versions of the film on Charlotte television – "right in the lap of the gathered national press corps."

What the document's authors hadn't foreseen was that it got leaked to the Democrats. Axe couldn't believe anyone was dumb enough to put such a plan into writing. Nevertheless, he realized that the plan, if executed, would steal the media spotlight away from the Democratic Convention. He was adamant they needed to slip it to the press as soon as possible, which would put the authors and their backers on the spot, killing the plan before it could be put into motion. But Axe didn't want his own fingerprints all over the disclosure, so they used a third party to funnel the document to *The New York Times*, where it was splashed all over the front page.[416]

After its disclosure, Axe got on Twitter to hammer the point home. With a link to the story, he wrote "Stunning! Will Mitt stand up…or allow the purveyors of slime to operate on his behalf?"[417]

Not only did the ensuing critical media coverage put an end to the whole scheme, it also made the Republican PACs look like they were engaging in down and dirty warfare. The incident seemed to confirm Axe's earlier warnings that the Republican PACs were nothing more than "contract killers." But the revelation did make it harder for the PACs to cross the line, without getting a pummeling in the press.

They Beat that into the American Psyche

In early summer, Axelrod and Plouffe decided they needed to ramp up the negative attacks. They went to Obama with a proposal to shift millions of dollars in advertising from the fall into the summer – just like Dick Morris had convinced Bill Clinton to do back in '96. The plan was to pummel Romney on his track record as an executive at Bain Capital, making Romney the poster boy of outsourcing, downsizing and enrichment of the super-rich – a man far removed from the life of ordinary Americans, fighting only for himself and his pals in the country club. It was another huge gamble because it would leave Obama to be overwhelmingly outspent in the fall. But Axe wanted to define Romney in the eyes of the voters before the airwaves were completely filled with political ads.

The President usually let Axe and the campaign generals handle such matters, but now he was uneasy. Afraid it would leave them without money and ammunition when the Republicans attacked in the last months of the campaign, he hesitated. Axe shared the President's understanding that it was a high-risk gamble, but still he persisted, insisting it was the right move.

Both the Obama campaign and the Democratic super PAC Priorities USA went into action. Some of the ads they released went viral. In "Stage," a former employee of a paper company that had been bought by Bain Capital told the story of being instructed to build a 30-foot stage. Once it was completed, the executives walked out onto it and told all the employees that the plant was to close and that they were all fired. The ad ends with the former employee saying;

> *We all just lost our jobs. We don't have an income. Mitt Romney made over a hundred million dollars by shutting down our plant - and devastated our lives. Turns out, when we built that stage, it was like building my own coffin.*

The gripping ad got millions of clicks online and received a lot of media attention.

In another ad, "Firms," Axe came up with the idea of using a video clip from the primaries where Romney sang "America the Beautiful" annoyingly off-key. The ad featured closed down factories, empty offices, and newspaper headlines about Bain shipping jobs overseas and Romney's foreign bank accounts and funds, all set to the soundtrack of his terrible rendition of the song echoing in the empty halls and office spaces of the closed down firms. The ad ended with two short sentences on a dark background: "Mitt Romney is not the solution. He's the problem."

In the polls, it soon became clear that the attacks were resonating with voters. The biggest single contribution to that came from Romney himself. At a private fundraiser in Palm Beach, Florida, Romney talked to a group of high-end contributors who wanted to know how he would convince people to rely less on the government. Naïvely thinking the remarks would remain private, not knowing he was actually being filmed by a disgruntled bartender, Romney told his supporters;

> There are 47 percent of the people who will vote for the president no matter what. There are 47 percent who are with him, who are dependent upon the government, who believe they are victims, who believe that government has a responsibility to care for them, who believe that they are entitled to health care, to food, to housing, to you name it... And my job is not to worry about those people. I'll never convince them they should take personal responsibility and care for their lives. What I have to do is convince the five to ten percent in the center...

The comment made Romney look uncaring and cold, pampering to his rich friends. It seemed to confirm everything Axe had been saying about him. When it broke, the damage was severe, propelling Obama into a lead in all the battleground states. Axe made sure the remark went viral, using every opportunity to portray Romney as an out-of-touch rich guy. Virginia governor Robert McDonnell, who during the campaign became one of Romney's leading surrogates, summed up the devastating effectiveness of Axe's strategy: "Early on, Mitt got brutally defined by the Obama attack machine: Here is a rich white guy who's out of touch with the middle class. They beat that into the American psyche."[418]

When Romney at the Republican National Convention got Paul Ryan nominated as his running mate, cementing his position as a candidate advocating large cuts in governmental programs and huge tax benefits for the rich, Axe was elated. The Republican candidate still didn't seem to get it.

A week later, at the Democratic National Convention, the time and energy invested in Bill Clinton paid off. The former president's credibility with middle class voters was impressive, especially so when it came to the economy. Axe wanted the former president to deliver a speech at the convention, placing Obama's name in nomination. Clinton enthusiastically obliged. As he strode out onto the podium smiling and waving, his old theme song "Don't Stop Thinking About Tomorrow" was blearing from the loudspeakers. Axe knew he had made the right choice. He had been nagging the Clintonites for a copy of the speech for a week but had just gotten a copy that afternoon. The speech was so good, Axe was taken aback.

Clinton held forth on stage, joking with the crowd, educating the troops, and attacking the Republicans. On point after point, he explained and defended Obama's accomplishments. Reframing Romneys argument for new economic stewardship, Clinton told the millions watching, "[At the RNC convention] the Republican argument against the president's re-election was actually pretty simple, pretty snappy. It went something like this: We left him a total mess. He hasn't cleaned it up fast enough. So, fire him and put us back in."

The crowd roared with laughter. Afterwards, Axe thought Clinton had hit it out of the ballpark. Michelle Obama also shone bright on stage, as did several other key speakers. The convention was a success.

While Axe's team were hammering their message home, Plouffe was fixated on the electoral map, focusing almost exclusively on the nine battleground states that really mattered. He imposed a fierce discipline in cultivating his approach throughout every part of the Obama machine. While Romney's main advisors saw the campaign in broad national terms, Plouffe's tactic was to run what was in effect something like nine governors' races in the battle states. He established nine intense campaign-within-the-campaign operations in Iowa, Florida, Wisconsin, New Hampshire, North Carolina, Colorado, Nevada, Virginia, and Ohio.

Plouffe made sure each of these individual campaigns always fit nicely into Axe's overall message and strategy.[419] Axelrod and Plouffe didn't gamble on building just a broad national message or just locally adjusted micro campaigns. They did both at the same time.

The Humorless Professor or the Passionate Champion?

They had soothed the electorate's angst about Obama's stewardship of the economy. They had built a state-by-state campaign. They had defined Romney as an out-of-touch rich guy, before the Republican machine understood what was happening. They knew they were on track to victory. Only one thing could derail the path to Obama's reelection-victory now: The debates.

Obama could be a great and inspiring orator, but the debates were another thing all together. With short straight-to-the-point answers and snappy replies, it was a format not immediately suited for a president who preferred to explain and deliberate every point he was making. Axe was part of the team of central advisors who tried their best to coach Obama. But the training sessions revealed that the President seemed totally off his game.

The biggest problem was that he simply didn't enjoy the smell of the battlefield.

"I hate this," he said. "I'm counting down the days until this is over." His attitude showed. He sounded like a humorless lecturing professor. Axe was genuinely concerned. But the President brushed him off saying, "When it's real, I'll dial it up."

At the first debate in Denver, Axe was anxious. Which Obama was going to show up? The fiery combatant that had won four years earlier or the phlegmatic professorial president who hated the debate circus?

As he met his Republican advisory for their first face to face duel, Obama showed little passion. It didn't take long to see that he wasn't in his fighting mode. He acted passive and was in obvious discomfort. Romney on the other hand crushed it. After getting blasted for his 47 percent remark and Axe's relentless Richie Rich ads, many voters had expected Romney to come off as an obnoxious out-of-touch presidential wannabe. Instead, Romney was passionate, warm, commanding and humorous – even joking with the President. While the millions watching grew more positive toward Romney, Obama struggled to connect.

It was torturous for Axe to watch as his candidate struggled and floundered. The President did so bad that when the debate finally came to an end, he knew the whole election could now be lost. Obama's third-rate performance came at the worst possible time, in an instant killing the momentum they had so diligently been building for months. A CNN poll of people watching showed 67 percent thought Romney had won the debate. CNN's Senior Political Analyst David Gergen summed up the effect of the debate: "A week ago, people were saying this was over. We've got a horse race now."[420]

As the first couple of days went by is became obvious that Gergen was right. The gap had closed, the two candidates were almost head-to-head in the polls. The next debate was scheduled only two weeks later in New York. Axe knew they had to get Obama back in his game before then. Frankly, he told the President in no uncertain terms to step up and do better.

"This is a performance," he told Obama, "Romney understood that. He was delivering lines. You were answering questions. I know it's a galling process, but it is what it is. It's part of the deal. You've done it before. We need you to do it again."[421]

The President got the message and worked on getting into the right mode. It paid off. A completely different Obama showed up on the debate stage in New York. Axe had pushed Obama to change. They had killed the phlegmatic professor, and in his place a champion slugger emerged. Obama hit Romney with everything he had, and he didn't let his opponent duck or slide away. He was everything Axe wanted him to be; forceful, commanding, passionate, presidential.

One highpoint came when Romney was pressing Obama on military spending.

"Our navy is smaller now than any time since 1917," Romney said, arguing the Navy needed more ships.

Obama shot back:

> I don't think Governor Romney has spent enough time looking at how our military works.
>
> You mentioned the Navy for example, that we have fewer ships than we had in 1916. Well Governor, we also have fewer horses and bayonets, because the nature of our military has changed. We have these things called aircraft carriers, with planes landing on them. We have ships that go under water, nuclear submarines. So the question is not a game of battleship where we are counting ships, but rather what are our capabilities.

It was funny and quick witted, and made Romney look like a chastened schoolboy. The immediate threat was over.

Going Out a Winner

With Obama back on track, Axe and the rest of the team could stay the course with the same strategy they had embraced all along. They kept hammering Romney as the representative of the mega rich, the out-of-touch guy who didn't care about the poorest half of the country. Axe just kept turning the heat up on Romney and never gave him room to change the agenda.

On election night, Axe, Obama and the president's speech writer Jon Favreau, laid their final hand on the President's victory speech. In the last week of the race, after Obama's comeback in the second debate, there really hadn't been any doubt that their strategy was working, and that they were on a path to victory. Axe felt confident. He had every reason to. The final tally gave the president 51.1 percent to Romney's 47.2 percent. That night, Obama told Axe's wife Susan; "I'm happy for David. He's going out a winner!"

For David Axelrod, Election Night 2012 was the crowning achievement of his career. It had taken a life of hard work to get there. The most important move had been choosing the right candidate, the right person, the right match for him – someone Axe could really believe in and sacrifice for.

"Barack Obama has been a great friend and a dream client," Axe wrote in his autobiography.

He had achieved the ultimate dream of any political consultant; he picked his candidate, set his strategy and did what only very few others had done before him – guided his candidate through the battlefield of two presidential campaigns, electing and reelecting the President of the United States.

To some, he is the knight wielding his axe for the greater good. To others, he is no more than a soulless mercenary, a man willing to do whatever it takes to win. Either way, no one can doubt his supreme strategic abilities and his historic achievements.

In January 2013, Axelrod established a bipartisan Institute of Politics at the University of Chicago, where he serves as director. He has also done campaign consulting for former Italian prime minister Mario Monti and the British Labour Party. He has worked for CNN as a senior political commentator, and during the 2020 campaign Axe co-hosted the popular podcast Hacks on Tap.

Axe had always been an extremely competitive, take-no-prisoners kind of guy. More than a few opponents had been subjugated to his vicious attacks and clever maneuverings. He won far more battles than he lost. Regardless of your political affiliation, one thing is certain: You should never underestimate the Axe.[422]

EPILOGUE

Six Men Shaped by Hardship and Loss

When I started working on this book, I was focused on the striking differences between these six masters of political strategy and communication. After all, they fought for very different visions and values. During the research for this book, however, I was time and time again struck by their similarities.

These six men are as complex and flawed as any of us. Perhaps even more so. And even in the climate of the highly partisan political warfare of today, we should still be able to recognize the anxieties, needs, and vulnerabilities of another human being – even if they themselves didn't always extend that courtesy to others. They were all geniuses in their own way. But the essential question is what made them so focused, so extremely competitive? What enabled them to win? One question in particular stands out: Is it a pure coincidence that they all had experienced profound loss and hardship?

Lee Atwater was haunted throughout his life by the screams of his little brother, in desperate pain, dying in front of him. He buried himself in his work as if to escape that horrific memory.

He was seen as fiercely competitive, driven, extremely focused. He ran 50 miles a week, no matter what the weather, no matter what the distractions. But it seems Lee was seldom at peace. So, he worked even harder and often overstepped normal boundaries.

Dick Morris' parents weren't especially interested in children. "Commenting on international affairs was the only way for me to get my parents' attention," he was to write. The boy had to act as an adult to get the basic attention that all kids crave. Such an upbringing is bound to create a certain pattern of behavior. In Morris, it fostered both recklessness and a boundless drive, a burning need for both recognition and bending the rules.

Roger Ailes suffered from ill-health. Being a hemophiliac, there were times when he almost didn't survive even smaller injuries. His father enforced strict rules, hitting young Roger with his belt to discipline him. Just after going to college, his parents broke up their marriage, but didn't tell him. He returned home for Christmas, only to find that his home and all his belongings were gone, sold off. His mother had gone off to California, he found his father depressed and downtrodden. So, he went back to college. He was on his own.

James Carville struggled for years, balancing on the edge of oblivion, desperately seeking his place in the world. Sometimes warm and congenial to those around him, sometimes demanding and merciless. His emotional ups and downs were swift and absolute. He struggled with ADHD for most of his adult life. Concluded friend Hillary Clinton, "A lot of people think James is a normal person trying to be eccentric. The truth is he is actually desperately trying to be normal." But he isn't normal. He is a political genius.

Karl Rove didn't grow up in the most stable emotional environment. His father held his feelings back, while his mother displayed them erratically. When his parents split up, the child support sent regularly by his father was withheld by his mother, who lied to Karl about never receiving it. He had to fend for himself. Eventually, Karl's mother took her own life. Losing your mother in such a way is bound to make you see life a little differently.

David Axelrod's mother was in his own words "subtle as a sledgehammer" and didn't have neither the time nor the emotional bandwidth for him. He spent as little time as possible at home and left as soon as he could. His father experienced hardships of his own and finally took his own life. "My father was dead. My mother, distant. I was completely on my own," he remembered. Later, he and his wife sat crying by the bedside of their little girl, while she had repeated seizures, again and again, coming around just long enough to grab her mother's hand and cry out, "Mommy, make them stop!" Who wouldn't be deeply affected by that?

The Bad Boy. The Gunslinger. The Master Communicator. The Ragin' Cajun. The Architect. The Axe. Six professional gladiators of the political arena. These were no knights in shining armor. They could play dirty, cajole, harass or bulldoze their way through opposition, leaving countless victims in their wake.

Still, they changed the world, and they managed to do so only because they all had a deep understanding on how to reach out and move people. They were experts in how to connect with the most basic of human emotions. They weren't born like this. All of them were profoundly shaped by the hardship and loss they experienced.

And maybe, just maybe, that became an essential part of their political genius.

SOURCES ALPHABETICALLY

All's Fair: Love, War and Running for President; Mary Matalin, James Carville; 1994.

All Too Human; George Stephanopoulos; 1999.

Answer this, James Carville; Patrick Gavin/Politico; 2011.

Bad boy; John Brady; 1997.

Barack Obama Announces Candidacy; AmericanRhetoric.com; 2007.

Barack Obama's Keynote Address at the 2004 Democratic National Convention; PBS NewsHour; 2004.

Behind the Oval Office; Dick Morris; 1997.

Believer; David Axelrod; 2015.

Bill Clinton Goes on the Attack; Ron Fournier/The Atlantic; 2016.

Bill Clinton's Convention Speech; The New York Times; 2008.

Boss Rove; Craig Unger; 2012.

Boy Genius; Lou Dubose, Jan Reid, Carl M. Cannon; 2003.

Bush Challenges Dukakis To Explain Stand on Crime; Gerald M. Boyd/The New York Times; 1988.

Bush Escalates Attack on Clinton For His Anti-Vietnam War Protests; Andrew Rosenthal/The New York Times; 1992.

Bush Faults House GOP Spending Plan; Terry M. Neal, Juliet Eilperin/The Washington Post; 1999.

Bush Hammers Dukakis On Crime; David Hoffman/The Washington Post; 1988.

Bush Is Hardly a Passive Fund-Raiser; Don Van Natta Jr/The New York Times; 1999.

Bush Questions Clinton's Account Of Vietnam-Era Protests and Trip; Andrew Rosenthal/The New York Times; 1992.

Bush, at Dinner for Giuliani, Praises 'America's Greatest Crime Fighter'; Frank Lynn/The New York Ties; 1989.

Bush's architect 'will be last man out the door'; the Sydney Morning Herald; 2004.

Bye Rove!; John B Judis/The New Republic; 2007.

Call-Girl Story Costs President A Key Strategist; Richard L. Berke / New York Times; 1996.

Campaign Almanac; A Narrow Lead; The New York Times; 1992.

Campaign Profile - Divining Clinton's Gut-Level Strategy; Peter Applebome/The New York Times; 1992.

Campaign Profile; Divining Clinton's Gut-Level Strategy; Peter Applebome/The New York Times; 1992.

Clinton and Bush in a sprint as race for White House ends; Michael Kelly/The New York Times; 1992.

Clinton Takes a Grilling in N.Y. and Gains an Audience; Douglas Jehl/Los Angeles Times; 1992.

Clinton wins the Carville primary; E Pianin, EJ Dionne /Washington Post; 1991.

Clinton's Staff Sees Campaign As a Real War; Michael Kelly/The New York Times; 1992.

Clintons Joined S&L Operator In an Ozark Real-Estate Venture; Jeff Gerth - The New York Times; 1992.

Connally: Coming on tough; Steven Brill/The New York Times; 1979.

Convention '96: Who is Dick Morris?; Eric Pooley/Time Magazine; 1996.

Courage and Consequence; Karl Rove; 2010.

Dark Genius; Kerwin Swint; 2008.

Democracy for Hire; Dennis W. Johnson; 2016.

Democracy for Hire: A History of American Political Consulting; Dennis W. Johnson; 2017.

Dick Morris Resigns In Wake of Scandal; The Wall Street Journal; 1996.

Dick Morris; David Brooks/The Weekly Standard; 1996.

Dirty Tricks, South Carolina and John McCain; Ann Banks/The Nation; 2008.

Documents Point to Bush Aides' Involvement in Prosecutor Firings; Eric Lichtblau, Eric Lipton /The New York Times; 2009.

Double Down; Mark Halperin, John Heilemann; 2013.

Driving W; Melinda Henneberger/New York Times; 2000.

Ex-Dinkins Worker Says He Used Campaign Money in Vote Effort; Frank Lynn/The New York Times; 1989.

Exclusive: Lee Atwater's Infamous 1981 Interview on the Southern Strategy; Rick Perlstein/The Nation; 2012.

G.O.P. Chairman Lee Atwater: Playing Hardball; Eric Alterman/The New York Time Magazine; 1989.

G.O.P. Race Focuses On South Carolina; Hedrick Smith/The New York Times; 1979.

Game Change; John Heilemann, Mark Halperin; 2010.

Getting away with murder; Robert Bidinotto/Readers Digest; 1988.

Giuliani Shifts 3 Top Advisers In G.O.P. Bid; Frank Lynn/The New York Times; 1989.

Giuliani Turns to Ailes to Boost his Mayoral Bid; Maralee Schwartz, Howard Kurtz/The Washington Post; 1989.

GOP 'Super PAC' Weighs Hard-Line Attack on Obama; Jeff Zeleny, Jim Rutenberg/The New York Times; 2012.

GOP Probes Official As Teacher of 'Tricks'; John Saar/The Washington Post; 1973.

Gumbo Yearbook, Class of 1963; Louisiana State University and Agricultural and Mechanical College.

Hatchet Man; The Rise of David Axelrod; Grant Pick/Chicago magazine; 1987.

How A Murderer And Rapist Became The Bush Campaign's Most Valuable Player; Roger Simon/The Baltimore Sun; 1990.

How Hillary Became Hillary; Robert Draper/The New York Times; 2016.

Humphrey's Heirs Lose; Douglas E. Kneeland/The New York Times; 1978.

Illinois Senate Campaign Thrown Into Prurient Turmoil; Stephen Kinzer/The New York Times; 2004.

Interview with Paul Begala on the Clinton Years; Chris Bury/Frontline PBS; 2000.

It's the middle class, Stupid; James Carville, Stan Greenberg; 2012.

Judge sentences 8 mafia leaders to prison terms; Arnold H. Lubasch/The New York Times; 1987.

Karl Rove and the Modern Money Machine; Kenneth P Vogel/POLITICO Magazine; 2014.

Karl Rove Laughs Last; Fred Barnes/the Weekly Standard; 2006.

Karl Rove The Architect; WGBH Educational Foundation/PBS Frontline; 2005.

Karl Rove; Dark Money Watch; 2019.

Lee Atwater, Master of Tactics For Bush and G.O.P., Dies at 40; Michael Oreskes/The New York Times; 1991.

Lew Lehrman's $7-million education; Michael Kramer/New York Magazine; 1982.

Living History; Hillary Rodham Clinton; 2003.

Man in the News, Fierce Ambition; Frank Bruni/The New York Times; 2001.

McCain's Moment; Nancy Gibbs/CNN; 2000.

Message Maven, Finds Fingers Pointing at Him; Mark Leibovich/The New York Times; 2010.

My Life; Bill Clinton; 2005.

New Breed of Arkansas Officials Taking Race Out Politics; Steven V. Roberts/The New York Times; 1978.

Obama – from promise to power; David Mendel; 2007.

Obama and Biden's Relationship Looks Rosy; Glenn Thrush/The New York Times; 2019.

Obama and Romney Campaigns Test Limits of Attacks; Michael Shear/The New York Times; 2012.

Obama Enters the League of Must-See TV; Lisa de Moraes/The Washington Post; 2008.

Obama holds key leads against Romney; Dan Balz, Jon Cohen/The Washington Post; 2012.

Obama Says Same-Sex Marriage Should Be Legal; Jackie Calmes, Peter Baker/The New York Times; 2012.

Obama Wins Nomination; Adam Nagourney/The New York Times; 2008.

Obama; Back of Divorce Files; Scott Fornek/Chicago Sun-Times; 2004.

October 11, 1992 Debate Transcript; CPD; 1992.

October 15, 1992 Debate Transcript; CPD; 1992.

Pennsylvania Elections: Statewide Contests from 1950-2004; John J Kennedy; 2006.

Perot is Back - Perot Undertoe Threatens Clinton; Pew Research Center; 1992.

Perot Quits Presidential Race; Edwin Chen/Los Angeles Times; 1992.

Perot Quits Race, Leaving two-man Field; Clinton wows change...; Robin Toner/The New York Times; 1992.

Political consultants' campaign role is expanding; Frank Lynn/The New York Times; 1982.

Political strategist Dick Morris reflects on his time advising Bill Clinton; Charlie Rose; 1997.

President's Guru Goes Public; Back Home, Dick Morris Tells Tales From the Clubhouse; Alison Mitchell/The New York Times; 1995.

Presidential Campaign Discourse; Kathleen E. Kendall; 1995.

Race for City Hall; Barry Bearak, Ian Fisher; 1997.

Rapidly Growing Arkansas Turns to Liberal Politicians; Wayne King/The New York Times; 1978.

Reagan Keeps Clean While Bush, Connally Sling Mud in S.C. Race; Bill Peterson/The Washington Post; 1980.

Reagan's Ad Aces; Elizabeth Bumiller/The Washington Post; 1984.

Rendezvous with Destiny: Ronald Reagan and the Campaign That Changed America; Craig Shirley; 2011.

Resurrection; How New Hampshire Saved the 1992 Clinton Campaign; Patrick Healy/The New York Times; 2016.

Rewinding the Kennedy-Nixon Debates; David Greenberg/ Slate; 2010.

Roger Ailes on Roger Ailes; Tom Junod/Esquire; 2011.

Roger Ailes, GOP Mastermind; Rolling Stone; 2011.

Roger Ailes: Master Maker of Fiery Political Darts; Josh Barbanel/The New York Times; 1989.

Roger Ailes: Master Maker of Fiery Political Darts; Josh Barbanel/The New York Times; 1989.

Roger Stone should be a footnote in history. Instead, his life shows our descent to shamelessness; Howard Fineman/ The Washington Post; 2019.

Romney takes debate to Obama over economy; Tom Cohen/CNNPolitics; 2012.

Rove Exposed; James Moore, Wayne Slater; 2005.

Rove's retirement a surprise to Kjellander, too; Bernard Schoenburg/the Harrisburg Register; 2007.

Strategy: A History; Lawrence Freedman; 2013.

Student Loan Interest Rates Loom as Political Battle; Tamar Lewin/The New York Times; 2012.

The 1991 election, Wofford Wins Senate Race, Turning Back Thornburgh; Michael Decourcy Hinds/The New York Times; 1991.

The ad campaign - The Two Faces of Clinton; Richard L. Berke/The New York Times; 1992.

The Ad Campaign; Clinton Focusing on the Economy; Gwen Ifill/The New York Times; 1992.

The Age Issue; James Reston - The New York Times; 1984

The Born-Again Battle; Tom Wicker/New York Times; 1980.

The busboy who cradled a dying RFK has finally stepped out

of the past; Steve Lopez /Los Angeles Times; 2015.

The Checkers speech; Richard Nixon; 1952.

The Color of Politics; Chris Danielson; 2013.

The Controller Karl Rove; Nicholas Lemann/The New Yorker; 2003.

The Controller; Nicholas Lemann/The New Yorker; 2003.

The Death of an Honorable Profession; Carl T. Bogus/Indiana Law Review; 1996.

The End of the Line - Politico Playbook 2012; Glenn Thrush, Jonathan Martin; 2012.

The Front Runner; Gerald M. Boyd/The New York Times; 1986.

The Majority Report from Congress on the Iran-Contra affair; 1987.

The Man behind the Message; Richard Stengel/CNN/Time; 1988.

The Obama Memos; Ryan Lizza/The New Yorker; 2012.

The Passionate Prosecutor; Richard Stengel; 2001.

The Political Legacy of Baaad Boy Atwater; Eleanor Randolph/The New York Times; 2008.

The politician; Andrew Young; 2010.

The Prime Time Players; Tom Morgentau, James Doyle/The Prime Time Players; 1980.

The Ragin' Cajun - Eccentric and Controversial; Bill Ellis/BraningforResults.com; 2015.

The Ragin' Cajun, Eccentric and Controversial, Authentic and Effective; Bill Ellis/BrandingForResults; 2015.

The Selling of the President; Joe McGinniss; 1969.

The Spot: The Rise of Political Advertising on Television; Edwin Diamond, Stephen Bates; 1984.

The Triumph of William McKinley: Why the Election of 1896 Still Matters; Karl Rove; 2015.

Truth Is a Casualty in Colorado's Bitter Senate Race; Lou Cannon/The Washington Post; 1978.

Two Texans dig deep for boat vet ads; John Frank/the Houston Chronicle; 2004.

U.S. jury convicts eight as members of mob commission; Arnold H. Lubasch/The New York Times; 1986.

Ultimatum Goes Out To Giuliani On Tactics; Celestine Bohlen/The New York Times; 1989.

US to Stop Deporting Some Immigrants; Julia Preston, John H Cushman Jr/The New York Times; 2012.

What Lee Atwater Knows About Winning; Jan Collins Stucker/Southern Magazine; 1989.

What Lee Atwater Learned; Tom Turnipseed/The Washington Post; 1991.

Who Is Jerry Brown? Voices From Past Show Why the Man Is an Enigma; Robert Reinhold/The New York Times; 1992.

Who Runs Gov – Karl Rove; Washington Post; printed 2019.

Why Are These Men Laughing?; Ron Suskind/Esquire; 2003.

With Ailes's Aid, Convict becomes 'Willie Horton' of N.Y. Campaign; Howard Kurtz; 1989.

Wofford Wins Senate Race, Turning Back Thornburgh; Michael Decourcy Hinds/The New York Times; 1991

You are the Message; Roger Ailes, Jon Kraushar; 1988.

REFERENCES

1 All's Fair: Love, War and Running for President; Mary Matalin, James Carville; 1994.

2 Bad boy; John Brady; 1997.

3 G.O.P. Chairman Lee Atwater: Playing Hardball; Eric Alterman/The New York Time Magazine; 1989.

4 G.O.P. Chairman Lee Atwater: Playing Hardball; Eric Alterman/The New York Time Magazine; 1989.

5 Bad boy; John Brady; 1997.

6 Bad boy; John Brady; 1997.

7 G.O.P. Chairman Lee Atwater: Playing Hardball; Eric Alterman/The New York Time Magazine; 1989.

8 G.O.P. Chairman Lee Atwater: Playing Hardball; Eric Alterman/The New York Time Magazine; 1989.

9 G.O.P. Chairman Lee Atwater: Playing Hardball; Eric Alterman/The New York Time Magazine; 1989.

10 Bad boy; John Brady; 1997.

11 The Controller Karl Rove; Nicholas Lemann/The New Yorker; 2003.

12 Rove Exposed; James Moore, Wayne Slater; 2005.

13 Rove Exposed; James Moore, Wayne Slater; 2005.

14 GOP Probes Official As Teacher of 'Tricks'; John Saar/The Washington Post; 1973.

15 What Lee Atwater Knows About Winning; Jan Collins Stucker/Southern Magazine; 1989.

16 Bad boy; John Brady; 1997.

17 Bad boy; John Brady; 1997.

18 Bad boy; John Brady; 1997.

19 Roger Stone should be a footnote in history. Instead, his life shows our descent to shamelessness; Howard Fineman/The Washington Post; 2019.

20 Bad boy; John Brady; 1997.

21 What Lee Atwater Knows About Winning; Jan Collins Stucker/Southern Magazine; 1989.

22 How the South Carolina 'Firewall' Fell Apart; Juian E. Zelizer/Politico; 2016.

[23] G.O.P. Race Focuses On South Carolina; Hedrick Smith/The New York Times; 1979.

[24] G.O.P. Race Focuses On South Carolina; Hedrick Smith/The New York Times; 1979.

[25] Reagan Keeps Clean While Bush, Connally Sling Mud in S.C. Race; Bill Peterson/The Washington Post; 1980.

[26] Adieu, Big John; John Stacks/Time; 1980.

[27] The Born-Again Battle; Tom Wicker/New York Times; 1980.

[28] The Political Legacy of Baaad Boy Atwater; Eleanor Randolph/The New York Times; 2008.

[29] What Lee Atwater Learned; Tom Turnipseed/The Washington Post; 1991.

[30] Lee Atwater, Master of Tactics For Bush and G.O.P., Dies at 40; Michael Oreskes/The New York Times; 1991.

[31] All's Fair: Love, War and Running for President; Mary Matalin, James Carville; 1994.

[32] Bad boy; John Brady; 1997.

[33] Strategy: A History; Lawrence Freedman; 2013.

[34] Strategy: A History; Lawrence Freedman; 2013.

[35] Reagan's Ad Aces; Elizabeth Bumiller/The Washington Post; 1984.

[36] Bad boy; John Brady; 1997.

[37] The Front Runner; Gerald M. Boyd/The New York Times; 1986.

[38] Bad boy; John Brady; 1997.

[39] The Front Runner; Gerald M. Boyd/The New York Times; 1986.

[40] The Front Runner; Gerald M. Boyd/The New York Times; 1986.

[41] The Majority Report from Congress on the Iran-Contra affair; 1987.

[42] Rather's Questioning of Bush Sets Off Shouting on Live Broadcast; Peter J. Boyer/The New York Times; 1988.

[43] Bad boy; John Brady; 1997.

[44] Bad boy; John Brady; 1997.

[45] Bad boy; John Brady; 1997.

[46] Getting away with murder; Robert Bidinotto/Readers Digest; 1988.

[47] How A Murderer And Rapist Became The Bush Campaign's Most Valuable Player; Roger Simon/The Baltimore Sun; 1990.

[48] Bush Challenges Dukakis To Explain Stand on Crime; Gerald M. Boyd/The New York Times; 1988.

[49] Bush Hammers Dukakis On Crime; David Hoffman/The Washington Post; 1988.

[50] Boss Rove; Craig Unger; 2012.

[51] Bush Attacks Dukakis As The 'Furlough King'; David Hoffman/The Washington Post; 1988.

[52] Race for the White House (TV series, episode on the 1992 election); CNN; 2016.

[53] Bad boy; John Brady; 1997.

[54] The Color of Politics; Chris Danielson; 2013.

[55] Bad boy; John Brady; 1997.

[56] All's Fair: Love, War and Running for President; Mary Matalin, James Carville; 1994.

[57] All's Fair: Love, War and Running for President; Mary Matalin, James Carville; 1994.

[58] All's Fair: Love, War and Running for President; Mary Matalin, James Carville; 1994.

[59] Adult Personality Development; Lawrence S. Wrightsman; 1994.

[60] Lee Atwater, Master of Tactics For Bush and G.O.P., Dies at 40; Michael Oreskes/The New York Times; 1991.

[61] Courage and Consequence; Karl Rove; 2010.

[62] Lee Atwater, Master of Tactics For Bush and G.O.P., Dies at 40; Michael Oreskes/The New York Times; 1991.

[63] Bad boy; John Brady; 1997.

[64] Call-Girl Story Costs President A Key Strategist; Richard L. Berke / New York Times; 1996.

[65] Dick Morris Resigns In Wake of Scandal; The Wall Street Journal; 1996.

[66] Statement on the Resignation of Political Consultant Dick Morris; GPO.gov; 1996.

[67] Dick Morris; David Brooks/The Weekly Standard; 1996.

[68] Behind the Oval Office - Winning The Presidency In The Nineties; Dick Morris; 1997.

[69] Behind the Oval Office - Winning The Presidency In The Nineties; Dick Morris; 1997.

[70] President's Guru Goes Public; Back Home, Dick Morris Tells Tales From the Clubhouse; Alison Mitchell/New York Times; 1995.

[71] President's Guru Goes Public; Back Home, Dick Morris Tells Tales From the Clubhouse; Alison Mitchell/New York Times; 1995.

[72] Behind the Oval Office - Winning The Presidency In The Nineties; Dick Morris; 1997.

[73] Political strategist Dick Morris reflects on his time advising Bill Clinton; Charlie Rose; 1997.

[74] Political strategist Dick Morris reflects on his time advising Bill Clinton; Charlie Rose; 1997.

[75] Political strategist Dick Morris reflects on his time advising Bill Clinton; Charlie Rose; 1997.

[76] Behind the Oval Office - Winning The Presidency In The Nineties; Dick Morris; 1997.

[77] First in His Class; David Maraniss; 1996.

[78] First in His Class; David Maraniss; 1996.

[79] New Breed of Arkansas Officials Taking Race Out Politics; Steven V. Roberts/The New York Times; 1978.

[80] First in His Class; David Maraniss; 1996.

[81] New Breed of Arkansas Officials Taking Race Out Politics; Steven V. Roberts/The New York Times; 1978.

[82] Behind the Oval Office - Winning The Presidency In The Nineties; Dick Morris; 1997.

[83] First in His Class; David Maraniss; 1996.

[84] Behind the Oval Office - Winning The Presidency In The Nineties; Dick Morris; 1997.

[85] Political strategist Dick Morris reflects on his time advising Bill Clinton; Charlie Rose; 1997.

[86] Living History; Hillary Rodham Clinton; 2003.

[87] Living History; Hillary Rodham Clinton; 2003.

[88] First in His Class; David Maraniss; 1996.

[89] How Hillary Became Hillary; Robert Draper/The New York Times; 2016.

[90] First in His Class; David Maraniss; 1996.

[91] Political consultants' campaign role is expanding; Frank Lynn/The New York Times; 1982.

[92] Behind the Oval Office - Winning The Presidency In The Nineties; Dick Morris; 1997.

[93] First in His Class; David Maraniss; 1996.

[94] First in His Class; David Maraniss; 1996.

[95] Behind the Oval Office - Winning The Presidency In The Nineties; Dick Morris; 1997.

[96] Bill Clinton Goes on the Attack; Ron Fournier/The Atlantic; 2016.

[97] My Life; Bill Clinton; 2005.

[98] Behind the Oval Office - Winning The Presidency In The Nineties; Dick Morris; 1997.

[99] Boogie Man - documentary film; Stefan Forbes; 2008.

[100] Living History; Hillary Rodham Clinton; 2003.

[101] Behind the Oval Office - Winning The Presidency In The Nineties; Dick Morris; 1997.

[102] Behind the Oval Office - Winning The Presidency In The Nineties; Dick Morris; 1997.

[103] Behind the Oval Office - Winning The Presidency In The Nineties; Dick Morris; 1997.

[104] Behind the Oval Office - Winning The Presidency In The Nineties; Dick Morris; 1997.

[105] Behind the Oval Office - Winning The Presidency In The Nineties; Dick Morris; 1997.

[106] Political strategist Dick Morris reflects on his time advising Bill Clinton; Charlie Rose; 1997.

[107] Double Down; Mark Halperin, John Heilemann; 2013.

[108] Behind the Oval Office - Winning The Presidency In The Nineties; Dick Morris; 1997.

[109] Political strategist Dick Morris reflects on his time advising Bill Clinton; Charlie Rose; 1997.

[110] Behind the Oval Office - Winning The Presidency In The Nineties; Dick Morris; 1997.

[111] Political strategist Dick Morris reflects on his time advising Bill Clinton; Charlie Rose; 1997.

[112] Back from the Dead; Evan Thomas, Karen Breslau, Debra Rosenberg, Leslie Kaufman, Andrew Murr; 1997.

[113] Behind the Oval Office - Winning The Presidency In The Nineties; Dick Morris; 1997.

[114] President's Guru Goes Public; Back Home, Dick Morris Tells Tales From the Clubhouse; Alison Mitchell/New York Times; 1995.

[115] Dick Morris Takes Aim at Hillary Clinton From a Tabloid Perch; Alessandra Stanley / New York Times; 2016.

[116] Roger Ailes on Roger Ailes; Tom Junod/Esquire; 2011.

[117] Roger Ailes on Roger Ailes; Tom Junod/Esquire; 2011.

[118] Roger Ailes on Roger Ailes; Tom Junod/Esquire; 2011.

[119] Roger Ailes on Roger Ailes; Tom Junod/Esquire; 2011.

[120] The Selling of the President 1968; Joe McGinniss; 1969.

[121] Dark Genius; Kerwin Swint; 2008.

[122] Rewinding the Kennedy-Nixon Debates; David Greenberg/Slate; 2010.

[123] Transcript of Nixon's News Conference on His Defeat by Brown in Race for Governor of California; New York Times; 1962.

[124] The Selling of the President 1968; Joe McGinniss; 1969.

[125] The Selling of the President 1968; Joe McGinniss; 1969.

[126] The Selling of the President 1968; Joe McGinniss; 1969.

[127] Dark Genius; Kerwin Swint; 2008.

[128] The Selling of the President 1968; Joe McGinniss; 1969.

[129] The Selling of the President 1968; Joe McGinniss; 1969

[130] The Spot: The Rise of Political Advertising on Television; Edwin Diamond, Stephen Bates; 1988.

[131] The Selling of the President 1968; Joe McGinniss; 1969

[132] Dark Genius; Kerwin Swint; 2008.

[133] The Spot: The Rise of Political Advertising on Television; Edwin Diamond, Stephen Bates; 1984.

[134] Truth Is a Casualty in Colorado's Bitter Senate Race; Lou Cannon/The Washington Post; 1978.

[135] Humphrey's Heirs Lose; Douglas E. Kneeland/The New York Times; 1978.

[136] The David Durenberger Papers; Minnesota Historical Society; Boxes 11 and 29.

[137] Memo to NRSCs Bob Moore about Ailes; Carnegie Mellon University

Libraries Digital Collections Portal; 1979.

[138] Dark Genius; Kerwin Swint; 2008.

[139] Connally: Coming on tough; Steven Brill/The New York Times; 1979.

[140] The Prime Time Players; Tom Morgentau, James Doyle/The Prime Time Players; 1980.

[141] Dark Genius; Kerwin Swint; 2008.

[142] Holtzman, Ehrenreich on Nader and Women's Rights; Elizabeth Holtzman/Womans eNews; 2000.

[143] Holtzman, Ehrenreich on Nader and Women's Rights; Elizabeth Holtzman/Womans eNews; 2000.

[144] Mama D'Amato; Editorial board New York Post; 2014.

[145] Dark Genius; Kerwin Swint; 2008.

[146] The Spot: The Rise of Political Advertising on Television; Edwin Diamond, Stephen Bates; 1988.

[147] Lew Lehrman's $7-million education; Michael Kramer/New York Magazine; 1982.

[148] The Age Issue; James Reston - The New York Times; 1984.

[149] Bare Knuckles and Back Rooms: My Life in American Politics; Ed Rollins; 1997.

[150] Dark Genius; Kerwin Swint; 2008.

[151] Dark Genius; Kerwin Swint; 2008.

[152] You are the Message; Roger Ailes, Jon Kraushar; 1988.

[153] Rather's Questioning of Bush Sets Off Shouting on Live Broadcast; Peter J. Boyer/The New York Times; 1988.

[154] The Man behind the Message; Richard Stengel/CNN/Time; 1988.

[155] Roger Ailes, GOP Mastermind; Rolling Stone; 2011.

[156] The Passionate Prosecutor; Richard Stengel; 2001.

[157] Judge sentences 8 mafia leaders to prison terms; Arnold H. Lubasch/The New York Times; 1987.

[158] Race for City Hall; Barry Bearak, Ian Fisher; 1997.

[159] Giuliani Shifts 3 Top Advisers In G.O.P. Bid; Frank Lynn/The New York Times; 1989.

[160] Giuliani Turns to Ailes to Boost his Mayoral Bid; Maralee Schwartz,

Howard Kurtz/The Washington Post; 1989.

[161] Roger Ailes: Master Maker of Fiery Political Darts; Josh Barbanel/The New York Times; 1989.

[162] Ex-Dinkins Worker Says He Used Campaign Money in Vote Effort; Frank Lynn/The New York Times; 1989.

[163] With Ailes's Aid, Convict becomes 'Willie Horton' of N.Y. Campaign; Howard Kurtz/The Washington Post; 1989.

[164] Ex-Dinkins Worker Says He Used Campaign Money in Vote Effort; Frank Lynn/The New York Times; 1989.

[165] Bush, at Dinner for Giuliani, Praises 'America's Greatest Crime Fighter'; Frank Lynn/The New York Ties; 1989.

[166] Giuliani maintains attack on Dinkins over Stock Deal; Sam Roberts/The New York Times; 1989.

[167] With Ailes's Aid, Convict becomes 'Willie Horton' of N.Y. Campaign; Howard Kurtz/The Washington Post; 1989.

[168] Ultimatum Goes Out To Giuliani On Tactics; Celestine Bohlen/The New York Times; 1989.

[169] Love and War; Mary Matalin, James Carville; 2013.

[170] It's the middle class, Stupid; James Carville, Stan Greenberg; 2012.

[171] Answer this, James Carville; Patrick Gavin/Politico; 2011.

[172] The Ragin' Cajun - Eccentric and Controversial; Bill Ellis/Braningfor-Results.com; 2015.

[173] It's the middle class, Stupid; James Carville, Stan Greenberg; 2012.

[174] All Fair: Love, War and Running for President; Mary Matalin, James Carville; 1994.

[175] Campaign Profile; Divining Clinton's Gut-Level Strategy; Peter Applebome/The New York Times; 1992.

[176] All Fair: Love, War and Running for President; Mary Matalin, James Carville; 1994.

[177] All Fair: Love, War and Running for President; Mary Matalin, James Carville; 1994.

[178] Gumbo Yearbook, Class of 1963; Louisiana State University and Agricultural and Mechanical College.

[179] All Fair: Love, War and Running for President; Mary Matalin, James Carville; 1994.

[180] Campaign Profile; Divining Clinton's Gut-Level Strategy; Peter Apple-

bome/The New York Times; 1992.

[181] All Fair: Love, War and Running for President; Mary Matalin, James Carville; 1994.

[182] All Fair: Love, War and Running for President; Mary Matalin, James Carville; 1994.

[183] All Fair: Love, War and Running for President; Mary Matalin, James Carville; 1994.

[184] All Fair: Love, War and Running for President; Mary Matalin, James Carville; 1994.

[185] Love and War; Mary Matalin, James Carville; 2013.

[186] Campaign Profile; Divining Clinton's Gut-Level Strategy; Peter Applebome/The New York Times; 1992.

[187] The Ragin' Cajun, Eccentric and Controversial, Authentic and Effective; Bill Ellis/BrandingForResults; 2015.

[188] All Fair: Love, War and Running for President; Mary Matalin, James Carville; 1994.

[189] All Fair: Love, War and Running for President; Mary Matalin, James Carville; 1994.

[190] The New York Times; The-Guru-Ad

[191] All Fair: Love, War and Running for President; Mary Matalin, James Carville; 1994.

[192] Wofford Wins Senate Race, Turning Back Thornburgh; Michael Decourcy Hinds/The New York Times; 1991

[193] Pennsylvania Elections: Statewide Contests from 1950-2004; John J Kennedy; 2006.

[194] Pennsylvania Elections: Statewide Contests from 1950-2004; John J Kennedy; 2006.

[195] Pennsylvania Elections: Statewide Contests from 1950-2004; John J Kennedy; 2006.

[196] The 1991 election, Wofford Wins Senate Race, Turning Back Thornburgh; Michael Decourcy Hinds/The New York Times; 1991.

[197] Campaign Profile - Divining Clinton's Gut-Level Strategy; Peter Applebome/The New York Times; 1992.

[198] Race for the White House (TV series, episode on the 1992 election); CNN; 2016.

[199] Interview with Paul Begala on the Clinton Years; Chris Bury/Frontline

PBS; 2000.

[200] Race for the White House (TV series, episode on the 1992 election); CNN; 2016.

[201] Clinton wins the Carville primary; E Pianin, EJ Dionne /Washington Post; 1991.

[202] Quest for the Presidency 1992; Peter Goldman, Thomas DeFrank, Mark Miller, Andrew Murr, Tom Mathews; 1994.

[203] Quest for the Presidency 1992; Peter Goldman, Thomas DeFrank, Mark Miller, Andrew Murr, Tom Mathews; 1994.

[204] Race for the White House (TV series, episode on the 1992 election); CNN; 2016.

[205] Quest for the Presidency 1992; Peter Goldman, Thomas DeFrank, Mark Miller, Andrew Murr, Tom Mathews; 1994.

[206] All's Fair: Love, War and Running for President; Mary Matalin, James Carville; 1994.

[207] All's Fair: Love, War and Running for President; Mary Matalin, James Carville; 1994.

[208] Race for the White House (TV series, episode on the 1992 election); CNN; 2016.

[209] All's Fair: Love, War and Running for President; Mary Matalin, James Carville; 1994.

[210] Resurrection; How New Hampshire Saved the 1992 Clinton Campaign; Patrick Healy/The New York Times; 2016.

[211] Race for the White House (TV series, episode on the 1992 election); CNN; 2016.

[212] Resurrection; How New Hampshire Saved the 1992 Clinton Campaign; Patrick Healy/The New York Times; 2016.

[213] Race for the White House (TV series, episode on the 1992 election); CNN; 2016.

[214] Resurrection; How New Hampshire Saved the 1992 Clinton Campaign; Patrick Healy/The New York Times; 2016.

[215] Quest for the Presidency 1992; Peter Goldman, Thomas DeFrank, Mark Miller, Andrew Murr, Tom Mathews; 1994.

[216] All's Fair: Love, War and Running for President; Mary Matalin, James Carville; 1994.

[217] All's Fair: Love, War and Running for President; Mary Matalin, James Carville; 1994.

[218] Quest for the Presidency 1992; Peter Goldman, Thomas DeFrank, Mark Miller, Andrew Murr, Tom Mathews; 1994.

[219] Clintons Joined S&L Operator In an Ozark Real-Estate Venture; Jeff Gerth - The New York Times; 1992.

[220] Quest for the Presidency 1992; Peter Goldman, Thomas DeFrank, Mark Miller, Andrew Murr, Tom Mathews; 1994.

[221] Quest for the Presidency 1992; Peter Goldman, Thomas DeFrank, Mark Miller, Andrew Murr, Tom Mathews; 1994.

[222] Quest for the Presidency 1992; Peter Goldman, Thomas DeFrank, Mark Miller, Andrew Murr, Tom Mathews; 1994.

[223] Who Is Jerry Brown? Voices From Past Show Why the Man Is an Enigma; Robert Reinhold/The New York Times; 1992.

[224] Who Is Jerry Brown? Voices From Past Show Why the Man Is an Enigma; Robert Reinhold/The New York Times; 1992.

[225] Quest for the Presidency 1992; Peter Goldman, Thomas DeFrank, Mark Miller, Andrew Murr, Tom Mathews; 1994.

[226] New York Battle Gains in Intensity as Brown Surges; Robin Toner/The New York Times; 1992.

[227] Quest for the Presidency 1992; Peter Goldman, Thomas DeFrank, Mark Miller, Andrew Murr, Tom Mathews; 1994.

[228] New York Battle Gains in Intensity as Brown Surges; Robin Toner/The New York Times; 1992.

[229] Clinton Admits Experiment With Marijuana in 1960's; Gwen Ifill/The New York Times; 1992.

[230] Quest for the Presidency 1992; Peter Goldman, Thomas DeFrank, Mark Miller, Andrew Murr, Tom Mathews; 1994.

[231] Clinton Takes a Grilling in N.Y. and Gains an Audience; Douglas Jehl/Los Angeles Times; 1992.

[232] All's Fair: Love, War and Running for President; Mary Matalin, James Carville; 1994.

[233] Race for the White House (TV series, episode on the 1992 election); CNN; 2016.

[234] Entrepreneurial Genius: The Power of Passion; Gene N. Landrum; 2003.

[235] Entrepreneurial Genius: The Power of Passion; Gene N. Landrum; 2003.

[236] Entrepreneurial Genius: The Power of Passion; Gene N. Landrum;

2003.

[237] Perot Quits Race, Leaving two-man Field; Clinton wows change...; Robin Toner/The New York Times; 1992.

[238] Quest for the Presidency 1992; Peter Goldman, Thomas DeFrank, Mark Miller, Andrew Murr, Tom Mathews; 1994.

[239] Quest for the Presidency 1992; Peter Goldman, Thomas DeFrank, Mark Miller, Andrew Murr, Tom Mathews; 1994.

[240] All's Fair: Love, War and Running for President; Mary Matalin, James Carville; 1994.

[241] All's Fair: Love, War and Running for President; Mary Matalin, James Carville; 1994.

[242] Clinton's Staff Sees Campaign As a Real War; Michael Kelly/The New York Times; 1992.

[243] All's Fair: Love, War and Running for President; Mary Matalin, James Carville; 1994.

[244] Quest for the Presidency 1992; Peter Goldman, Thomas DeFrank, Mark Miller, Andrew Murr, Tom Mathews; 1994.

[245] All's Fair: Love, War and Running for President; Mary Matalin, James Carville; 1994.

[246] Quest for the Presidency 1992; Peter Goldman, Thomas DeFrank, Mark Miller, Andrew Murr, Tom Mathews; 1994

[247] The ad campaign - The Two Faces of Clinton; Richard L. Berke/The New York Times; 1992.

[248] All's Fair: Love, War and Running for President; Mary Matalin, James Carville; 1994.

[249] All's Fair: Love, War and Running for President; Mary Matalin, James Carville; 1994.

[250] Quest for the Presidency 1992; Peter Goldman, Thomas DeFrank, Mark Miller, Andrew Murr, Tom Mathews; 1994.

[251] All's Fair: Love, War and Running for President; Mary Matalin, James Carville; 1994.

[252] Race for the White House (TV series, episode on the 1992 election); CNN; 2016.

[253] All's Fair: Love, War and Running for President; Mary Matalin, James Carville; 1994.

[254] Quest for the Presidency 1992; Peter Goldman, Thomas DeFrank, Mark Miller, Andrew Murr, Tom Mathews; 1994.

[255] Bush Escalates Attack on Clinton For His Anti-Vietnam War Protests; Andrew Rosenthal/The New York Times; 1992.

[256] Quest for the Presidency 1992; Peter Goldman, Thomas DeFrank, Mark Miller, Andrew Murr, Tom Mathews; 1994.

[257] Bush Questions Clinton's Account Of Vietnam-Era Protests and Trip; Andrew Rosenthal/The New York Times; 1992.

[258] Quest for the Presidency 1992; Peter Goldman, Thomas DeFrank, Mark Miller, Andrew Murr, Tom Mathews; 1994.

[259] Bush Questions Clinton's Account Of Vietnam-Era Protests and Trip; Andrew Rosenthal/The New York Times; 1992.

[260] All's Fair: Love, War and Running for President; Mary Matalin, James Carville; 1994.

[261] Perot Quits Presidential Race; Edwin Chen/Los Angeles Times; 1992.

[262] Quest for the Presidency 1992; Peter Goldman, Thomas DeFrank, Mark Miller, Andrew Murr, Tom Mathews; 1994.

[263] Perot is Back - Perot Undertoe Threatens Clinton; Pew Research Center; 1992.

[264] Clinton Campaign Rally; C-SPAN; 1992.

[265] Quest for the Presidency 1992; Peter Goldman, Thomas DeFrank, Mark Miller, Andrew Murr, Tom Mathews; 1994.

[266] October 11, 1992 Debate Transcript; CPD; 1992.

[267] October 11, 1992 Debate Transcript; CPD; 1992.

[268] Race for the White House (TV series, episode on the 1992 election); CNN; 2016.

[269] October 15, 1992 Debate Transcript; CPD; 1992.

[270] October 15, 1992 Debate Transcript; CPD; 1992.

[271] Race for the White House (TV series, episode on the 1992 election); CNN; 2016.

[272] Presidential Campaign Discourse; Kathleen E. Kendall; 1995.

[273] Quest for the Presidency 1992; Peter Goldman, Thomas DeFrank, Mark Miller, Andrew Murr, Tom Mathews; 1994.

[274] All's Fair: Love, War and Running for President; Mary Matalin, James Carville; 1994.

[275] Quest for the Presidency 1992; Peter Goldman, Thomas DeFrank, Mark Miller, Andrew Murr, Tom Mathews; 1994.

[276] Campaign Almanac; A Narrow Lead; The New York Times; 1992.

[277] Quest for the Presidency 1992; Peter Goldman, Thomas DeFrank, Mark Miller, Andrew Murr, Tom Mathews; 1994.

[278] All's Fair: Love, War and Running for President; Mary Matalin, James Carville; 1994.

[279] The War Room (documentary/movie); Directed by Donn Alan Penne-baker, Chris Hegedus; 1993.

[280] The War Room (documentary/movie); Directed by Donn Alan Penne-baker, Chris Hegedus; 1993.

[281] Clinton and Bush in a sprint as race for White House ends; Michael Kelly/The New York Times; 1992.

[282] Love and War; Mary Matalin, James Carville; 2013.

[283] Love and War; Mary Matalin, James Carville; 2013.

[284] Campaign Profile - Divining Clinton's Gut-Level Strategy; Peter Apple-bome/The New York Times; 1992.

[285] Courage and Consequence; Karl Rove; 2010.

[286] Boy Genius; Lou Dubose, Jan Reid, Carl M. Cannon; 2003.

[287] Courage and Consequence; Karl Rove; 2010.

[288] Courage and Consequence; Karl Rove; 2010.

[289] Rove's retirement a surprise to Kjellander, too; Bernard Schoenburg/the Harrisburg Register; 2007.

[290] Courage and Consequence; Karl Rove; 2010.

[291] The Controller; Nicholas Lemann/The New Yorker; 2003.

[292] Boss Rove; Craig Unger; 2012.

[293] GOP Probes Official As Teacher of 'Tricks'; John Saar/The Washington Post; 1973.

[294] The Controller; Nicholas Lemann/The New Yorker; 2003.

[295] Boy Genius; Lou Dubose, Jan Reid, Carl M. Cannon; 2003.

[296] Courage and Consequence; Karl Rove; 2010.

[297] Boy Genius; Lou Dubose, Jan Reid, Carl M. Cannon; 2003.

[298] Courage and Consequence; Karl Rove; 2010.

[299] The Controller Karl Rove; Nicholas Lemann/The New Yorker; 2003.

[300] Driving W; Melinda Henneberger/New York Times; 2000.

[301] Boy Genius; Lou Dubose, Jan Reid, Carl M. Cannon; 2003.

[302] Driving W; Melinda Henneberger/New York Times; 2000.

[303] Driving W; Melinda Henneberger/New York Times; 2000.

[304] Courage and Consequence; Karl Rove; 2010.

[305] Courage and Consequence; Karl Rove; 2010.

[306] Boy Genius; Lou Dubose, Jan Reid, Carl M. Cannon; 2003.

[307] Man in the News, Fierce Ambition; Frank Bruni/The New York Times; 2001.

[308] Boy Genius; Lou Dubose, Jan Reid, Carl M. Cannon; 2003.

[309] Boy Genius; Lou Dubose, Jan Reid, Carl M. Cannon; 2003.

[310] The Triumph of William McKinley: Why the Election of 1896 Still Matters; Karl Rove; 2015.

[311] Bush Is Hardly a Passive Fund-Raiser; Don Van Natta Jr/The New York Times; 1999.

[312] The God Strategy: How Religion Became a Political Weapon in America; David Domke, Kevin Coe; 2007.

[313] McCain's Moment; Nancy Gibbs/CNN; 2000.

[314] Dirty Tricks, South Carolina and John McCain; Ann Banks/The Nation; 2008.

[315] McCain's Moment; Nancy Gibbs/CNN; 2000.

[316] Courage and Consequence; Karl Rove; 2010.

[317] Bush Faults House GOP Spending Plan; Terry M. Neal, Juliet Eilperin/The Washington Post; 1999.

[318] Courage and Consequence; Karl Rove; 2010.

[319] Courage and Consequence; Karl Rove; 2010.

[320] Courage and Consequence; Karl Rove; 2010.

[321] Man in the News, Fierce Ambition; Frank Bruni/The New York Times; 2001.

[322] Managing the President's Message; Martha Joynt Kumar; 2007.

[323] Karl Rove Laughs Last; Fred Barnes/the Weekly Standard; 2006.

[324] Courage and Consequence; Karl Rove; 2010.

[325] Bye Rove!; John B Judis/The New Republic; 2007.

[326] Why Are These Men Laughing?; Ron Suskind/Esquire; 2003.

[327] Courage and Consequence; Karl Rove; 2010.

[328] Bye Rove!; John B Judis/The New Republic; 2007.

[329] Courage and Consequence; Karl Rove; 2010.

[330] Swift Vets Top Contributors, 2004 Cycle; opensecrets.org.

[331] Two Texans dig deep for boat vet ads; John Frank/the Houston Chronicle; 2004.

[332] Karl Rove Laughs Last; Fred Barnes/the Weekly Standard; 2006.

[333] Bush's architect 'will be last man out the door'; the Sydney Morning Herald; 2004.

[334] Bush's architect 'will be last man out the door'; the Sydney Morning Herald; 2004.

[335] Who Runs Gov – Karl Rove; Washington Post; printed 2019.

[336] Documents Point to Bush Aides' Involvement in Prosecutor Firings; Eric Lichtblau, Eric Lipton /The New York Times; 2009.

[337] The Controller Karl Rove; Nicholas Lemann/The New Yorker; 2003.

[338] Karl Rove and the Modern Money Machine; Kenneth P Vogel/POLITICO Magazine; 2014.

[339] Karl Rove; Dark Money Watch; 2019.

[340] The busboy who cradled a dying RFK has finally stepped out of the past; Steve Lopez /Los Angeles Times; 2015.

[341] Believer; David Axelrod; 2015.

[342] Believer; David Axelrod; 2015.

[343] Believer; David Axelrod; 2015.

[344] Believer; David Axelrod; 2015.

[345] Believer; David Axelrod; 2015.

[346] Obama – from promise to power; David Mendel; 2007.

[347] Believer; David Axelrod; 2015.

[348] Game Change; John Heilemann, Mark Halperin; 2010.

[349] David Axelrod remembers Harold Washington on 30th anniversary of death; ABC7chicago.com; 2017.

[350] David Axelrod remembers Harold Washington on 30th anniversary of death; ABC7chicago.com; 2017.

[351] Believer; David Axelrod; 2015.

[352] Believer; David Axelrod; 2015.

[353] Believer; David Axelrod; 2015.

[354] Believer; David Axelrod; 2015.

[355] The Obama Memos; Ryan Lizza/The New Yorker; 2012.

[356] Obama – from promise to power; David Mendel; 2007.

[357] Obama – from promise to power; David Mendel; 2007.

[358] Believer; David Axelrod; 2015.

[359] Obama; Back of Divorce Files; Scott Fornek/Chicago Sun-Times; 2004.

[360] Ryan file a bombshell; John Chase, Liam Ford/Chicago Tribune; 2004.

[361] Obama – from promise to power; David Mendel; 2007.

[362] Illinois Senate Campaign Thrown Into Prurient Turmoil; Stephen Kinzer/The New York Times; 2004.

[363] Ryan Drops Out of Ill. Senate Race; Fox News; 2004.

[364] Obama – from promise to power; David Mendel; 2007.

[365] Barack Obama's Keynote Address at the 2004 Democratic National Convention; PBS NewsHour; 2004.

[366] Obama – from promise to power; David Mendel; 2007.

[367] Believer; David Axelrod; 2015.

[368] PoliticsPA.com; 2012

[369] Believer; David Axelrod; 2015.

[370] Believer; David Axelrod; 2015.

[371] Barack Obama Announces Candidacy; AmericanRhetoric.com; 2007.

[372] Believer; David Axelrod; 2015.

[373] The Candidate; Samuel L. Popkin; 2012.

[374] The Candidate; Samuel L. Popkin; 2012.

[375] Game Change; John Heilemann, Mark Halperin; 2010.

[376] The Obama Memos; Ryan Lizza/The New Yorker; 2012.

[377] Barack Obama Speech at the Jefferson-Jackson Dinner; AmericanRhetoric.com; 2007.

[378] The Candidate; Samuel L. Popkin; 2012.

[379] Believer; David Axelrod; 2015.

[380] Bill Clinton's Convention Speech; The New York Times; 2008.

[381] Game Change; John Heilemann, Mark Halperin; 2010.

[382] Game Change; John Heilemann, Mark Halperin; 2010.

[383] Axelrod and Penn; Matt Bai/The New York Times; 2008.

[384] Game Change; John Heilemann, Mark Halperin; 2010.

[385] Believer; David Axelrod; 2015.

[386] Game Change; John Heilemann, Mark Halperin; 2010.

[387] Game Change; John Heilemann, Mark Halperin; 2010.

[388] Believer; David Axelrod; 2015.

[389] Obama and Biden's Relationship Looks Rosy; Glenn Thrush/The New York Times; 2019.

[390] Obama and Biden's Relationship Looks Rosy; Glenn Thrush/The New York Times; 2019.

[391] Believer; David Axelrod; 2015.

[392] Obama Wins Nomination; Adam Nagourney/The New York Times; 2008.

[393] Game Change; John Heilemann, Mark Halperin; 2010.

[394] Believer; David Axelrod; 2015.

[395] Palin's Start in Alaska: Not Politics as Usual; William Yardley/The New York Times; 2008.

[396] Game Change; John Heilemann, Mark Halperin; 2010.

[397] Game Change; John Heilemann, Mark Halperin; 2010.

[398] Game Change; John Heilemann, Mark Halperin; 2010.

[399] Obama Enters the League of Must-See TV; Lisa de Moraes/The Washington Post; 2008.

[400] Game Change; John Heilemann, Mark Halperin; 2010.

[401] Game Change; John Heilemann, Mark Halperin; 2010.

[402] Message Maven, Finds Fingers Pointing at Him; Mark Leibovich/The New York Times; 2010.

[403] Message Maven, Finds Fingers Pointing at Him; Mark Leibovich/The New York Times; 2010.

[404] Message Maven, Finds Fingers Pointing at Him; Mark Leibovich/The New York Times; 2010.

[405] Double Down; Mark Halperin, John Heilemann; 2013.

[406] Double Down; Mark Halperin, John Heilemann; 2013.

[407] Double Down; Mark Halperin, John Heilemann; 2013.

[408] Add Watch: What is Mitt Romney hiding; The Wall Street Journal; 2012.

[409] Double Down; Mark Halperin, John Heilemann; 2013.

[410] Obama holds key leads against Romney; Dan Balz, Jon Cohen/The Washington Post; 2012.

[411] US to Stop Deporting Some Immigrants; Julia Preston, John H Cushman Jr/The New York Times; 2012.

[412] Student Loan Interest Rates Loom as Political Battle; Tamar Lewin/The New York Times; 2012.

[413] Obama Says Same-Sex Marriage Should Be Legal; Jackie Calmes, Peter Baker/The New York Times; 2012.

[414] Double Down; Mark Halperin, John Heilemann; 2013.

[415] Obama and Romney Campaigns Test Limits of Attacks; Michael Shear/The New York Times; 2012.

[416] GOP 'Super PAC' Weighs Hard-Line Attack on Obama; Jeff Zeleny, Jim Rutenberg/The New York Times; 2012.

[417] Twitter account of @davidaxelrod, 2012.

[418] The End of the Line - Politico Playbook 2012; Glenn Thrush, Jonathan Martin; 2012.

[419] The End of the Line - Politico Playbook 2012; Glenn Thrush, Jonathan Martin; 2012.

[420] Romney takes debate to Obama over economy; Tom Cohen/CNNPolitics; 2012.

[421] Double Down; Mark Halperin, John Heilemann; 2013.

[422] Hatchet Man; The Rise of David Axelrod; Grant Pick/Chicago magazine; 1987.